Civil Military Operation

Civil Military Operation

Capt. Prem Singh

Prashant Publishing House
DELHI - 110094 (INDIA)

PRASHANT PUBLISHING HOUSE
C-34, 28 Foota Road, Gali No. 3
West Karawal Nagar, Delhi-110094
Phone : 9810396373, 22963970

Civil Military Operation

First Published : 2009

ISBN : 978-81-908282-1-5

PRINTED IN INDIA

Published by Mr. R. K. Jha M/s. Prashant Publishing House, Delhi and Printed at H.S. Offset Press, Delhi.

Preface

This book addresses the operational context of information operations (IO), relevant terminology, and the environment of information operations. It supports battle command and provides guidelines for commanders that conduct IO to support all phases of the force-projection operating environment, including planning and executing early entry and force-projection operations in joint and multinational settings.

Military operations occur in peace and war. The traditional focus when discussing information and C2 was electronic warfare (EW), electronic countermeasure (ECM), and electronic counter countermeasure (ECCM) operations that take place during war. The focus of this manual is on command and control warfare (C2W), public affairs (PA), and civil affairs (CA). All are operations that the Army currently uses to gain and maintain information dominance as well as effective C2. Successful operations require effective C2 to transform military capabilities into applied military power. The more effective the force's C2 system, the more completely its capabilities can be realized in peace or war.

This doctrine applies to the total Army--active and reserve components and Army civilians. It is specifically oriented at the operational and tactical levels of military operations. It may be useful to other services, nonmilitary agencies, and allies involved in such operations.

— *Author*

Preface

Contents

1

Indo-Pakistani War of 1971

The Indo-Pakistani War of 1971 was a major military conflict between India and Pakistan. The war is closely associated with the Bangladesh Liberation War (sometimes also referred to as the Pakistani Civil War). Although there is some disagreement about the exact dates of the war, hostilities between India and Pakistan commenced officially on the evening of December 3, 1971. The armed conflict on India's western front during the period between 3 December 1971 and 16 December 1971 is called the "Indo-Pakistani War" by both the Bangladeshi and Indian armies. The war ended in the surrender of the Pakistani military after armed hostilities on two fronts.

BACKGROUND

The Indo-Pakistani conflict was sparked by the Bangladesh Liberation war, a conflict between the traditionally dominant West Pakistanis and the majority East Pakistanis. The Bangladesh Liberation war ignited after the 1970 Pakistani election, in which the East Pakistani Awami League won 167 of 169 seats in East Pakistan and secured a simple majority in the 313-seat lower house of the Majlis-e-Shoora (Parliament of Pakistan). Awami League leader, Sheikh Mujibur Rahman, presented the Six Points to the President of Pakistan and claimed the right to form the government.

After the leader of the Pakistan Peoples Party, Zulfikar Ali Bhutto, refused to yield the premiership of Pakistan to Mujibur, President Yahya Khan called out the military, which was made up largely of West Pakistanis.

Mass arrests of dissidents began, and attempts were made to disarm East Pakistani soldiers and police. After several days of strikes and non-cooperation movements, the Pakistani military cracked down on Dhaka on the night of March 25, 1971. The Awami League was banished, and many members fled into exile in India. Mujib was arrested and taken to West Pakistan. On 27 March 1971, Ziaur Rahman, a rebellious major in the Pakistani army, declared the independence of Bangladesh on behalf of Mujibur. In April, exiled Awami League leaders formed a government-in-exile in Boiddonathtola of Meherpur. The East Pakistan Rifles, an elite paramilitary force, defected to the rebellion. A guerrilla troop of civilians, the Mukti Bahini, was formed to help the Bangladesh Army.

INDIA'S INVOLVEMENT IN BANGLADESH LIBERATION WAR

On 27 March 1971, the Prime Minister of India, Indira Gandhi, expressed full support of her government to the Bangladeshi struggle for independence. The Bangladesh-India border was opened to allow Bangladeshi Refugees safe shelter in India. The governments of West Bengal, Bihar, Assam, Meghalaya and Tripura established refugee camps along the border. Exiled Bangladeshi army officers and voluntary workers from India immediately started using these camps for recruitment and training of Mukti Bahini guerrillas. As violence in East Pakistan escalated, an estimated 10 million refugees fled to India, causing financial hardship and instability in the country. The United States, a long and close ally of Pakistan, promised to ship arms and supplies to West Pakistan. In the early autumn of 1971, Indira Gandhi launched a diplomatic offensive with a tour of Europe. She was successful in getting both the United Kingdom and France to break with the United States to block any pro-Pakistan directives in the United Nations security council. Gandhi's greatest coup was on 9 August when she signed a twenty-year treaty of friendship and co-operation with the Soviet Union, greatly shocking the United States, and decreasing the possibility that the People's Republic of China would become involved in the conflict. China, an ally of Pakistan, had been providing moral support, but little military aid, and did not advance troops to its border with India. Operation of the Mukti Bahini caused severe casualties to the Pakistani Army, which was in control of all district headquarters. As the flow of refugees swelled to a tide, the economic costs for India began to escalate. India began providing support including weapons and training for the Mukti Bahini.

INDIA'S OFFICIAL ENGAGEMENT WITH PAKISTAN

By November, war seemed inevitable; a massive buildup of Indian forces on the border with East Pakistan had begun. The Indian military waited for winter, when the drier ground would make for easier operations and Himalayan passes would be closed by snow, preventing any Chinese intervention. On 23 November, Yahya Khan declared a state of emergency in all of Pakistan and told his people to prepare for war.

On the evening of Sunday, 3 December, the Pakistani air force launched sorties on eight airfields in north-western India. This attack was inspired by the Arab-Israeli Six Day War and the success of the Israeli preemptive strike. At, 5:30 PM that day, General Yahya Khan ordered the Pakistan Air Force to bomb Indian Forward Airbases. Pakistan started flying sorties towards India within fifteen minutes of the order. Pakistan launched attacks against eight Indian airfields on the Western front including Agra which was 300 miles (480 km) from the border. These attacks could only achieve partial success. Unlike the Israeli attack on Arab airbases in 1967 which involved a large number of Israeli planes, Pakistan flew no more than 50 planes to India. Indian runways were non-functional for several hours after the attack. India reacted strongly and declared war on Pakistan. India started flying sorties to Pakistan by midnight. On the Eastern front, the Indian Army joined forces with the Mukti Bahini to form the Mitro Bahini ("Allied Forces"); the next day the Indian forces responded with a massive coordinated air, sea, and land assault on the West Pakistani Army in East Pakistan.

India mounted its troops mainly on the East Pakistan Border. Pakistan had two objectives during the war: 1)To hold Indian forces from East Pakistan to the maximum extent. It was not easy for Indian troops to go long into Bangladesh as Bangladesh had many rivers and subrivers separating the land. Transporting the entire army and artillery across these rivers was not easy. 2)To occupy as much territory as possible on the western side of India. Pakistan expected that all India could achieve was a stalemate. In the end, a cease fire would be ordered and the territory procured prior to the stalemate would be theirs. The main Indian Objective on the western front was to prevent Pakistan from entering its soil. It had no intention of occupying Pakistan.

Pakistan attacked at several places along India's western border with Pakistan, but the Indian army successfully held their lines. The Pakistan Army suffered a defeat at Battle of Longewala, where a 2000-3000 strong assault force of the 51st Infantry Brigade of the Pakistani Army, backed by the 22nd Armoured Regiment, was repulsed by the 120-odd soldiers of Indian 'A' company, 23rd Bn, Punjab Regiment. The Indian Army quickly responded to the Pakistan Army's movements in the west and made some initial gains, including capturing around 5,500 square miles (14,000 km^2) of Pakistan territory (land gained by India in Pakistani Kashmir, Pakistani Punjab and Sindh sectors was later ceded in the Simla Agreement of 1972, as a gesture of goodwill).

At sea, the Indian Navy achieved success in Operation Trident, the name given to the attack on Karachi's port, which resulted in the destruction of 2 Pakistani destroyers and a minesweeper. This operation was followed by Operation Python. The waters in the east were also secured by the Indian Navy.

The Indian Air Force flew 4,000 sorties in the west while its counterpart, the PAF put up little retaliation, partly because of the paucity of non-Bengali technical personnel. This lack of retaliation has also been attributed to the deliberate decision of the PAF High Command to cut its losses as it had already incurred huge losses in the conflict. In the east, the small air contingent of Pakistan Air Force No. 14 Sqn was destroyed, resulting in Indian air superiority.

The Indian campaign employed "blitzkrieg" techniques, exploiting weakness in the enemy's positions and bypassing opposition, and resulted in a swift victory. Faced with insurmountable losses, the Pakistani military capitulated in less than a fortnight. On December 16, the Pakistani forces in East Pakistan surrendered. The next day Pakistan surrendered.

AMERICAN AND SOVIET INVOLVEMENT

The United States supported Pakistan both politically and materially. Nixon, backed by Henry Kissinger, feared Soviet expansion into South and Southeast Asia. Pakistan was a close ally of the People's Republic of China, with whom Nixon had been negotiating a rapprochement and where he intended to visit in February 1972. Nixon feared that an Indian invasion of West Pakistan would mean total Soviet domination of the region, and that it would seriously undermine the global position of the United States and the regional position of America's new tacit ally, China. In order to demonstrate to China the bona fides of the United States as an ally, and in direct violation of the US Congress-imposed sanctions on Pakistan, Nixon sent military supplies to Pakistan, routing them through Jordan and Iran, while also encouraging China to increase its arms supplies to Pakistan.

The Nixon administration also ignored reports it received of the 'genocidal' activities of the Pakistani Army in East Pakistan, most notably the Blood telegram. When Pakistan's defeat in the eastern sector seemed certain, Nixon sent the USS Enterprise to the Bay of Bengal, a move deemed by the Indians as a nuclear threat. The Enterprise arrived on station on December 11, 1971. On 6 December and 13 December, the Soviet Navy dispatched two groups of ships, armed with nuclear missiles, from Vladivostok; they trailed U.S. Task Force 74 into the Indian Ocean from 18 December 1971 until 7 January 1972. The Soviets also sent a nuclear submarine to ward off the threat posed by USS Enterprise in the Indian Ocean. American policy towards the end of the war was dictated primarily by a need to restrict the escalation of war on the western sector to prevent the 'dismemberment' of West Pakistan.6 Years after the war, many American writers criticized the White House policies during the war as being badly flawed and ill-serving the interests of the United States. The Soviet Union sympathized with the Bangladeshis, and supported the Indian Army and Mukti Bahini during the war, recognizing that the independence of Bangladesh would weaken the position of its rivals the United States and China. The USSR gave assurances to India that if a confrontation with the United States or China developed, it would take counter-measures. This assurance was enshrined in the Indo-Soviet friendship treaty signed in August 1971.

EFFECTS

The war ended with the surrender of the Pakistani military to the allied forces of India and Bangladesh, jointly known as the Mitro Bahini. Bangladesh became an independent nation, the world's third most populous Muslim state. Loss of East Pakistan demoralized the Pakistani military. President Yahya Khan resigned, to be replaced by Zulfiqar Ali Bhutto. Mujibur Rahman was released from a West Pakistani prison, returning to Dhaka on January 10, 1972. The extent of casualties in East Pakistan is not known. R.J. Rummel cites estimates ranging from one to three million people killed.8 Other estimates place the death toll lower, at 300,000. On the brink of defeat around December 14, the Pakistani Army, and its local collaborators. systematically killed a large number of Bengali doctors, teachers and intellectuals,910 part of a pogrom against the Hindu minorities who constituted the majority of urban educated intellectuals.1112 Young men, especially students, who were seen as possible rebels were also targeted. The cost of the war for Pakistan in monetary and human resources was high. In the book Can Pakistan Survive? Pakistan based author Tariq Ali writes, "Pakistan lost half its navy, a quarter of its airforce and a third of its army." India took approximately 90,000 prisoners of war, including Pakistani soldiers and their East Pakistani civilian supporters. 79,676 prisoners were uniformed personnel, of which 55,692 were Army, 16,354 Paramilitary, 5,296 Police, 1000 Navy and 800 PAF.13 The remaining prisoners were civilians - either family members of the military personnel or collaborators (razakars). The Hameedur Rahman Committee Report instituted by Pakistan lists the Pakistani POWs as follows:

Branch	Number of captured Pakistani POWs
Army	54,154
Navy	1,381
Air Force	833
Paramilitary including police	22,000
Civilian personnel	12,000
Total:	90,368

The war resulted in one of the largest surrenders of forces since World War II. Although India originally wished to try some 200 prisoners for war crimes for the brutality in East Pakistan, the government eventually acceded to releasing all prisoners as a gesture of reconciliation. The Simla Agreement signed the following year, also resulted in control of Pakistani territory (more than 15,000 km^2) that had been captured during the war being given back to Pakistan, in order to create a "lasting peace" between the two nations and to affirm that India had no territorial ambitions.

IMPORTANT DATES

- March 7, 1971: Sheikh Mujibur Rahman declares that, "The current struggle is a struggle for independence", in a public meeting attended by almost a million people in Dhaka.
- March 25, 1971: Pakistani forces start Operation Searchlight, a systematic plan to eliminate any resistance. Thousands of people are killed in student dormitories and police barracks in Dhaka.
- March 26, 1971: Major Ziaur Rahman declares independence from Kalurghat Radio Station, Chittagong. The message is relayed to the world by Indian radio stations.
- April 17, 1971: Exiled leaders of Awami League form a provisional government.
- December 3, 1971: War between India and Pakistan officially begins when West Pakistan launches a series of preemptive airstrikes on Indian airfields.
- December 6, 1971: East Pakistan is recognized as Bangla-Desh by India.
- December 14, 1971: Systematic elimination of Bengali intellectuals is started by Pakistani Army and local collaborators.11
- December 16, 1971: Lieutenant-General A. A. K. Niazi, supreme commander of Pakistani Army in East Pakistan, surrenders to the Allied Forces (Mitro Bahini) represented by Lieutenant General Aurora of Indian Army at the surrender. Bangladesh gains victory

- January 12,1972: Sheikh Mujibur Rahman comes to power.

MILITARY AWARDS

For bravery, a number of soldiers and officers on both sides were awarded the highest military award of respective countries. Following is a list of the recipients of the Indian award Param Vir Chakra, Bangladesh award Bir Sreshtho and the Pakistani award Nishan-E-Haider:

INDIA

Recipients of the Param Vir Chakra:

- Lance Naik Albert Ekka (Posthumously)
- Flying Officer Nirmal Jit Singh Sekhon (Posthumously)
- Second Lieutenant Arun Khetarpal (Posthumously)
- Major Hoshiar Singh

BANGLADESH

Recipients of the Bir Sreshtho:

- Captain Mohiuddin Jahangir (Posthumously)
- Lance Naik Munshi Abdur Rouf (Posthumously)
- Sepoy Hamidur Rahman (Posthumously)
- Sepoy Mostafa Kamal (Posthumously)
- ERA Mohammad Ruhul Amin (Posthumously)
- Flight Lieutenant Matiur Rahman (Posthumously)
- Lance Naik Nur Mohammad Sheikh (Posthumously)

PAKISTAN

Recipients of the Nishan-E-Haider:

- Major Muhammad Akram (Posthumously)
- Pilot Officer Rashid Minhas (Posthumously)
- Major Shabbir Sharif (Posthumously)
- Sowar Muhammad Hussain (Posthumously)
- Lance Naik Muhammad Mahfuz (Posthumously)

2

History of the Civil War in Sri Lanka

INTRODUCTION

The Democratic Socialist Republic of Sri Lanka was known as Ceylon before 1972; it used to be a colony of Great Britain until it obtained political independence in 1948. Its civil war is an ongoing conflict between the government of Sri Lanka and the Liberation Tigers of Tamil Eelam, or the LTTE. This conflict is due to ethnic discrimination of minority group, the Tamils, by the majority group, the Sinhalese. It has caused over 60,000 death tolls since 1983 when the war began.

The War up to the end of 2002 can be divided into five distinct phases: escalation, 1983-1987 (Eelam War I); Indian intervention, 1987-1989; the reign of Ranasinghe Premadasa, 1989-1993 (Eelam War II); and the attempt to find a negotiated solution, 1993-1994; and Eelam War III, 1995-2002. (1) This essay will cover from the origins of the war to the most recent news and then discuss the future prospects with possible solutions.

Origins of the Sri Lankan Civil War

The origins of the Sri Lankan civil war lie in sharp disagreements over language, access to universities, and riots between Sinhalese and Tamils. These gradually escalated from the 1920s until the outbreak of civil war in 1983.

During the colonial period by the British, Tamils had benefited from favoritism under Britain and many agree that this "divide and rule" policy caused the roots of the conflict. After the independence in 1948, the minority Tamils no longer had support from the British.

Official Language Policy

In 1956, the SLFP began the "Sinhala Only" campaign, which claimed Sinhala as the only official language of Sri Lanka. The bill was quickly enacted after the party's electoral victory, despite a bitter objection from the Left. This meant unemployment for many Tamils who were not fluent in Sinhala. The Government faced demonstrations from Tamils, which were repressed brutally by the Sinhalese nationalist gangs. By most Tamils the "Sinhala Only Act" is seen as a watershed and the foundation of the current civil war in the country.

The Universities Act of 1978

Under the British, Tamils who lived in northern and eastern regions gained easier access to English-medium education. Therefore, a large portion of students enrolled in universities were English speaking Tamils. During the 1970es university admissions were standardized in order to rectify disparities created in university enrolment during colonial rule, the main piece of the legislation being the Universities Act no.16 of 1978. Once the policy was enacted, the benefits enjoyed by Sinhalese students meant significantly less Tamil students gaining tertiary education.

Riots

There were two major riots before the civil war began; the first one in 1958 and the other in 1977. In both cases, Tamils were the major victims.

In 1958, the government resettled 400 unemployed Tamil laborers in Polonaruwa district, which angered the Sinhalese people. In May 25th, over 70 Tamil laborers in Polonnaruwa farms were murdered by a Sinhalese mob. The violence spread all over the country especially in Colombo and Panadura until 27th when the government finally declared state of emergency and restored order. Nearly 12,000 Tamil refugees had fled to camps near Colombo.

Riots broke out again in 1977, in response to an alleged assault on Sinhalese policemen. Up to 300 Tamils were killed and 25,000 fled their homes. These riots shattered the trust between communities and convinced the Tamil youths that armed insurrection was the only way..

Other Reasons

The number of other policies and events by the Sinhalese that were discriminatory to Tamils include: Denial of citizenship to estate Tamils; Sinhala colonisation of Tamil areas; Banning of Tamil media and literature importation; and destruction of the Jaffna Public Library. All of those contributed to set fire on the events of the Black July in 1983, and encouraged the Tamils to form militant groups that would start the civil war.

Escalation, 1983-1987; Eelam War I

Outbreak of the Civil War

The most prominent militant group was the LTTE. On 22nd July 1983, an attack on the military by the LTTE, which killed 13 Sinhalese soldiers, sparked riots by Sinhalese in Colombo, the capital. The official death toll was 367, but unofficial estimates are as high as 3,000 , including the 53 Tamil political prisoners in the Wlikada Prison. The mobs created 135,000 Tamil refugees and damage of US$ 100 million. It is claimed that the government was using the dead soldier's funeral to instigate the riot.

Escalation of Violence

Throughout the 1980s, increased violence accumulated death tolls. Emergency Regulation 15A enabled security forces to dispose of bodies without inquest proceedings, which facilitated extrajudicial killings.

On the first anniversary of the 1983 riots, Tamil guerillas killed 95 people. In August 2, a suitcase bomb exploded in airport, killing 32 people. In the same month, LTTE ambushed security forces, leaving estimated 100 people dead. In revenge, 100 Tamil shops and homes were destroyed. A week later, six soldiers died when their jeep ran over a land mine. Armed forces retaliated killing two Tamils and destroying 123 buildings. Chunnakam police station near Jaffna was destroyed, killing 19 Tamil prisoners, which both sides blamed on the other. In May 14, 146 Sinhala civilians were massacred at Anuradhapura. Between June 14 1983 and April 20, 1986, 272 Tamils were arrested by members of the security forces and were never seen again. Violence also broke out between Plantation Tamils and Kandyan Sinhalese in the early 1986. In the same year May, LTTE emerged as the most powerful extremist faction after killing around 150 members of TELO. In 1987, government troops pushed the LTTE fighters to the northern city of Jaffna. In July, LTTE carried out their first suicide attack when a member drove a truck with explosives into Sri Lankan army camp, reportedly killing forty soldiers. At this point the conflict reached its peak, as both sides engaged in a series of mass murder.

Attempts of Negotiation

There were three periods of negotiations before the Indian Intervention: a yearlong All-Parties Conference in 1984; eight months of a poorly maintained ceasefire from June 1985 to January 1986; and agreement conceded under pressure from CWC in 1986. The LTTE requested for a separate state of Tamil - a politically impossible task - but Sinhalese nationalists objected to any proposal that gave Tamil more powers of administration in All-Parties Conference. In 1985, the Tamils produced the four "Thimpu Principles" but only one: citizenship for all Tamils in Sri Lanka, was conceded by the government in 1986. The other three: recognition of Tamil as a distinct national entity; an identified Tamil homeland with guaranteed integrity; and their right to self-determination, were rejected.

Indian Intervention (1987-1989)

India is geographically a neighboring country to Sri Lanka. During the colonial period, many Tamils who lived in Indian state of Tamil Nadu had moved to Sri Lanka. This caused deep sympathy for the discrimination against Sri Lankan Tamils. At the same time, the Indian government wanted to project India as the regional power in the area.

India became actively involved in 1987 when the Indian Air Force airdropped food parcels to Jaffna while it was under siege by Sri Lankan forces. Relations between the two nations were extremely strained until the announcement of Indo-Sri Lanka Peace Accord on July 29, 1987, which Sri Lanka was too weak to refuse. This accord demanded Sri Lankan government to grant official status for the Tamil language and LTTE to surrender their arms to the Indian Peace Keeping Force (IPKF) sent to Jaffna. In October 1987, 17 heavily armed LTTE members were captured by IPKF and were turned over to the Lankan army. The members attempted mass suicide; killing 12 of them, and LTTE restarted its massacres of Sinhalese villagers. Within days, IPKF tried to demobilize the LTTE by force. Violence escalated between LTTE and IPKF and they ended up in a full-scale conflict. Due to the 'peace keeping' nature, the IPKF were unable to defeat the outnumbered LTTE. Simultaneously, nationalist sentiment opposed the presence of Indian in Sri Lanka. By the end of March 1989, IPKF was called back to India.

Later in 1991 when a member of LTTE assassinated the prime minister of India, Rajiv Gandhi, India dismantled its aid network, and support for the LTTE among the Tamil politicians evaporated.

The Administration of Ranasinghe Premadasa (1989-1993), Eelam War II

The LTTE took significant parts of the north as the IPKF withdrew. After a tentative ceasefire held in 1990, in which both major combatants had established their power bases, they turned on each other again. The government with Ranasinghe Premadasa as president, aimed to retake Jaffna. This Phase of war is called the Eelam War II.

During this period, both sides showed that they were capable of inflicting major damage on the enemy and civilians. Yet, neither displayed any hope of winning the war. The government placed an embargo on food and medicine entering the Jaffna. The air force relentlessly bombed the area, destroying the Naguleswaram, one of the five ancient holiest Hindu Shiva temples. The LTTE responded by attacking Sinhalese and Muslim civilians. The government death squads killed anybody suspected of being LTTE sympathizers. LTTE used 'ethnic cleansing' strategy of Muslim districts and massacred 120 Muslims at prayer. Lankan military attacked LTTE in the east successively. Security forces captured Pooneryn from the LTTE in 1992, and the LTTE captured it back the next year. The sight of burning bodies became a common feature along roadsides in the north and east. The largest battle of war was in July 1991, when the 5,000 LTTE troops tried to capture Elephant Pass, which cut Jaffna off from the rest of the island. It was resisted and kept by government after a month-long siege, losing over 2,000 men on each side. In February 1992, government offensives failed to capture Jaffna when military operations commander Major General Denzil Kobbekaduwa was killed by a land mine. In September 1993, Government troops began another major offensive in the northern Sri Lanka but were ambushed by LTTE, resulting in over 150 deaths.

In May 1, 1993, while mingling with a crowd of supporters, President Premadasa was assassinated by a youth who approached him and exploded a bomb strapped to his body.

Attempt to Find a Negotiated Solution (1993-1994)

In the 1994 parliamentary elections, the UNP (9) was defeated. Amidst great hope, the SLFP came to power on a peace platform. In October 1994, the LTTE made four demands: lifting the embargo on nonmilitary goods to Jaffna, ending the ban on sea fishing, dismantling of the army base at Pooneryn, and allowing armed LTTE cadres to move freely in the Eastern Province. The government conceded the first two and said the other two could only occur after the cessation of hostilities. The LTTE accepted a cease-fire in January 1995, but at this point, neither side was willing to risk peace for fear of losing power to their internal rivals. Both sides began preparing for war.

Eelam War III (1995-2002)

The LTTE broke the ceasefire on April 19, 1995. Although started as a stalemate, Eelam war III took six years of another bloody fighting before a cease-fire was possible.

The LTTE suffered its biggest defeat in the war in July in the Weli Oya region. Weli Oya is the largest Sinhalese colonist in Eastern Province. Unlike in 1993 when the LTTE had successively destroyed the army base that was without a commander, this time, the army was prepared and killed hundreds of guerillas with little loss of life.

The new government then pursued a policy of "war for peace". The government troops had succeeded in bringing Jaffna under government control by December 1995, but holding the city tied down many of the government forces and weakened them elsewhere.

After March 1997, the government pushed a campaign to open a military supply route to the Jaffna Peninsula. If successful, the offensive would have split the LTTE forces and strengthen the government's bargaining position both with the LTTE and Sinhalese extremists. The result was a total failure. Government troops of 20,000 were simply not capable of doing what 50,000 men from IPKF had failed to do. The campaign created a great hardship for the people of the region and left another thousand young men dead.

In the meantime, LTTE terrorist attacks continued throughout Eelam War III. Bombs were exploded numerous times in populated cities. Among the 241 suicide bombers were one who attacked the central bank in Colombo in January 1996, one who bombed Sri Lankan World Trade Center in October 1997, one who detonated a truck bomb in Kandy in January 1998, damaging one of the holiest Buddhist shrines in the world, and those who committed suicide assault on Sri Lanka's international airport in July 24, 2001, causing $1billion worth of damage. Terrorism not only intimidates the Sinhalese, it provokes a military and civilian backlash against innocent Tamils, which helps drives Tamils into their hands.

In response to this bombing, the Sri Lankan government outlawed the LTTE and in July 1996, several leading countries, led by the U.S. declared the LTTE to be a terrorist organization. Especially after September 11, 2001, U.S. anti-terrorist activities not only put increased pressure on LTTE but also significantly interfered with their fund-raising activities.

In February 2000, Norway was asked to mediate by both sides. After a unilateral ceasefire from December 2000 to April 2001; LTTE launched another offensive. By the end of that month, the LTTE had further advanced northwards and secured the

Elephant Pass military complex. Exhaustion with the war was building. The Sri Lankan military continued to grow in number but weakened its will to fight. Up the end of 2002, the army had 5,141 deserters. It was becoming increasingly difficult for the army and the rebels to find new recruits to fight a war that looked endless. The rebels and the government signed a cease-fire agreement in February 2002. And so the Eelam War III ended.

Recent News and Future Prospects

Ceasefire and Peace Talks

This time, the ceasefire not only actually worked, but also had number of other achievements. Thousands of internally displaced families have returned home, food and medical support was supplied, and buildings were reconstructed while the politicians were doing the peace talks.

Through six rounds of peace talks from September 2002 to April 2003, the situation made a dramatic progress. Although the government did not agree with LTTE's demand that they bcome an interim administration in the north and east, they agreed to share power within the federal system in which Tamils would have autonomy in the north and east of the country. The LTTE in turn, agreed to accept regional autonomy rather than a separate state. LTTE promised to stop taking on child soldiers.

Beginning of Eelam War IV (2006)

For the next few years, the Sri Lanka Monitoring Mission (SLMM) has been working to keep the cease-fire going but recorded increasing number of cease-fire violations by the LTTE, and the government did not keep their promise to withdraw troops. LTTE has lost its power since then. In March 2004, Colonel Karuna betrayed the LTTE and went under government's control. The tsunami of 2004 damaged much of their equipments but above all, it has lost the international support. After a few failures of two-party meetings in 2006, ceasefire violations rose to a point of low-intensity warfare by July. On April 25, a Tamil suicide detonated a bomb at Army Headquarters, and another in June that killed 64 people on a bus. The government retaliated by air strikes on LTTE territory. In the late July, there was a 'declaration of war' from Colombo and the ceasefire became 'null and void'. And so, the Eelam War IV began.

Future Prospects and Possible Solutions

As Sri Lanka headed toward Eelam War IV, diplomatic initiatives were underway by many countries, to prevent a resumption of all-out war and to encourage steps toward a peaceful resolution.

However, as LTTE committed numerous terrorist acts, there is little hope of reconciliation. The LTTE's stubborn demand for absolute independence of Tamils is worsening the situation. There is high probability that Eelam War IV will be another bloody conflict. On the brighter side, the government will try a wide range of diplomatic policies to put constant pressure on LTTE and at the same time, suggest various peace treaties.

In order to achieve the peace back in Sri Lanka, the government could adopt three possible options. The first policy option is to emphasize the inappropriateness of purely "majoritarian" decision-making in sharply divided societies.

It was the discrimination against minorities that resulted the civil war from the very beginning. Second, where sharp cleavages exist in societies, political stability should be ensured, if not guaranteed, by devising institutional arrangements giving minorities easy access to the highest decision-making processes. Third, stop the restrictions and minor discriminations against Tamils.

Today, Tamils are required to carry multiple forms of identification and are subject to searches and interrogation at any time. Non-Sinhalese areas are under the occupation of Sinhalese troops. These minor restrictions arouse antipathy among the people.

Even if the war is stopped and peace resettles, the problems ahead of Sri Lanka are vast. Tsunami reconstructions, removal of one million land mines, and fairer employment between the Tamils and Sinhalese are all just part of assignments left. Hope, is probably the best and the only word to describe my feelings toward the situation in Sri Lanka.

A BRIEF NAVAL CHRONOLOGY OF THE CIVIL WAR (1861-65)

Some Significant Events of 1861

12 April: Fort Sumter fired on by Confederate batteries -- the conflict begins.

19 April: President Lincoln issued proclamation declaring blockade of Southern ports from South Carolina to Texas.

20 April: Norfolk Navy Yard partially destroyed to prevent Yard facilities from falling into Confederate hands and abandoned by Union forces.

24 May: Commander S. C. Rowan, U.S.S Pawnee, demanded the surrender of Alexandria, Virginia; an amphibious expedition departed Washington Navy Yard and occupied the town.

3 August: John LaMountain made first ascent in a balloon from Union ship Fanny at Hampton Roads to observe Confederate batteries on Sewell's Point, Virginia.

29 August: Union forces under Flag Officer S. H. Stringham and General B. F. Butler received the unconditional surrender of Confederate-held Forts Hatteras and Clark, closing Pamlico Sound.

1 October: Confederate naval forces, including CSS Curlew, Raleigh, and Junaluska, under Flag Officer W. F. Lynch, CSN, captured steamer Fanny (later CSS Fanny) in Pamlico Sound with Union troops on board.

7 November: Naval forces under Flag Officer S. F. Du Pont captured Porr Royal Sound.

U S S Tyler, Commander H. Walke, and USS Lexington, Commander R. Stembel, supported 3,000 Union troops under General Grant at the Battle of Belmont, Missouri. and engaged Confederate batteries along the Mississippi River

8 November: USS San Jacinto, Captain C. Wilkes, stopped British mail steamer Trent in Old Bahama Channel and removed Confederate Commissioners James Mason and John Slidell.

11 November: Thaddeus Lowe made balloon observation of Confederate forces from Balloon-Boat G. W. Parke Curtis anchored in Potomac River.

12 November: Fingal (later CSS Atlanta), purchased in England, entered Savannah laden with military supplies -- the first ship to run the blockade solely on Confederate government account.

21 December: Congress enacted legislation providing for the Medal of Honor.

Some Significant Events of 1862

9 January: Flag Officer D. G. Farragut was appointed to command the Western Gulf Blockading Squadron -- the beginning of the New Orleans campaign.

16 January: Seven armored river gunboats were commissioned, thus providing the naval force for the overwhelming combined operations in the west.

6 February: Naval forces under Flag Officer A. H. Foote captured strategic Fort Henry on the Tennessee River. This breached the Confederate line and opened the flood gates for the flow of Union power deep into the South.

7-8 February: Joint amphibious expedition under Flag Officer L. M. Goldsborough and Brigadier General A. E. Burnside captured Roanoke Island -- the key to Albemarle Sound.

14 February: Gunboats under Flag Officer A. H. Foote attacked Fort Donelson on the Cumberland River in conjunction with troops under Brigadier General U. S. Grant. The fort capitulated on 16 February.

3 March: Forces under Flag Officer S. F. Du Pont took Fernandina, Florida, and the surrounding area in joint operations against the South Atlantic coast.

8 March: Ironclad ram CSS Virginia, Captain F. Buchanan, destroyed wooden blockading ships USS Cumberland and Congress in Hampton Roads.

9 March: USS Monitor, Lieutenant J. L. Worden, engaged CSS Virginia, Lieutenant C. ap R. Jones, in the historic first battle of ironclads.

14 March: Joint amphibious assault under Commander S. C. Rowan and Brigadier General A. E. Burnside captured New Bern, North Carolina -- "an immense depot of army fixtures and manufactures, of shot and shell..."

17 March: CSS Nashville, Lieutenant R. B. Pegram, ran the blockade out of Beaufort, North Carolina -- a "Bull Run of the Navy."

4 April: USS Carondelet, Commander H. Walke, dashed past Confederate batteries on Island No. 10 to support Major General J. Pope's assault on the island.

7 April: Island No. 10, vital to the Confederate defense of the upper Mississippi, surrendered to the naval forces of Flag Officer A. H. Foote.

24 April: Flag Officer D. G. Farragut's fleet ran past Forts Jackson and St. Philip, destroyed the defending Confederate flotilla below New Orleans, and, next day, compelled the surrender of the South's largest and wealthiest city.

10 May: Confederates destroyed the Norfolk and Pensacola Navy Yards in actions caused by the forced Southern withdrawal from her coasts.

11 May: CSS Virginia was blown up by her crew off Craney Island to prevent her capture by advancing Union forces.

15 May: The James River Flotilla under Commander J. Rodgers advanced unsupported to within eight miles of Richmond before being turned back at Drewry's Bluff by batteries manned in part by Confederate Navy and Marine personnel.

6 June: Gunboats under Captain C. H. Davis and rams under Colonel C. R. Ellet Jr., destroyed the upper Mississippi portion of the Confederate River Defense Fleet under Captain J. E. Montgomery at the Battle of Memphis. The Tennessee city surrendered.

28 June: Flag Officer D. G. Farragut's fleet successfully passed the heavy Vicksburg batteries; three days later, 1 July, his forces were joined by those of Flag Officer C. H. Davis: the fresh and salt-water fleets met for the first time.

1-2 July: Flag Officer L. M. Goldsborough's fleet covered the withdrawal of Major General G. B. McClellan's army after the battle of Malvern Hill.

15 July: CSS Arkansas, Lieutenant I. N. Brown, engaged and ran through the Union fleet above Vicksburg, partially disabling USS Carondelet and Tyler.

16 July: David Glasgow Farragut promoted to Rear Admiral, the first officer to hold that rank in the history of the U.S. Navy.

24 August: Commander R. Semmes assumed command of celebrated raider CSS Alabama.

26 August: Franklin Buchanan promoted to Admiral, ranking officer in the Confederate Navy.

25 September: USS Kensington and Rachel Seaman and mortar schooner Henry James bombarded Sabine City, Texas, and forced Confederate troops to withdraw from the city.

1 October: The Western Gunboat Fleet was transferred from the War Department to the Navy.

31 October: During October the Confederate Torpedo Bureau was established under Lieutenant H. Davidson, continuing work pioneered by Commander M. F. Maury.

3 November: CSS Cotton and shore batteries engaged Union squadron at Berwick Bay, Louisiana. The squadron suffered considerable damage before the gallant Confederate gunboat expended all its ammunition and was compelled to withdraw.

12 December: USS Cairo, Lieutenant Commander T. O. Selfridge, was sunk in the Yazoo River, the first ship to be destroyed by a Confederate torpedo.

31 December: USS Monitor, Commander J. P. Bankhead, foundered and was lost at sea off Cape Hatteras.

Some Significant Events of 1863

1 January: CSS Bayou City and Neptune engaged the Union fleet at Galveston, forcing the North's withdrawal from that foothold on the Texas coast. USS Harriet Lane was captured and USS Westfield was destroyed.

9-11 January: Gunboats under Rear Admiral D. D. Porter, with troops embarked, compelled the surrender of Fort Hindman (Arkansas Post) on the Arkansas River.

11 January: CSS Alabama, Captain R. Semmes, engaged and sank USS Hatteras, Lieutenant Commander H. C. Blake, off Galveston.

14 January: Joint Army-Navy forces attacked Confederate positions at Bayou Teche, Louisiana, compelling a Southern withdrawal and the subsequent destruction of gunboat CSS Cotton.

17 January: CSS Josiah Bell and Uncle Ben captured USS Morning Light and Velocity, temporarily lifting the blockade of Sabine Pass, Texas.

30 January: USS Commodore Perry and Army troops severed Confederate supply lines to Richmond via the Perquimans River, North Carolina.

31 January: CSS Palmetto State and Chicora attacked the blockading fleet off Charleston; USS Mercedita and Keystone State were heavily damaged and struck their flags.

14 February: USS Queen of the West grounded in the Black River and was abandoned under heavy fire.

24 February: CSS William H. Webb and Queen of the West engaged and sank ram USS Indianola below Warrenton, Mississippi.

28 February: USS Montauk, Wissahickon, Seneca, and Dawn shelled and destroyed blockade runner Rattlesnake (formerly CSS Nashville) under the guns of Fort McAllister, Georgia. For more than a month, Union ironclads had been bombarding the fort guarding the approaches to Savannah.

11 March: Ships of the Yazoo Pass Expedition, begun in February with the objective of cutting off Vicksburg in the rear, engaged Fort Pemberton, Mississippi. The expedition ultimately had to retire without achieving its purpose.

14 March: Rear Admiral D. G. Farragut passed the heavy batteries at Port Hudson with USS Hartford and Albatross to establish an effective blockade of the vital Red River supply lines.

31 March: Confederate troops opened a sustained attack on Union forces at Washington, North Carolina, but Northern warships, moving swiftly to the support of the soldiers, halted the assault.

7 April: Rear Admiral S. F. Du Pont's ironclad squadron engaged strong Confederate forts in Charleston harbor in an attempt to penetrate the defenses and capture the city. The ironclads were heavily damaged and the attack was broken off; USS Keokuk sank the next day.

16-17 April: Gunboats under Rear Admiral D. D. Porter escorting Army transports successfully passed the Vicksburg batteries preparatory to attacking Grand Gulf.

3 May: Rear Admiral Porter's force and troops under Major General U. S. Grant forced the evacuation of Grand Gulf. Porter reported: "The Navy holds the door to Vicksburg."

17 June: CSS Atlanta, with two wooden steamers in company, engaged USS Weehawken and Nahant in Wassaw Sound, Georgia. The heavy Confederate warship grounded and was compelled to surrender.

4 July: Vicksburg surrendered after a lengthy bombardment and siege by Union naval and land forces. President Lincoln wrote: "The Father of Waters again goes unvexed to the sea."

9 July: Port Hudson, Louisiana, surrendered after prolonged attack by Northern sea and land forces. The Union had won the war in the West.

10 July: Rear Admiral J. A. Dahlgren's ironclads renewed the bombardment of Charleston defenses, opening on Fort Wagner, Morris Island.

13 July: Yazoo City, Mississippi, was captured by a joint Army-Navy expedition.

1 August: Rear Admiral D. D. Porter relieved Rear Admiral D. G. Farragut of command of the lower half of the Mississippi and assumed command of the River from New Orleans to the headwaters.

5 August: USS Commodore Barney was severely damaged by Confederate electric torpedo in the James River above Dutch Gap, Virginia.

29 August: Confederate submarine H. L. Hunley, Lieutenant J. A. Payne, CSN, sank for the first time in Charleston harbor after making practice dives preparatory to attacking the blockading fleet.

6 September: Morris Island, Charleston harbor, was evacuated by Confederate forces after nearly 2 months of intensive bombardment from afloat and ashore.

8 September: CSS Uncle Ben and shore batteries turned back a Union expedition to take Sabine Pass, Texas. USS Clifton and Sachem were disabled and surrendered.

5 October: CSS David, Lieutenant W. T. Glassell, exploded a spar torpedo against USS New Ironsides in an attempt to destroy the heavy blockader off Charleston. New Ironsides was damaged but not destroyed.

15 October: Submarine H. L. Hunley sank for the second time in Charleston harbor. The part owner for whom she was named and a crew of seven perished in the accident, but she was again recovered and a third crew volunteered to man her.

31 October: During October, instruction began for 52 midshipmen at the Confederate States Naval Academy on board CSS Patrick Henry in the James River.

2-4 November: Naval forces convoyed and supported Army troops at Brazos Santiago, Texas, where the Union secured a valuable position on the Mexican border. As a result of this operation, Brownsville, Texas, was also evacuated.

7 December: Steamer Chesapeake en route Portland, Maine, was seized off Cape Cod by Confederates disguised as passengers and carried to Nova Scotia.

Some Significant Events of 1864

2 February: Confederate boat expedition led by Commander J. T. Wood captured and destroyed USS Underwriter in the Neuse River, North Carolina.

17 February: Confederate submarine H. L. Hunley sank Union blockader Housatonic off Charleston -- the first submarine to sink a ship in combat.

12 March: Ships of Rear Admiral D. D. Porter's Mississippi Squadron moved up the Red River to commence the unsuccessful Army-Navy campaign to gain a foothold in the Texas interior.

19 April: CSS Albemarle, Commander J. W. Cooke, sank USS Southfield and forced the remainder of the Union squadron at Plymouth, North Carolina, to withdraw. Having gained control of the waterways in the area, the Confederates were able to capture Plymouth on 20 April.

5 May: USS Sassacus, Wyalusing, and Mattabesett engaged CSS Albemarle off the mouth of the Roanoke River as the Union sought in vain to regain control near Plymouth.

6 May: Confederate torpedo destroyed USS Commodore Jones in the James River, Virginia, one of several losses the Union suffered from torpedoes during the year.

13 May: The last of Rear Admiral Porter's squadron, after being trapped by low water, dashed through the hurriedly constructed Red River dams to safety below the Alexandria rapids.

19 June: USS Kearsarge, Commander J. A. Winslow, sank CSS Alabama, Captain R. Semmes, off Cherbourg, France, ending the career of the South's most famous commerce raider.

5 August: Rear Admiral D. G. Farragut's fleet steamed by Forts Morgan and Gaines, through the deadly torpedo field blocking the channel, and into Mobile Bay. In the fierce engagement with the forts and Admiral F. Buchanan's small squadron, Farragut won a victory worthy of his great name.

6 August: CSS Tallahassee, Commander J. T. Wood, put to sea from Wilmington, launching a brief but highly successful cruise against Northern shipping.

23 August: Fort Morgan, the last of the three forts at Mobile Bay to remain in Confederate hands, capitulated.

7 October: USS Wachusett, Lieutenant N. Collins, captured CSS Florida, Lieutenant C. M. Morris, at Bahia, Brazil. Thus, in the same year were the cruises of the dread raiders Alabama and Florida ended.

19 October: CSS Shenandoah, Lieutenant J. I. Waddell, commissioned off the Madeira Islands.

27 October: Torpedo launch commanded by Lieutenant W. B. Cushing destroyed ram CSS Albemarle in the Roanoke River, assuring the North of renewed control of the waters around Plymouth, North Carolina.

4 November: Confederate raiders captured small gunboats USS Key West, Tawah, and Elfin near Johnsonville on the Tennessee River.

13 December: Rear Admiral Farragut arrived in New York

City, for a period of rest after his arduous duty in the Gulf of Mexico and was acclaimed as a conquering hero. Ten days later he was promoted to the newly established rank of Vice Admiral.

21 December: Flag Officer W. W. Hunter destroyed the last of the Confederate Savannah Squadron to prevent its capture by the advancing forces of General W. T. Sherman.

24-25 December: A joint Army-Navy operation under Rear Admiral Porter and Major General B. F. Butler unsuccessfully attempted to take the Confederate stronghold of Fort Fisher, Wilmington, by amphibious assault.

Some Significant Events of 1865

13-15 January: The joint amphibious assault under Rear Admiral David D. Porter and Major General Alfred H. Terry took Fort Fisher, the key in the defense of Wilmington, North Carolina, which was the last port by which supplies from Europe could reach General Lee's troops at Richmond.

23-24 January: The Confederate fleet under Flag Officer John K. Mitchell attempted to dash down the James River to attack General Grant's headquarters at City Point, Virginia. The bold attack was thwarted when the heaviest of the ironclads ran aground.

17-18 February: Charleston, confronted by General William T. Sherman's soldiers approaching from the rear and a Navy-supported amphibious assault from Bull's Bay, was evacuated.

18 February: CSS Shenandoah, Lieutenant James I. Waddell, departed Melbourne to resume her commerce raiding career in the Pacific.

22 February: Wilmington, North Carolina, was evacuated as Rear Admiral Porter's ships steamed up the Cape Fear River and General Terry's soldiers marched on the city.

24 March: CSS Stonewall, Captain Thomas J. Page, put to sea from Ferrol, Spain, en route to Havana. The ironclad was intended to raise the blockade of one or more southern ports.

28 March: Rear Admiral Porter joined Generals Grant and Sherman for a conference with President Lincoln on board steamer River Queen at City Point, Virginia. They discussed the strategy to be followed in the closing days of the war and how the South would be treated at the close of the conflict.

2-4 April: CSA Secretary of the Navy Stephen R. Mallory ordered the destruction of the Confederate James River Squadron and directed its officers and men to join General Lee's troops then in the process of evacuating Richmond and retreating westward toward Danville.

3 April: Midshipmen at the Confederate Naval Academy, under the command of Lieutenant William H. Parker, escorted the archives of the government and the specie and bullion of the treasury from Richmond to Danville and southward.

4 April: Rear Admiral Porter accompanied President Lincoln up the James River to Richmond on board flagship Malvern. Vice Admiral David G. Farragut had already arrived in the Confederate capital.

9 April: General Lee met General Grant at Appomattox Courthouse and formally surrendered the Army of Northern Virginia.

11-12 April: Batteries Tracy and Huger, up the Blakely River from Spanish Fort, fell to Union forces and Confederate troops evacuated Mobile, which was surrendered by the mayor.

14 April: President Lincoln was shot shortly after 10 p.m. while watching "Our American Cousin" at Ford's Theatre, Washington. He died at 7:22 a.m. the next morning.

14 April: Major General Anderson, Commander of the Union Army garrison at Fort Sumter on 14 April 1861, raised above Sumter's ruins "the same United States flag which floated over the battlements of that fort during the rebel assault...."

23-24 April: CSS Webb, Lieutenant Read, dashed from the Red River and entered the Mississippi in a heroic last-ditch effort to escape to sea.Trapped below New Orleans, Webb was grounded and fired to avoid capture.

27 April: The body of John Wilkes Booth, President Lincoln's assassin, was delivered on board USSMontauk, anchored in the Anacostia River off the Washington Navy Yard.

3 May: CSA Secretary of the Navy Mallory submitted his resignation to President Davis at Washington, Georgia.

10 May: President Jefferson Davis was captured by Union troops near Irwinville, Georgia.

19 May: CSS Stonewall, Captain T. J. Page, was turned over to Cuban officials at Havana.

2 June: Terms of surrender of Galveston were signed on board USS Fort Jackson by Major General E. Kirby Smith on behalf of the Confederacy.

22 June: Secretary Welles announced to the naval forces that France and Great Britain had "withdrawn from the insurgents the character of belligerents", and that the blockade of the coast of the United States would soon be lifted.

28 June: This date marked the most successful single day CSS Shenandonh, Lieutenant Waddell, enjoyed as a commerce raider during her long cruise that spanned 13 months and covered 58,000 miles.On this field day Waddell captured 11 American whalers near the narrows of the Bering Strait.

18 July: Rear Admiral Louis M. Goldsborough arrived at Flushing, in the Netherlands, where he hoisted his flag on USS Colorado and assumed command of the reinstated European Squadron. The East India Squadon was reactivated on 31 July.

2 August: Lieutenant Waddell, CSS Shenandoah, spoke the English bark Barracouta and for the first time learned positively that the war was over. He determined to make a nonstop voyage to Liverpool, England, via Cape Horn.

12 August: Brazil Squadron reactivated under Rear Admiral Godon in flagship Susquehanna.

11 September: Emperor Maximilian approved the "Regulations and Instructions" prepared by Matthew Fontaine Maury to encourage emigration of Southerners to Mexico. The Emperor also appointed Maury director of the proposed National Observatory.

3 November: Secretary Welles ordered all naval vessels to resume rendering honors when entering British ports and to begin again exchanging official courtesies with English men of war.

6 November: CSS Shenandoah, Lieutenant Waddell, arrived at Liverpool, England, 123 days and 23,000 miles from the Aleutians.Waddell lowered the last official Confederate flag, and his ship was ultimately turned over to American authorities.

4 December: Secretary Welles announced that the West India Squadron was to be re-established under Commodore James S. Palmer, in that area "where we have so large a trade, owing to the proximity of the islands to our shores, it is essential that we cultivate friendly relations."

31 December: In his annual report to the President, Secretary Welles wrote: "It is still wise -- the wisest -- economy to cherish the navy, to husband its resources, to invite new supplies of youthful courage and skill to its service, to be amply supplied with all needful facilities and preparations for efficiency, and thus to hold within prompt and easy reach its vast and salutary power for the national defence and self- vindication."

Sri Lanka's warring factions are divided along ethnic lines. The majority of the Sri Lankan population is Sinhalese and have resided on the island nation for millennia. The Tamils are the largest minority group and are separated into the northern Tamils, who are descendants of Tamil invaders from India from many centuries past, and the plantation Tamils, who were brought to the island to work British tea plantations in the nineteenth century.

The roots of the current war can be found in the British colonial practices. The British gained the island of Sri Lanka in 1798 as a Crown colony after a short struggle with the previous Dutch rulers. Tea and rubber estates were developed and Tamils were imported from India to work the plantations. The Sinhalese residents refused to work for the slave wages offered by the British. However, as the colonial occupation continued, the Sinhalese who had refused to work for the British found themselves passed over for education and employment opportunities which went to the Tamils. The result of British rule was the domination of the island's economic and political life by the Tamil minority.

In 1948, Sri Lanka was granted independence and a Sinhalese government was appointed. This government quickly passed legislation discriminatory against Tamils, allowing the Sinhalese greater access to land, education, and employment. Some plantation Tamils were even deported to India. The legalized discrimination continued through the 1970s, when two major Tamil parties joined to form the Tamil United Front, which would later become the Tamil United Liberation Front (TULF) and would press for creation of a separate state "Tamil Eelam", from within the system. Other Tamils, more militant than the TULF, chose the path of terrorism and became the LTTE and other guerrilla groups. These Tamils concentrated their efforts on murdering Sinhalese officials and civilians until 1983.

The War

In July 1983, the LTTE killed thirteen soldiers with a land mine. This explosion sparked three days of anti-Tamil rioting across Sri Lanka by the Sinhalese. Rioters rampaged through Tamil neighbourhoods, burning them to the ground and killing any Tamils they found. By the time the government took action to calm the rioting, some 400 Tamils had been massacred. The government was accused of not acting fast enough to stop the rioting, and this accusation, coupled with a tradition of official discrimination against Tamils, turned many to assisting the Tamil guerrillas.

Armed with popular support among their people, the guerrillas stepped up their guerrilla and terrorist activities. In one such attack in May 1985, Tamil guerrillas dressed as government soldiers entered Anuradhapura and went on a killing spree. They attacked the Bodhi Tree shrine, a sacred site to Buddhist Sinhalese, and then rampaged through the town. At least 150 civilians died in the hour-long attack.

Civilian massacres and atrocities continued unabated until July 1987, when a negotiated peace settlement was worked out under Indian mediation. The agreement called for an Indian peacekeeping force (IPKF) to disarm the guerrillas in exchange for a full amnesty for the guerrillas and limited autonomy for Tamils. Unfortunately, the Tamils refused to be disarmed, and fighting broke out again, this time involving the IPKF. After months of fighting, the IPKF were able to remove control of the city of Jaffna from LTTE hands.

Terrorist attacks continued during the resurgence in fighting following the arrival of the peacekeeping force, and in 1987, an old terror group was resurrected. This old group was the Janatha Vinukthi Peramuna (JVP) and was composed of Sinhalese extremists who felt that the government had made too many concessions to the Tamils. The JVP, in a previous incarnation, had tried to take over the government in the short 1971 revolution. In its present incarnation, the JVP has launched terrorist attacks against Tamils and government personnel, including a bombing attack on the presidential palace that almost killed then-President Jaywardene. A counter-insurgency campaign in late 1989 was thought to have effectively wiped out the JVP.

The IPKF bore the brunt of the fighting against the Tigers until 1989, when souring relations between the Sri Lankan and Indian governments and continued heavy fighting caused the recall of the 50,000 member force. The last Indian troops left on March 24, 1990.

This war, like many others, has fallen into a pattern of repeated ceasefires and combat. A thirteen-month cease fire was broken in June 1990 when a Tamil complained to the LTTE of police brutality. During 1990, several battles took place between LTTE and Government forces and Government forces discovered that the LTTE had used the ceasefire to build strong fortifications on the Elephant Pass which linked Jaffna to the rest of Sri Lanka. Combat continued until January 1991, when a week-long ceasefire occurred.

1991 saw continued military and guerrilla activity with LTTE forces attacking military bases. Terrorist activities also continued, with the assassination of Defence Minister Wijerante in a bomb blast on March 2. The war goes on.

Prospects for Sri Lanka are dismal. The hatred of the Sinhalese and Tamils for each other is simply too strong and too many civilians have been slaughtered to allow the mutual hate and fear which has existed since colonial times to be wiped out in a short time. Until one side either gives up the struggle, or gains enough strength to wipe out the other, the war will continue. At this point, the differences between the LTTE and the Government are irreconcilable.

Forces

The war in Sri Lanka is primarily fought between the Army and the LTTE, with some other groups joining the battle until being wiped out by either of the first two groups.

The Army in Sri Lanka is a large conventional force with a strong infantry base. Some 40,000 people serve in the Army, although this may have increased through repeated calls for enlistment by the regime. They are organized into 5 infantry brigades, 2 reconnaissance regiments, and 5 support regiments. Infantry weapons are mainly the AK-47 assault rifle, Bren L4 machinegun, and the M2HB heavy machinegun although other weapons can be found in service. Artillery support is provided by several small-calibre howitzers including the 25 Pounder, the 85mm Type-56, and the 76mm M-48 and this is supplemented by a small number of 106mm M-40 and 82mm M-60 recoilless launchers. Mortars include the Soviet 82mm M-37, 107mm M-38, and the 120mm M-43. Finally, Armoured units have a number of wheeled AFVs, including Saladins, Ferrets, Dingos, BTR-152s, and armoured SAMIL 100s.

Small local militia or Home Guard units provide support for the military and attempt to keep local peace along with police forces. Both the militia and police use civilian small arms, but the police may have access to military-style weapons. There also exist paramilitary Special Task Force Units, which seem to be internal security forces.

On the opposing side are the LTTE. Little is known of their structure or armaments, but they may follow a Soviet-style organization as all Sri Lankan guerrilla groups have received training either from the Palestinians in Lebanon or the Indian government. The LTTE is also believed to have received weapons from the Indian government and possibly other Marxist nations. So, speculation on likely arms for the LTTE would produce a list encompassing AK-47s and older model Soviet support weapons such as RP-46 and RPD machineguns. Photographs have also shown them fielding L7A2 GPMGs. Weapons such as DShKs and RPG-7Vs are also likely to be found, but would be rare. Rounding out the LTTE armouries would be large quantities of civilian and military rifles, pistols, and shotguns.

Other Tamil guerrilla groups would mimic the LTTE in weapons, but not numbers. The LTTE is large enough to have held off both the Sri Lankan Army and the Indian Peace Keeping Force (IPKF) while at the same time fighting the other Tamil groups to eliminate rivals. On several occasions, the LTTE has almost wiped out its rivals. These other Tamil groups include the LTTE-allied Eelam Revolutionary Organization (EROS), a terrorist group and the Three Star Group, which is a rival to the LTTE. The Three Star Group consists of the Eelam People's Revolutionary Liberation Front (EPRLF), the People's Liberation Organization of Tamil Eelam (PLOT), and the Tamil Eelam Liberation Organization (TELO).

The final guerrilla group is the Sinhalese Janatha Vinukthi Peramuna (JVP), or People's Liberation Front. These are Marxist insurgents who are fighting against the government which they see as having given too many concessions to the Tamils. Their weapons likely mirror the LTTE.

Of these last groups, only the LTTE currently remains a viable guerrilla organization. The others have been either wiped out by counterinsurgency efforts of the government or by LTTE attacks. Those fragments which remain have chosen terrorist tactics to continue their struggle.

3

Global Civil War Overview

Introduction

In an effort to provide an overview to the much-debated era of human history known as the Global Civil War, I have been requested to compile the various materials and documents available into a single comprehensive document. The purpose of this document is two-fold; first it will piece together evidence and first-person sources concerning the war, and second, it will provide clarity to alien races that wish to study human history prior to the First Robotech War. This document will attempt to make an impartial overview of the war, without taking sides by vilifying one side over another. An unfortunately common practice in some historical documents is to portray the loser in a conflict in a negative light either by exaggerating details or omitting details that may vilify the victors. The facts speak for themselves and it is up to the reader to draw their own conclusions.

The World in the Post Cold War Era

The Cold War dominated the world in the decades following World War II. On one side was the "West", dominated by the capitalist United States of America and acting mainly through the North Atlantic Treaty Organization (NATO), while on the other side was the "East", dominated by the communist United Soviet Socialists Republic (Soviet Union or USSR). The two sides were opposed ideologically, both in government styles and financial systems, and geographically. Nearly all events that occurred in the world during this time, such as the Vietnam War and the war in Afghanistan, became an exercise of will between the two super powers, the US and the USSR. The threat of a total nuclear war that will end life on Earth hung over the world during this era, even though neither side wanted to use their large nuclear arsenals.

The Soviet Union, after losing nearly 20 million people during World War II, was determined that it would never again be invaded and built the world's largest military at the time. While it did rely on numbers over technology, they still built some of the most advanced war machines in the world, and many were as good, if not better, than those of the more technologically advanced western countries. Realizing that they could never realistically match the Soviet Union in military size for any great period of time, NATO decided to use nuclear weapons as a deterrent for war. Most NATO countries built and maintained a large stockpile of nuclear arms, which were significantly cheaper to maintain then a large standing army. This caused the Soviet Union to respond by building its own large stockpile of nuclear weapons, but their numbers of lower than NATO's.

During the 1980's, the Soviet Union suffered a demoralizing setback when their military failed to defeat rebel factions in Afghanistan and increased military spending was tearing the country's economy to shreds. NATO and the United States did not realize the extent of collapse in the Soviet Union until in 1989 they allowed the reunification of Germany, which had been split into two countries following World War II, one side controlled by NATO, the other by the Soviet Union. Soon after, the entire Soviet Union collapsed leaving many former republics independent for the first time ever and a much weaker Russian Republic.

The now democratic Russia was suffering from economic collapse and many western countries were too used to viewing the Russians as enemies to offer any help. This forced the Russians, and many of the independent Republics to sell many of their weapons to third world countries, such as China, the Middle East, and many countries in Africa. Some of the weapons sold were even rumored to be nuclear warheads, which would garner a huge price on the black market.

In contrast, this was an impressive time for the western countries: they had easily won a war in the Middle East against Iraq and advances in space technology allowed the concept of a space station become a reality. Since Russia had one of the world's largest space agencies and the world's only existing space station, they were reluctantly included in the US dominated international space agency. As computers became widespread, information became more accessible to those that opposed the world's current notion of peace. With the Cold War over, and with many countries looking forward to a time of real pace, many powerful countries forgot that most of the world had been dominated by only a few countries and that with the collapse of colonialism, imperialism, and the end of the Cold War many of these countries were truly free for the first time ever. These countries, particularly China, India, Iran, and several countries in Africa, did not appreciate that the world had decided that there would be no more wars, no more taking from other countries what you wanted, which is exactly what the current Super Powers had done to achieve their power.

Tensions would rise continuously throughout the early half of the 1990's, as many countries fought the "world powers" both in the United Nations General Assembly, and in world markets to achieve what they believed was their fair share. Support ebbed and waned for international cooperation throughout the world and many countries felt cheated by the United States, as the US would treat them as partners with one hand and as enemies with the other.

New alliances were formed throughout the world, such as a growing bond between Islamic countries in the Middle East, between former enemies in Africa, and between China and India, but the United States viewed these alliances as strategic threats that it could not counter with traditional methods. A new world order was being built around the United States claiming the world had moved past imperialism and other countries finally moving into positions where they could execute their own imperialist goals. The International Space Station, named Freedom Station, was the focal point for the anger that had grown among the countries of the world.

Freedom Station: Excuse or Justification?

Freedom Station had cost over 100 billion American dollars to construct and had taken over three years to finish. When it was completed on February 16, 1996, the members of the International Space Agency cheered and looked forward to using the station for research into survival in space and industrial applications of space. Almost overnight, NASA had risen in importance in the American public's eyes and its popularity skyrocketed, but this was nearly overshadowed by criticisms from several countries that complained that they would not be given a fair portion of the station's facilities. China led the criticisms against the International Space Agency, when it had announced that Freedom Station's crew would be made up of Americans and Russians. While some countries, mainly other NATO members, would be given access to the station's laboratories through remote control, countries such as China, which had contributed several billion dollars to the project, would be refused access to the station during the first few years of the project. China also claimed that the United States had stated that the Chinese would be considered invaders if they tried to dock with the station without permission. China, India, and several other countries withdrew from the International Space Agency.

Tensions rose between the countries of the world, but nothing could stop the momentum that the Freedom Station incident had caused, all the world needed was an excuse to start a war. The excuse soon presented itself through a simple accident. The Russian complement of Freedom Station had already arrived at the station and was waiting for the American complement, when a routine diagnostic caused a mysteriously explosion that destroyed the Chinese module of the station. The Chinese were furious; they had spent billions of dollars and years of research to build the laboratory module, and claimed that the Russians had destroyed it on purpose as a warning to the Chinese. Allegations of sabotage were thrown around in the United Nations Security Council and on May 1, 1996, the Chinese declared war on the Russian Republic.

Opening Stages of World War III

China quickly consolidated its forces and declared the existence of the Sino-South East Asian Alliance. Members of the alliance included North Korea, Vietnam, Indonesia, and nearly all other countries in South East Asia, with the exception of Taiwan, Japan, and South Korea. The Chinese-led alliance quickly launched its armies against Taiwan and South Korea and before the end of the second month both countries were firmly under the control of the Chinese. The United States of America, living up to its position of defense for both South Korea and Taiwan, declared war on what became known as the Sino Alliance.

With the United States distracted in the Far East, several Arab countries in the Middle East declare war on Israel and several neighboring former Russian Republics. As part of their war effort, these countries cut the world off from all oil produced they produced and force the surrender of all European, American, or Canadian forces within their borders. This sent oil prices skyrocketing and world economy began to collapse, but many western countries instituted special war bonds to keep their economies running for the war efforts. To assist Israel, NATO organized an expeditionary force and sent it to the Middle East through the Persian Gulf, but the fleet was intercepted by a carrier group from India. Not wishing to start a war with India at this stage, NATO withdrew its expeditionary force from the Indian Ocean. The United States pulls most of its forces into the Pacific Ocean to wage its war against the Sino Alliance, but it has little chance of defeating the huge Chinese army.

Africa descends into chaos as several countries, bolstered by military arms sold by the former Soviet Union, declare war on their neighbors. Old tribal feuds, hidden for decades, resurface as leaders feel that the present is a perfect time for revenge.

As the interests of the United States pull it away from the interests of the European countries, NATO becomes sidetracked and the European countries give their full support into the European Union. As part of this new support, a common currency is brought into effect, as is the European Union Reaction Force.

China launches its invasion of Siberia and quickly captures Vladivostok. The degradation of the Russian military is exposed, as more troops run away from the Chinese army then try to fight it. China contains Japan by blockading the island by sea and constantly attacking the island with its massive air force. The United States is forced to operate further and further away from China, as the island bases it maintained since World War II are systematically destroyed by long range cruise missile attacks from

China. Fortunately, the United States is using its own cruise missiles to directly attack China's industrial centers.

The War Grows

In September 1996, India joined the Sino Alliance and brought its army to bear against the nuclear-armed Pakistan. For unknown reasons, the government of Pakistan surrenders to the invading Indians without much of a fight. India proceeded to invade Bangladesh and Sri Lanka before moving its army into Kazakhstan. The Indian navy completely takes control of the Indian Ocean, forcing the remaining NATO ships to fall back into the Pacific and Atlantic Oceans. The European Union forms an alliance with the Russian Republic and deploys a large portion of the EU Reaction Force into Siberia to slow the advancing Chinese army. In an effort to increase the effectiveness of their troops, the United States, in conjunction with the Japanese and the Canadian, develop several prototype power armor suits, although many of these crude designs are eventually copied by the Sino Alliance.

After successfully completing their invasion of Israel, the Arab countries of Egypt, Saudi Arabia, Kuwait, Iran, Jordan, Syria, and Lebanon form the United Arab Empire. The United Arab Empire proceeds to invade the rest of the Arabian Peninsula and Iraq, which requires only two months to finish. Afterwards, the United Arab Empire turns its attention against Europe and begins its invasion through Turkey and into the Balkans. The European Union recalls much of its force back from Russia to stop the invasion from the Middle East.

The Tides of War Begin to Change

Advances in technology continue to shift the war in favor of the United States and the European Union. The European Union Reaction Force easily overpowers the invasion from the Middle East and successfully forces the United Arab Empire to pull back its troops. The EU is once again able to send its forces, now equipped with power armor designed in the United States and Canada, into Russia to slow the advancing Chinese army.

Through superior technology and tactics, the Americans are able to gain total supremacy in the Indian and Pacific Ocean, allowing them to increase their raids against the industrial centers of India, China, and the United Arab Empire. While the Chinese army is slowing in central Siberia and the Indian army is heavily engaged in Kazakhstan, the Americans are continuing to systematically destroy the industrial capabilities of both countries, and it is beginning to have a serious impact on their abilities to continue the war.

With the decreasing support from their industries back in China, the Chinese army is forced to stop its advance and begin to fall back as supplies begin running out along the Siberian front. While not quite the same feet as the storming of the beach at Normandy, the Americans and Canadians succeed in landing an army in northern Russia, which places the army behind the main Chinese army. The American and Canadian army is able to liberate Vladivostok and begin an invasion of northern China, where it finally meets resistance from hastily assembled Chinese reserves.

In February 1998, an experimental nuclear fusion reactor is successfully tested in Princeton University in the United States of America. This new reactor will allow for more powerful military equipment to be built, from tanks and airplanes to ocean ships and power armor. Seeing increasing opportunities for cooperation, the European Union, the Unites States, and Canada begin to coordinate their military actions through NATO.

The second-generation power armor troops from NATO land in Sri Lanka and capture it from the occupying Indian forces. This, coupled with disastrous defeats in Kazakhstan, forced the Indian government to reevaluate its position in the Sino Alliance and it begins to seek a way to end its involvement in the war. The main Chinese army fell back far enough that it had to engage the advancing Russian / European Union army and the American / Canadian army simultaneously.

The Visitor Arrives

It appears that at the current rate, the Sino Alliance would have been forced out of Siberia, but whether the advancing armies would have been able to successfully invade China itself is highly questionable. Even without the actual invasion of China, many soldiers had been killed in the three-year conflict, but nowhere near as bad as the wars that continued to tear Africa apart. What changed the course of the war and the destiny of humankind was a strange visitor from the stars. It passed through the atmosphere above the east coast of the United States and proceeded on a low orbit trajectory towards its final resting place on Macross Island. In its wake, every area that it passed over was devastated; the visitor accomplished in a single night what the Sino Alliance could not accomplish after three years of missile attacks. Hundreds of thousands of people died in the United States as the result of atmospheric disturbances, floods, and earthquakes that followed the visitor during its journey across the sky. The visitor leveled entire cities and the chaos that followed led to the deaths of thousands more.

An immediate ceasefire was called and World War III suddenly ended as the United Nations Security Council learned of a worse danger, a danger from the stars. But in the seeds of the armistice that ended World War III, laid the seeds for many new conflicts that would haunt the world struggling to rebuild and prepare for an invasion from above. As part of the armistice the Sino Alliance withdrew from Russia and Mongolia, but China still retained direct control over Taiwan, Hong Kong, and Macau. Also, India withdrew from the Sino Alliance and all of territory that it had conquered, which included Pakistan, Bangladesh, and most of central Asia. Many of countries in central Asia, already devastated by war, turned to the United Arab Empire to provide them with protection. The only change in the United Arab Empire, besides gaining new territory in central Asia, is the liberation of Israel and the formation of Palestine from the Gaza Strip, the West Bank, and East Jerusalem.

The United Earth Government

After the end of the Cold War, great efforts were made to integrate the world together in a process known as globalization. The end result would be that all parts of the world would be integrated economically so that no one would want for anything. Unfortunately, after only a few years of globalization it became apparent that this would not occur at least for many years. Many companies shut down factories in prosperous counties and relocated them to poor countries where worker wages were lower and less money had to be spent on environmental protection or safety regulations.

This process was mostly put on hold during the Third World War, but it still continued in certain areas. For example, North American companies, cut off from the Asian market, turned to South America, Central America, and Mexico to establish low cost facilities, and over the course of the war, the general technological level in those areas rose dramatically. This culminated with the completion of one of the most advanced semiconductor factory in Costa Rica.

After the armistice that ended the World War III was signed and the true nature of the Visitor was revealed to the permanent members of the United Nations Security Council, serious talks began about creating a permanent defense force that would be controlled by the United Nations. This plan met with immediate problems, as countries that faced each other in war only months earlier attempted to decide how such a defense force would be controlled. After a long period of negotiations between the Sino Alliance, the European Union, the United States, Canada, and a coalition representing the countries of South America, a new international body called the United Earth Government (UEG) was established. This body would be responsible for controlling the new United Earth Defense Force, which would be used to protect the Earth from the alien invaders. The first Prime Minister of the UEG was a former democratic senator from the United States named Harlan J. Niven.

One of the major differences between the United Nations and the United Earth Government was its organization. The United Nations was organized as a collection of governments that were working together to create international committees, whereas the UEG was organized as a government, with a two tiered legislative body and headed by a Prime Minister. The first level of the body was called the Assembly and consisted of 3141 seats that would be distributed based on population to every country in the world with a population over one million and the second level was called the Senate and each country with a population of over a million was given two seats and each country with a population less then one million was given only one seat.

This two-tiered system created some balance, because together, the Sino Alliance and India held a third of the seats in the Assembly, but only four seats in the Senate. The only restriction on who could serve in the Assembly and the Senate is that they must have authority to make independent action. This restriction greatly sped up decisions within the United Earth Government. The Prime Minister was chosen from the Senate, but had to be approved by the Assembly. How the members of the Assembly and Senate were chosen was up to each individual country, but the disposition of seats in the Assembly was calculated every five years, corresponding with the global census held in the years 2000, 2005, and 2010 CE and a new Prime Minister was to be chosen at that time. The Prime Minister was chosen by first establishing a list of candidates, each of which must have been nominated by at least four other countries, and then having an election to choose the top two candidates, and then finally a second election was held to determine which of the two would become the new Prime Minister. Prime Ministers were only allowed to serve a single term, although former Prime Ministers could remain in the Senate for as long as their country of origin chose to allow it.

During this time, the United Earth Defense Force was beginning construction on the Apollo Moon Base in 2000 and Mars Base Sara in 2001, and the decision had been made to use the Visitor, now called the Alien Space Ship-1 (ASS-1), as the flagship for a space fleet to protect the Earth and restoration efforts were beginning and a military base and a community for workers had been built on Macross Island, where the ship had crashed. Also, the United Earth Defense Force had acquired plans to build space ships capable of combat from the United States. These plans would eventually evolve into the Oberth Class Space Destroyer. Among the other technological discoveries related to the ASS-1 were the ground-combat anti-giant weaponry, or "Destroid System," and the all-purpose variable combat system, which would eventually become the Veritech Fighters. Major construction efforts by the United Earth Defense Force include their headquarters in a remote part of Alaska, and the Grand Cannons, which were located in Alaska, Australia, Brazil, the Central African Republic, and Luna (the moon) and began construction in 2002, 2004, 2004, 2005, and 2006 respectively.

The Formation of the Anti-Unification Movement

Within a span of a year, the UEG had established its presence on the world and built its headquarters in Sweden. The United Earth Defense Force was quickly becoming a force to be reckoned with and was spreading across the globe to ensure that every place was protected from alien invaders. But everything was not as perfect as it appeared to be. Across the globe those that had battled against globalization, fought against losing their independence as a country, and fought against becoming friends with those they considered to be their enemies, found that they all faced the same entity, the United Earth Government.

As these groups began joining together and staging protests, rallies, and demonstrations, a movement known as the Anti-Unification Movement was established. This movement was never a single group, but many groups sometimes working independently, sometimes working separately, and sometimes even working against each other. The movement located places in the world where they could gather and use as staging areas, these areas were in Africa and in the Middle East.

The United Arab Empire refused to participate in the United Earth Government in any way and sent its military might against Islamic countries of Northern and Central Africa, such as Libya, Sudan, and Somalia, that also refused to join the UEG. The rest of Africa was still struggling with chaos and many refused to join the United Earth Government if it meant working with their enemies. To combat the situation in Africa, the UEG authorized the use of the United Earth Defense Force to invade the most violent and aggressive countries in hopes of convincing the weaker countries that joining the UEG was better then any other alternative. Unfortunately, the UEG was divided on how to deal with the United Arab Empire, so instead of military action, a trade embargo was established. Unfortunately, the trade embargo created a perfect place for the Anti-Unification Movement to establish a presence outside of UEG jurisdiction.

Outside of the efforts of the United Arab Empire, three major anti-unification groups were formed and laid the foundation for the peak of the movement, which would occur in 2005. The first group, known as Liberty Front, was an amalgamation of several militia groups in the United States and it was well supplied by dissident members of the United States military. The second group had no official name, but it was an ultra-violent faction of the Chinese military that broke from the People's Liberation Army following the end of the Third World War. The group, under the command of Colonel Long, was able to leave the Sino Alliance with a full strength brigade, including tanks, helicopters, and soldiers, and escaped into what was once Afghanistan, but now under the control of the United Arab Empire. The third group, and perhaps the most important, operated from deep within the European Union. The group, known only as the Black Group, consisted of many high ranked political figures throughout the European Union, and with their influence to secretly organize riots and protests.

The Rise of the Anti-Unification Movement

The first major action of the Anti-Unification Movement was staged in May of 2002, when a special-forces company from the United Arab Empire landed on Macross Island and attempted to destroy the ASS-1. The battle lasted several days, and while the soldiers were able to cause severe damage to the facilities around the ship, all of their efforts to actually damage the ASS-1 failed and they were eventually captured or killed by the United Earth Defense Force. This attack created a huge political nightmare for the United Arab Empire; the United Earth Government had evidence that the United Arab Empire had engaged in an act of war. The danger that the UEG was invade hung over the United Arab Empire for many months after the incident, but no invasion occurred as the United Earth Defense Force was still too occupied in Africa.

In 2003, the United Earth Defense Force established a special sub-division called the Robotech Defense Force (RDF), which would command all military forces that utilized the advanced alien technology, called Robotechnology. The RDF would control the new Destroids, the variable fighters, and even the space fleet, but the United Earth Defense Force retained command over the Grand Cannon projects and all suits of power armor. While 2004 saw a rise in violence against the United Earth Government, such as riots in Kazakhstan, Europe, and North America, and several military actions in Africa by the United Arab Empire, the Anti-Unification Movement peaked in 2005. During the month of January, the United Arab Empire sent another military force against Macross Island, and while this group was also destroyed, it cause much more damage to the island and the facilities located there. This battle also marked the first use of Destroids in a real combat situation. In April, 2005, just prior to the election for a new Prime Minister, the current Prime Minister, Harlan J. Niven, was assassinated by people working for the Black Group. Niven's chosen successor, Robert A. Rhysling from Britain, announced that the United Earth Defense Force would not rest until all anti-unification terrorists were stopped.

In July, 2005, Liberty Front began a campaign against the United States government. The group was responsible for attacks against military, political, and commercial targets in over 30 states and is directly responsible for the deaths of thousands. Because of secret internal support for Liberty Front within the US Government, the President called the RDF into America to deal with the terrorist group.

By September, 2005, threats from several anti-unification groups forced the UEG to shut down Mars Base Sara to protect the population of the base. Much of the population of the base was brought onboard the Oberth, the first Oberth Class Space Destroyer, for the journey back to Earth. Unfortunately, the Black Group orchestrated the hijacking of the third Oberth Class Destroyer, the Koroljev, and used it to destroy the Oberth while it was still carrying the people from Mars Base Sara. On its way back to Earth, the Koroljev was attacked and destroyed by the Goddard, under the command of Captain Gloval, who would go on to command the ASS-1 / SDF-1. Suddenly exposed, nearly all members of the Black Group were quickly arrested by the United Earth Defense Force. The European Union also organized a massive internal investigation to clean out any remaining elements of the Black Group.

Following closely after the incident involving the Koroljev, the United Arab Empire launched an attack against the incomplete Grand Cannon II in Australia and the Grand Cannon IV in the

Central African Republic. Both unfinished cannons were destroyed, but the United Arab Empire suffered huge riots protesting the current violence against the United Earth Government. Many groups operating against the regime in control of the United Arab Empire also began receiving secret aid from the United Earth Defense Force.

THE COLLAPSE OF THE ANTI-UNIFICATION MOVEMENT

After many early successes in the United States, Liberty Front was forced into hiding by the Robotech Defense Force. Realizing that Liberty Front had supporters within the government, the President of the United States declared martial law. During the first few months of 2006, the President cleaned the government and congress of all those supporting Liberty Front or other anti-unification terrorists. By June, 2006, Liberty Front had been disbanded and its leaders were captured. Soon after, the President of the United States ordered an end to martial law and resigned from office.

Showing himself for the first time since he abandoned the Sino Alliance, Colonel Long began a three month long siege of Macross Island starting in April of 2006. His forces had occupied nearly all of the surrounding islands and established bases of operations for their attacks. Long's campaign against the United Earth Defense Force and the Robotech Defense Force almost succeed, except for the presence of the CVS-101 Prometheus and the SLV-101 Daedalus, which allowed the United Earth Defense Force to systematically capture each of Long's island bases. By the end of the siege, Colonel Long was killed and his forcers were captured or destroyed by the combined efforts of the Earth Defense Force and the Robotech Defense Force.

In September 2006, the last elements of the Black Group, now completely cut off from all support and hunted by the European Union and the United Earth Government, traveled to the Russian Republic with a small tactical nuclear weapon. The weapon was detonated in the city of St. Petersburg, Russia, and killed hundreds of thousands of people.

By the end of 2006, the last remaining countries in Africa that were rebelling against the UEG put down their weapons and negotiations begin to bring them peacefully into the Organization of African Unity and the United Earth Government.

Throughout 2007 the United Arab Empire struggled with internal dissident elements that were opposing the increasingly oppressive regime. Slowly, country after country separated from the United Arab Empire and declared its independence. Most of these countries sought immediate admittance into the United Earth Government and the Islamic League was formed within the United Earth Government. By the end of the 2007, the United Arab Empire had completely collapsed and from the ashes of the empire came many of the countries that had originally formed it.

Conclusion

The Global Civil War always consisted of two separate parts that have become merged into a single event in the eyes of history. The first part, World War III, was never actually stopped, and many sides were unsatisfied with the results of the war, but found a way to release these feelings through the Anti-Unification Movement, which forms the second part. It is strange to see, but the Anti-Unification Movement was almost successful in pulling apart the UEG. Nearly all militaries on Earth contributed to the movement, but never at the same time.

If it had not been for the Zentraedi Holocaust, which killed 98% of all Humans on Earth, the United Earth Government might have collapsed within a few years of the completion of the SDF-1. As we see from events following the start of the First Robotech War, even the United Earth Defense Force gained a life of its own and was positioning itself for a coup d'état to stay in power if it felt threatened. The only international organization that was successful was the RDF, which had NATO working side by side with former members of the Chinese, Indian, and Russian militaries. It is therefore fortunate that the RDF is one of the few organizations that withstood the Zentraedi Holocaust and served as a model for a world struggling to survive.

4

Hearing on U.S.-India Civil Nuclear Cooperation Initiative

INTRODUCTION

Mr. Chairman and members of the Committee, thank you for inviting Under Secretary Joseph and me to discuss the current state of our relations with India and, specifically the development of full civil nuclear energy cooperation between India and the U.S. The July 18 visit of Indian Prime Minister Manmohan Singh to Washington marked a watershed in our ties with the world's most populous democracy.

President Bush's desire to transform relations with India is based on his conviction that, as he has said, "This century will see democratic India's arrival as a force in the world." We believe it is in our national interest to develop a strong, forward-looking relationship with India as the political and economic focus of the global system shifts toward Asia. We know that many in Congress embrace this view. And the time is right. The Cold War, when India was the ultimate non-aligned nation and the United States the ultimate aligned nation, is long past. It is time to shift our U.S.-India relationship to a new, strategic partnership for the decades ahead. India is a rising global power with a rapidly growing economy. Within the first quarter of this century, it is likely to be included among the world's five largest economies. It will soon be the world's most populous nation, and it has a demographic distribution that bequeaths it a huge, skilled and youthful workforce. India's military forces will continue to be large, capable and increasingly sophisticated. Just like our own, the Indian military remains strongly committed to the principle of civilian control. Above all else, we know what kind of country India will be decades from now. Like the United States, India will thrive as a multi-ethnic, multi-religious and multi-lingual democracy, characterized by individual freedom, rule of law and a constitutional government that owes its power to free and fair elections.

Under Secretary Joseph and I are here as part of a consultation process with both houses of Congress to seek eventually the adjustment of U.S. laws to accommodate civil nuclear trade with India. We are at the very beginning of that process. We will work closely with Congress to determine the best way ahead.

Since President Bush agreed with Prime Minister Singh on this nuclear initiative on July 18, we have discussed with many of you individually where best to begin the decision-making process with Congress. Both of us testified before the House International Relations Committee in September. Secretary Rice has briefed the Senate and House leadership on this initiative. She is eager to engage with you in more detailed discussions in the coming months. We have already had extensive briefings of House and Senate staff, and we even invited House staff to attend with us the meeting of the Nuclear Suppliers Group in Vienna two weeks ago dealing with the Indian civil nuclear issue. In short, we have shared with the Congress our rationale for the July 18 agreement and have consulted consistently and in detail on our discussions with the Indian government since that time.

Secretary Rice, Under Secretary Joseph and I look forward to continuing this dialogue. We recognize that the pace and scope of the initiative requires close consultation with Congress and we welcome your suggestions and advice as we move forward.

Indeed, we cannot go forward on this initiative without the express consent of Congress. The advent of full U.S. civil nuclear cooperation with India requires adjustments in U.S. law. I had the privilege of negotiating the July 18 agreement for the U.S. and remain the principal negotiator with the Indian government. Based on my visit to New Delhi two weeks ago, it is clear that it will take some time for the Indian government to fulfill all of the commitments it made in the July 18 agreement. The actions India committed to undertake are difficult, complex and time-consuming. The Administration thus believes it is better to wait before we ask Congress to consider any required legislative action until India is further along in taking the necessary steps to fulfill our agreement. I believe that will likely be in early 2006.

Our judgment is that it would not be wise or fair to ask Congress to make such a consequential decision without evidence that the Indian government was acting on what is arguably the most important of its commitments - the separation of its civilian and military nuclear facilities. I told the Indian leadership in Delhi two weeks ago that it must craft a credible and transparent plan and have begun to implement it before the Administration would request Congressional action. My counterpart, Foreign Secretary Shyam Saran, assured me that the Indian government will produce such a plan. He stressed last week to a domestic audience at the New Delhi-based Institute of Defense Studies and Analyses, "It makes no sense for India to deliberately keep some of its civilian facilities out of its declaration for safeguards purposes, if it is really interested in obtaining international cooperation on as wide a scale as possible." As India begins to meet its commitments under our agreement, we will propose appropriate language that would be India-specific and would demonstrate our dedication to a robust and permanent partnership.

I have invited Foreign Secretary Saran to Washington in December to continue our talks, and I intend to return to India in January to further our understanding of India's plans to separate its civil and military nuclear facilities. We will, of course, keep the Congress fully apprised of all these discussions. We hope very much that India can make the necessary progress to allow us to refer legislation to Congress by early 2006.

THE CIVIL NUCLEAR COOPERATION INITIATIVE

Mr. Chairman, you requested that we answer three questions in this hearing: first, why is it necessary to draw closer to India; second, how would U.S. concerns about India's nonproliferation policies be addressed by this agreement; and, third, will our proposed policy change apply to countries other than India. Under Secretary Joseph and I will respond to each of your questions.

When Secretary Rice set out last spring to develop the structure of such a partnership, we knew we would have to deal with the one issue that has bedeviled U.S.-India relations for the last 30 years - the nuclear issue. We determined from the start that we could not recognize India as a nuclear weapons state. Such a step would weaken fundamentally the nuclear Nonproliferation Treaty (NPT) and would be logically inconsistent with U.S. policy under the last seven American presidents. It was equally clear that India would not become a party to the NPT as a non-nuclear weapons state.

We also knew that we would have to confront the more difficult and complex issue of whether to work with India on full civil nuclear cooperation. India had made this the central issue in the new partnership developing between our countries. As you know, past Administrations had decided to forego such civil cooperation with India due to India's nuclear weapons program and its status outside the nonproliferation regime. We had to decide whether this policy remained consistent with U.S. interests in building a strong nonproliferation regime and with our obvious priority of improving relations with the world's largest democracy.

Because India developed nuclear weapons outside the regime, we had no existing cooperation between our civil nuclear energy industries and, as such, no real influence on India's adherence to the critical international nonproliferation standards that are the bedrock of our efforts to limit the spread of nuclear technology. While not formally part of the NPT regime, India has demonstrated a strong commitment to protect fissile materials and nuclear technology. Indeed, as other responsible countries with advanced nuclear technology, India has resisted proposals for nuclear cooperation with nuclear aspirants that could have had adverse implications for international security.

We weighed the pros and cons of whether or not to seek changes to U.S. policy and ask Congress for authorization to begin full civil nuclear energy cooperation.

We decided that it was in the American interest to bring India into compliance with the standards and practices of the international nonproliferation regime. And, we decided that the only way to reach that goal was to end India's isolation and begin to engage it. India will soon have the largest population in the world, and to consign it to a place outside that system did not appear to bestrategically wise and has not proven effective.

Withoutsuch an agreement, India, with its large and sophisticated nuclear capabilities, would continue to remain outside the international export control regimes governing commerce in sensitive nuclear and nuclear-related technologies. With this agreement, given India's solid record in stemming and preventing the proliferation of its nuclear technology over the past 30 years, the U.S. and the international community will benefit by asking India to open up its system, to separate its civil and military nuclear facilities, and to submit to international inspections and safeguards on its civil facilities, thus allowing it to bring its civil nuclear program into effectiveconformity with international standards.

India will assume the same nonproliferation responsibilities as other responsible nations with civil nuclear energy and will protect against diversion of items either to India's weapons program or to other countries. U.S.-Indian cooperation on nuclear energy will therefore help strengthen the international order in a way that advances widespread international equities in nuclear nonproliferation. It also will allow India to develop much more quickly its own civilian nuclear power industry, thus reducing demands on the world energy market and in a way that provides clean energy for the future.

This was not an easy choice. We do not live in an ideal world. We concluded we had a better chance to have India meet international nonproliferation standards if we engaged rather than isolated it. We believe the resulting agreement advances our strategic partnership and is a net gain for nonproliferation. We do not plan to offer such cooperation to any other country.

In addition to aligning ourselves with a country that shares our democratic values and commitment to a multi-ethnic, multi-religious society, developing civil nuclear cooperation with India will bring concrete benefits to the U.S. and to the international community more broadly. Under Secretary Joseph will address this initiative in detail, but let me outline here some of the key reasons why we believe this initiative makes excellent sense:

- Security Benefits: All the steps that India pledged on July 18 strengthen the international nonproliferation regime, and all align with our efforts to prevent the spread of weapons of mass destruction. India's September vote in the International Atomic Energy Agency (IAEA) that found Iran in noncompliance with its nuclear obligations reflects India's coming of age as a responsible state in the global nonproliferation mainstream.
- Environmental Benefits: Nuclear energy is one of the few proven sources of energy that does not emit greenhouse gases, and thus can help India modernize in an environmentally friendly manner that does not damage our common atmosphere and contribute to global warming.
- Commercial Benefits: As a result of our involvement in India's civil nuclear industry, U.S. companies will be able to enter India's lucrative and growing energy market, potentially providing jobs for thousands of Americans.
- Energy Benefits: India's expertise in basic science and applied engineering will add significant resources and substantial talent in the development of fusion as a cheap energy source if India can participate in the International Thermonuclear Experimental Reactor (ITER) program and help make the next generation of reactors safer, more efficient and more proliferation-resistant as a member of the Generation-IV Forum (GIF).

The Broader Relationship

Although our civil nuclear initiative has garnered the most attention, it is only part of a much broader and deeper strategic partnership with India, something that has not really been possible until now. In late June, Defense Minister Pranab Mukherjee and Secretary of Defense Donald Rumsfeld signed a New Defense Framework that will guide our defense relations for the next decade. We're planning to enlarge defense trade, improve cooperation between our armed forces, and co-produce military hardware. The brilliant cooperation of our two militaries during the response to the Tsunami disaster last December was a remarkable testament to how far we have come, and the great potential we have for the future. A strong, democratic India is an important partner for the United States. We anticipate that India will play an increasingly important leadership role in 21st Century Asia, working with us to promote democracy, respect for human rights, economic growth, stability and peace in that vital region. By cooperating with India now, we accelerate the arrival of the benefits that India's rise brings to the region and the world.

By fostering ever-closer bilateral ties, we also eliminate the possibility that our two nations might overlook their natural affinities and enter into another period of unproductive estrangement as was so often the case during the Cold War period. By challenging India today, with a full measure of respect for its ancient civilization, traditions and accomplishments, we can help it realize its full potential as a natural partner in the struggle against the security challenges of the coming generation, and the global threats that are flowing over, under and through our respective national borders.

I visited New Delhi two weeks ago and held an extensive series of discussions with senior Indian officials on the range of our foreign policy interests. While there, I had broad-ranging discussions on many issues, everything from HIV/AIDS to the situation in Nepal to our concerns about Iran. The July 18 Joint Statement calls for government-to-government joint cooperation in many areas, including civil nuclear cooperation; a U.S.-India Global Democracy Initiative; an expanded U.S.-India Economic Dialogue focusing on trade, finance, the environment, and commerce; continued cooperation in science and technology; an Energy Dialogue to strengthen energy security and promote stable energy markets, an Agricultural Knowledge Initiative, an Information and Communications Technology Working Group; Space Cooperation; a U.S.-India Disaster Response Initiative; and the U.S.-India HIV/AIDS Partnership.

Foreign Secretary Saran and I have already begun working on the joint ventures that the President and Prime Minister Singh had asked us to undertake and plan to further our cooperation in the fields of education, in agriculture, in science and technology, and in space. We very much would like to welcome an Indian astronaut to fly on the space shuttle. I think it is clear that our interests converge on all these issues. With this ambitious agenda, our two countries are becoming, in effect, global partners.

Cooperation in several of these areas has already begun and is yielding results. Just last month, the U.S.-India Treaty on Mutual Legal Assistance in Criminal Matters entered into force, providing for enhanced, streamlined and more effective law enforcement cooperation between our two countries. On October 17, Secretary Rice and Indian Science and Technology Minister Sibal signed an umbrella Science and Technology Agreement that will strengthen U.S. and Indian capabilities and expand relations between the extensive scientific and technological communities of both countries This agreement includes a substantive Intellectual Property Rights (IPR) provision -- another indication of India's increasing recognition of the need to respect intellectual property.

The Challenges We Face

We have accomplished much, but we have just scratched the surface of our partnership with India. Ambassador Mulford and his outstanding team in New Delhi, aided by frequent high-level visitors to the sub-continent over the next several months, will continue to pursue this expanding agenda.

We want the U.S. and India to work together more effectively than we have in the past to become more effective global partners. Let me provide a few examples. On the political side of the ledger, we will be seeking early tangible progress with India towards:

o Creating a closer U.S.-India partnership to help build democratic institutions in the region and worldwide. During the Prime Minister's visit to Washington, our two leaders agreed for the first time to work together to promote democracy worldwide. Both countries have contributed to the UN's Democracy Fund. We will seek ways to work together in strengthening democratic institutions and practices in specific countries. India's experiment in democracy has been a success for over half a century, and its 2004 national polls were the largest exercise in electoral democracy the world has ever seen. We share a belief that democracy and development are linked, that effective democratic governance is a precondition to healthy economic development. In this regard, we hope India will share its democratic experience with Central

Asian nations, which are having a difficult time making the transition from authoritarianism to democracy, and assist them in building institutions necessary to the success of democracy and the advancement of human rights.

- o Advancing our shared interest in reform at the United Nations. Members of this Committee know well the President's deep desire to promote reform at the United Nations. This is a top priority for this Administration, and India as well. We want a far more vigorous Indian engagement with us in the ongoing process of reforming the UN into an organization that serves the interests of its members. I think both our countries would agree that this process should neither be politicized nor subjected to the sort of country bloc calculations that prevailed during the Cold War. India has much to offer in moving reform efforts ahead.
- o Indian participation in the Proliferation Security Initiative. India boasts one of the world's largest commercial maritime fleets and a Navy that demonstrated its rapidly growing expeditionary capacity in responding to the December tsunami. Indian support for the multi-national Proliferation Security Initiative (PSI) would be a boon to the participating nations' goal of tracking and interdicting dangerous terrorist and weapons of mass destruction (WMD) cargoes world-wide. We hope India will choose to join PSI.
- o U.S.-India cooperation for regional peace and stability. India is one of the largest international donors to Afghanistan's reconstruction and works closely with us in the areas of road construction, public health, education, telecommunications, and human resource development. India and the United States share the goal of a return to democracy in Nepal and a defeat of the Maoist insurgency. In Sri Lanka, we both support the government's efforts to recover from the tsunami and return to the peace process. We should do more to promote human rights and democracy in autocratic Burma. Our two countries should work more closely to promote peace and stability in Asia.

o Convincing Iran to return to negotiations. India and the U.S. have found an increasingly positive dialogue on Iran. We are both dedicated to the goal of an Iran that lives in harmony in its region, ends support of terrorist groups and does not seek nuclear weapons. We welcomed India's vote with us at the IAEA in September to find Iran in noncompliance with its international obligations. We appreciate India's belief that Iran should not acquire a nuclear weapons capability, and India's continuing cooperation with the U.S. and Europe is essential to convince Iran to return to negotiations.

We and India also need to focus on a number of important economic challenges, both bilateral and global. Since the early 1990s, India has progressed far in liberalizing its tariff regime and investment environment, and these major changes have fueled the growth and increased prosperity of recent years. Any quick survey of India's economic landscape provides thousands of examples of innovation and excellence. India is increasingly a global competitor in knowledge-based industries such as information and communications technology and biotechnology research and development. Despite its impressive record of economic growth during the last decade, India still struggles with many of the persistent challenges faced by developing countries: insufficient and underdeveloped infrastructure, inefficient markets for goods and services, and minimal access of credit and capital among the urban and rural poor. In addition, India also suffers from a shortage of foreign capital and investment, which can bring in key, new technologies, create jobs, and modernize industries. In this new partnership, the U.S. and India have a great opportunity to work together to overcome these challenges, toward the continued prosperity of our peoples, and to play a positive role in shaping the world's economic future. The ongoing negotiations in the World Trade Organization (WTO) in the Doha Development Round offer the perfect opportunity to work on our shared goals of trade, development, and prosperity.

Both India and the United States stand to gain from the increasing liberalization of trade in goods and services, and in convincing our trading partners to do the same. There is no reason why India and the U.S. should not be partners in this forum, whose success is so crucial to our common future. We plan to work closely with India on proposals that can translate the promise of the WTO's mission - and the new era of U.S.-India relations - into reality. This effort will take hard work on both sides, and we look forward to this opportunity to engage India seriously, to the economic betterment of both our people. As we build closer economic relations, we look forward to India's agreement to purchase American civil and military aircraft and to open its doors further to trade with our country.

Building People-to-People and Private Sector Cooperation between India and the U.S.

The new U.S.-India partnership is not and cannot be just between governments. We have seen an equally powerful expansion of our people-to-people ties and business growth. The immense power of the India-U.S. people-to-people network goes deeper than anyone could have ever imagined. We find thousands of Americans in Delhi, in Mumbai and Bangalore, and even more Indians in New York, Washington and Los Angeles. Over 85,000 Americans are living in India, lured by its growing economy and the richness of its culture. There are 2 million persons of Indian origin in the United States, citizens and legal permanent residents. They are operating businesses in our country, running for political office and building bridges back to India. There are more Indian students in the United States today than from any other country in the world -- 80,000. We have, in essence, the development of a true, comprehensive, across the board, engagement between India and the United States, our governments, our societies and our peoples. This engagement by individuals and businesses will propel and sustain the formal ties between our governments.

CONCLUSION

I am pleased to have had the opportunity to share with you the many elements of this strategic transformation that we are witnessing in the U.S.-India relationship. Both President Bush and Prime Minister Singh have shown the confidence and vision to pursue a common vision for the world together. We hope the Congress will help us make that vision a reality.

5

India China War

THE WESTERN SECTOR

The disputed territories between China and India are located at a no-man's land, where nothing grows and no one lives, on high altitude Himalayas, one of the most barren regions of the world. For centuries, the Himalayas was the focal point of military and political maneuvers between the three empires, the Russians in the north, the British on the subcontinent and the Chinese over the other side of the Himalayas. A constant and basic British aim was to keep the Russians as far as possible from the plains of India. The British and Russians made Afghanistan to play as buffer between them to avoid collision, but their attempts to make China as a buffer failed as the Chinese refused to cooperate.

In 1846, after the British took Kashmir and set it up as the northern frontier, they tried to demarcate a boundary with Tibet at Ladakh, which lay in the valley of the upper Indus at an altitude of twelve thousand feet or more. It had been part of Tibet up to the tenth century, when it became an independent kingdom. In the sixteenth century, it became a tributary state of the Mongol Empire, and in the nineteen century, it was regarded as part of Tibet again. In 1846, since neither the Chinese nor Tibetans cooperated with Britain, no demarcation of the Tibet-Ladakh boundary took place. In 1846 and 1847, the British commissioners drew boundaries in north of the Pangong Lake and stopped at the Karakoram Pass but could not correctly define the northwest boundaries of Tibet. Aksai Chin, which became the heart of contention between India and China a century later, lay between the Lake and the Pass. At 17,000 feet elevation, the desolation of Aksai Chin had no human importance other than an ancient trade route that crossed over it, providing a brief pass during summer for caravans of yaks from Sinkiang to Tibet that carried silk, jade, hemp, salt or wool.

By the 1860s, the Russians forced China to sign the treaties of Aigun and Peking. China lost a great tract of territory in Central Asia to Russia, which took all the north of the Amur River and east of its tributary, cutting off China from the Sea of Japan. China decided not to negotiate boundary settlements from a weak position, and persisted with this approach until the middle of the 1950s. In early 1880s, China and India agreed the Karakoram Pass as the fixed point of boundary, while leaving both sides of the pass indefinite. In the mid-1890s, China claimed Aksai Chin as its territory, and voiced the claim to Macartney in 1896, who drew part of the British boundary in the Himalayas. Macartney presented the claim to the British who agreed with his comment that part of Aksai Chin was in China and part in the British territory. Meanwhile, the forward school of British strategist in London suggested that the British should not only include the whole of Aksai Chin, but also all the territory given to Kashmir in 1865.

In 1899, however, the British proposed a boundary demarcation with the Macartney-MacDonald line, which gave China the whole of the Karakash Valley, and almost all of Aksai Chin proper while pushing the British boundary forward on the Karakoram range, but China never replied to the proposal. By the first decade of the twentieth century, the British adhered to the 1899 proposal and aimed at making Aksai Chin as part of Tibet, rather than Sinkiang. In 1911, the collapse of the Chinese power in central Asia prompted the British to revise its objective of keeping Russia away from the plains of India. The British had long expected the Russian annexation of Sinkiang. The forward school of strategist recommended to place Aksai Chin outside Russia but within British territory. The London Government ignored the recommendation, and held to the 1899 proposal and in the Simla Convention in 1914 still placed Aksai Chin as part of Tibet. Up until the end of British rule, Britain had never attempted to exert authority on Aksai Chin or establish posts in it.

For the first decade of the twentieth century, Britain attempted to establish exclusive influence over Tibet. When the British first arrived, Nepal, Sikkim, and Bhutan were all in various degrees of dependence upon or allegiance to China. Nepal was created by a Hindu hill-people invading Tibet in the eighteen century. In 1792, the Chinese troops defeated their invasion of Tibet and left Nepal a tributary of China. Lhasa took Sikkim as a Tibetan dependency, and periodically asserted suzerainty over Bhutan. The British considered the Tibetan, and indirectly the Chinese, dominance as a challenge to its rule. In the nineteenth century, Britain achieved the reversal of the allegiance of the Himalayan states by converting Nepal, Sikkim, and Bhutan as a chain of protectorates. With that, the British were content comfortably with their boundary beneath the Himalayan foothills.

To the east of Bhutan lay another no-man's land, demarcating the boundary and presented as both worry and temptation for the British India. In 1873, the British drew a line at the foothills called "Inner Line" to protect the zone beneath the hills. The international boundary comprised of the Outer Line, which ran along the southern border of Bhutan and the foothills leading to the Tibetan tableland. Around the British territory in the northwest, Tawang was the only salient wedge of territory, administered through the great monastery of Tawang in the north and populated by Buddhist tribes deeply influenced the Tibetan culture. In 1907, Britain entered into an agreement with Russia in an Anglo-Russian Convention and set up Tibet as a buffer state, like Afghanistan. The British viewed China as a passive or almost neutral element in its diplomacy. But in the first decade of the twentieth century, as the Manchu dynasty ended, Chinese policy changed sharply in Tibet.

Military presence was extended through central Tibet, and more modern institutions replaced the theocratic and ancient machinery of administration, which reducing the role of the Dalai Lama and the power of the monastic orders. By 1910, China had established effective power in Tibet, and the buffer for India to keep Russia away was lost, as the Morning Post in London wrote: "A great Empire, the future military strength of which no man can foresee, has suddenly appeared on the North-East Frontier of India."

The British was concerned that China would pose a strategic threat to India, and the forward school recommended more active patrolling in the hills beyond the frontier. It was decided that if China attacked India, Britain would attack China from the sea. The Chief of the General Staff warned of the dangerous pressure through Tawang Tract, and recommended bringing not only Tawang but also a sizeable slice of Tibet into India. From 1911, the Indian government embarked on a deliberate advance of the northeastern boundary. In order not to invite a vigorous Chinese protest, the Indian military made secrete expeditions into the Tibetan tribal belts of Assam which British took for India twenty years ago, bypassing the Parliament's permission. Although it was outside of the external frontiers, the official British maps showed it as part of the frontier. The officials fobbed that "it is not intended to increase the area administered by" the Indian government. The statement was literally true since the Inner Line was not changed, but it was the Outer Line that was advanced.

In 1911-12, the Chinese power in Tibet suddenly collapsed. The British decided that it was in their strategic and political interest to exclude effective Chinese power from Tibet. In 1913, British convoked a conference at Simla which was aimed at making Tibet a buffer state between Britain and China, like the buffer effect to keep the Russians away. McMahon, the Foreign Secretary of the Indian government, led the British delegation to attend the Simla Conference. The British made open effort to make China accept a division of Tibet into Inner and Outer Tibet, as the agreement made by China and Russia in the case of Mongolia. China would have suzerainty over the whole of Tibet, but would have no administrative rights in Outer Tibet, thereby keeping back from the borders of India. The coercive diplomatic methods of Britain brought the weak and unwilling China to the conference.

The Chinese representatives stressed the paramount importance of Tibet and resisted its zonal division, keenly aware of the British effort to separate Tibet or at least a great part of it from China. In April 1914, McMahon induced the Chinese official, Ivan Chen, to initiate a draft treaty, but the Chinese government repudiated the unauthorized compliance immediately. McMahon presented the draft to the British, which plainly cancelled its validity. In July, the conference was closed without Chinese signing the convention. London had instructed McMahon all along not to sign bilaterally with Tibetans if China refused, but McMahon proceeded to sign with the Tibetan representative while Ivan Chen was sent to the next room.

Chen was not told of what was being signed and the declaration was kept as secret for many years. Although all this provided much fertile ground for international lawyers, the results of the conference were clear, and was accepted as such by the British Government at the time: the Simla Conference produced no agreement to which the government of China was a party. McMahon admitted this himself: "It is with great regret that I leave India without have secured the formal adherence of the Chinese Government to a Tripartite Agreement." China had emphatically and repeatedly denied that Tibet enjoyed sovereign identity and that China would not recognize any bilateral agreement between Tibet and Britain.

A covert byproduct of the Simla Conference was the McMahon Line. It came as a result of the secret discussions, without the Chinese participation or knowledge, which took place in Delhi between the British and the Tibetans in February and March of 1914. These meetings breached not only the Anglo-Chinese Convention of 1906, in which Britain was to "engage not to annex Tibetan territory," but also of the Anglo-Russian Convention of 1907, in which Britain was to engage "not to enter into negotiations with Tibet except through the intermediary of the Chinese Government." The British moved the line progressively to the north of Tawang, which was still short of the goal proposed by the Chief of the General Staff to annex some two thousand square miles of Tibetan territory. McMahon Line essentially pushed the boundary northward about sixty miles, and moved it from the foothills to the crest line of the Assam Himalayas.

In doing so, McMahon accomplished for British India what other officials attempted twenty years ago on the Afghan frontier, and brought the tribal no-man land under nominal British sovereignty. China forcefully repudiated the convention and denied the validity of the map, and the Tibetans in practice ignored the Line. In 1919, the British tried once more to induce China to resume the tripartite negotiations. After China refused, the British began providing military aid to Tibetans, including arms, ammunitions, and training in their use. When the British relinquished the Indian Empire in 1947, they started to translate the McMahon Line from the maps as the effective northwest boundary of India, despite that the Line appeared on its maps only ten years before. As the British departed, the new Indian government assured that they would complete their work: "If anything, they intended to pursue an even more forward policy than had the British."

COLLISION COURSE

The Course is Set

With their independence on August 14, 1947, the status of the boundaries of India changed from the pawns for the British to play with their imperial rivals, to become the cell walls of a new national identity. The Indian government followed closely the footsteps of the British colonists. In 1949, India sent troops during an uprising in Sikkim and brought the state as a protectorate. In the same year, India signed a treaty to take over Britain's rights to guide Bhutan in foreign affairs. In 1950, India increased its control over Nepal and consolidated the "chain of protectorates" in the Himalayan states. Towards Tibet, the new Indian Government followed the British mission in encouraging Tibetan separatism. In its strategic and geopolitical thinking inherited from the British, the Indian Government continued the exclusion of China's authority from Tibet and attempted to increase the Indian influence. The Tibetans hoped that the transfer of British power to the Indians would give them an opportunity to regain the territory that British took from them a century before. In October 1947, they formally requested India to return their territory from Ladakh to Assam, and including Sikkim. The Indians in return simply asked Tibet to continue the relationship on the basis of the previous British Government.

The Indian plan to continue with British policy was met with major challenges. The absence of the British power and emergence of a strong central authority with the establishment of the Communist China reversed the power balance. With the announcement of Chinese military marching into Tibet, India reacted sharply and threatened that it would support the position of the Nationalist rump on Formosa rather than the People's Republic of China in the United Nations. A few days later, Chinese army entered Tibet, and Indian government headed by the Prime Minister Nehru issued an angry protest, deploring the "invasion" of Tibet. China replied sharply: "Tibet is an integral part of China, and the problem of Tibet is entirely a domestic problem of China," and warned that it would not tolerate foreign interference.

In response to India's avowal that the use of military would injure China's reputation in the world, China stated that any governments that interfere with China's sovereign rights in Tibet as a pretext to obstruct China's membership in the UN would further demonstrate their hostility. Indian government changed the China's "sovereignty" to "suzerainty" over Tibet and hoped that China would leave domestic affairs to Tibetans like what Indians did in Bhutan. China viewed the Indian desire to have semi-independence in Tibet as a preliminary attempt to draw Tibet under Indian influence, an inference neither far-fetched nor unfair. When China later established diplomatic relations with Nepal, China became an open competitor in what India regarded as diplomatic reserve. In 1950, after its failed attempt to have some degrees of Tibetan independence and buffer, the Indian government adopted a pragmatic policy of pursuing friendship with China, a central element in India's foreign policy formulated by Nehru. As China confirmed its authority in Tibet, India did not support the appeal of Tibet to the UN.

The presence of Chinese power in the northern borders alarmed the political rights in India, who feared the Communist China the most. The Opposition criticized the Tibet policy of Nehru and the Government, and accused them of complacency and vacillation. Fundamental reappraisal of China policy was proposed, and India was to deploy forces to guard potentially disputed areas. While maintaining the policy of friendship to China and advocating on behalf of China in the United Nations, Nehru ordered Indian administration to extend at the tribal belt beneath the McMahon Line through the North-East Frontier Agency. In a year, twenty posts were extended into NEFA, and several hundreds porters and escorts moved into Tawang without challenging the Tibetan administration there. The Indian government decided not to modify McMahon Line and push their boundary up from Se La to the McMahon Line. In response to the protests of the Tibetan authorities in Lhasa, the Indian officials stated that India was taking over Tawang. The Tibetans protested again that they "deeply regret and absolutely cannot accept' what the Indian government "seizing as its own what did not belong to it." The Indian government ignored the protests, forced the Tibetan administration out, and stayed on in Tawang, as the British did in Dirang Dzong in 1944.

With this, the Indian government overcame the "dangerous wedge" of Tibetan/Chinese territory that so concerned the British General Staff. Having their verbal resistance ignored, the Tibetans took a toll in blood the Indian extension. One of the Tibetan tribes warmly welcomed a strong patrol comprising seventy-four riflemen and civilians from Assam. The Tibetans feasted and gave them shelter, and then massacred all but one. Nehru ordered an overwhelming show of force, rather than burning the villages or imprisoning the Tibetans as would have done by the British. The McMahon Line was formally transported from the maps to the ground, and was set as the de facto northeast boundary of India. To deal with China about the repudiated McMahon Line, the British provided part of the solution, that India would simply treat McMahon Line as the boundary and leave it to China to protest. Indian Government decided to push the boundary settlement from diplomacy to an absolutist approach, that "India would refuse to open the question to negotiation when or if the Chinese did raise it." In November 1950, the Government unilaterally declared the McMahon Line as their boundary, "map or no map" we will not allow anybody to come across that boundary," as Nehru declared.

In September 1951, the Chinese Prime Minister Chou En-lai, proposed to the Indian ambassador to stabilize the Tibetan frontier through discussions between India, China and Nepal, confirming that China had decided to accept the McMahon Line as India's northwest boundary. But India passed the opportunity to formalize the McMahon Line. In July 1952, when China proposed to settle "pending problems" related to commercial intercourse and trade in Tibet, the boundary question was not raised. There was doubt in India about the decision not to raise the boundary questions with China. But it was decided that McMahon Line might be the "scars left by Britain in the course of her aggression against China" and that to "seek to heal or ease this scar" was not in the liking or interest of India. The Indian government was fully aware that China, "never having accepted "as the frontier between Tibet and us," would not regard the McMahon Line as the settled boundary. They decided to treat the Line as the boundary and leave it for China to either agree or ignore the statement. In 1954, when the Indian delegation went to negotiate trade and intercourse in Tibet, they even went out of their way to avoid the subject.

The agreement stated the famous "Five Principles of Peaceful Co-existence," or "Panch Sheel" as Indians called them, the first of which was "mutual respect for each other's territorial integrity and sovereignty." China's sovereignty in Tibet was unequivocally recognized, and the British attempts and latter Indian attempts to treat Tibet as independent were formally buried. India formed a crucial China policy that India would make clear and treat what India regarded as proper boundary, leaving it to China to protest, and then "refuse to reopen the question." Based on the first principal of the Panch Sheel, China would have not choice but to accept the boundary. It was understood, based on Chinese acquiescence in the 1951 Indian takeover of Tawang, that China was going to accept the McMahon Line. The decision not to renegotiate transformed a boundary problem into a dispute, which then progressed into a border war. China maintained that parts of the boundaries were undetermined and to be negotiated. Indians held that the boundaries were already determined and decided to establish checkposts all along them.

In 1954, the official Indian map made sharp changes in the northern boundaries. The British earlier made Aksai Chin a strategic area to keep Russian advance from India, but never proposed it as a boundary and reflected in the extension of administration, which was far beyond the British capacity. However, India categorically claimed Aksai Chin as part of the northern border and Nehru ruled it as "a firm and definite one which was not open to discussion with anybody." Thus far, the claim remained on the official map change and not reflected on the ground. The Indian posts were set in Ladakh, far short of Aksai Chin. In September 1954, it was decided that border posts should be advanced as far as possible into the disputed areas.

The forward move into the middle sector brought prompt Chinese protests that Indian troops had intruded into Chinese territory and violated the principles of non-aggression and friendly co-existence. The Indian government responded that the territory belonged to India and asked China to keep the personnel out. The Tibetans had so far controlled the middle sectors of the boundary passes, and an annual race occurred to get to the high point before the other side. The Indian government accused China of aggression, while in fact the two border forces came into contact as a result of the forward move made by the Indians, a fact that Nehru confirmed to the Parliament years later. The reversed accusation by India, that it was China who "probe forward," took place before the ink was dry on the Panch Sheel agreement and was universally believed.

Aksai Chin was easily accessible from the Chinese side as an ancient trade route wedging from Sinkiang across the plateau to Tibet. It was more difficult for the Indians to reach, as it led to nowhere for them. Through the first half of the 1950s, China used the Aksai Chin route to supply western Tibet and built a total length of seven hundred and fifty miles of road, of which one hundred and twelve crossed the territory claimed by India. By 1958, on the east, the Indians completed the unfinished work left by the British in claiming the McMahon Line as boundary and asserting administration over the tribal territory from Tawang, which was renamed as North-East Frontier Agency (NEFA) listed as Indian territory. On the west, the road built across Aksai Chin had become the main traffic artery between Sinkiang and Tibet. The two sides left each other alone, and the boundary problem went faraway from resolving itself.

From 1950 on, Nehru had no peers in the Indian government and acted as the Prime Minister, Defense Minister, and took on the presidency of the Congress Party, and retained the portfolio of External Affairs until his death in 1964. Nehru often made crucial foreign policy decisions without the awareness of the committees or the Cabinet. One Finance Minister resigned in 1956 after complaining Nehru's "cavalier and unconstitutional" methods. Nehru visited China in 1939 and again in 1954, and was much impressed by the "terrifying strength," the energy and discipline that the Chinese demonstrated in their nation building. The domestic oppositions attacked Nehru for his China policy as appeasement. But in the middle 1950s, the resentment at the assertion of Chinese authority in Tibet died down and was replaced with the popular policy of Hindee Chinee bhai-bhai, or India-China brotherhood.

In 1956, Chou En-lai returned Nehru's visit and was cheered by large crowds. Chou raised the subjects of the McMahon Line. Nehru warned Chou that the Burmese were displeased about the two big neighbors and suggested China to take steps to remove Burma's misgivings. Chou told Nehru that China had accepted the McMahon Line, albeit established by the British imperialists as unfair, as the boundary with Burma because of the friendly relations between China, India and other countries concerned. Chou reaffirmed that the Chinese Government approached the alignment established by former imperialist neighbors as effective boundary, including the Sino-Russian boundary on the Ussuri and Amur Rivers. The Indians made the McMahon Line as the de facto boundary only five years ago, but China treated the "accomplished fact" as effective boundary. This was the only practical way for China to go on without creating intractable and poisonous disputes with every neighbor. However, China would not simply confirm the McMahon Line that had no treaty basis, but was prepared to accept the alignment in negotiation with India.

In October 1958, after discovering the Aksai Chin road, the Indian Government claimed that the territory had been "part of the Ladakh region of India for centuries." India expressed "surprise and regret" to Peking that the Chinese government constructed "a road through indisputably Indian territory without first obtaining the permission of the Government of India." The note further inquired of a missing Indian patrol. China counter complained that an Indian armed personnel was detained for having intruded into Chinese territory, and asked India to comply with the five principles of peaceful co-existence. With conflict of claims over Aksai China came into open, the Indian Government replied that it was "a matter in dispute," the only time it conceded of the disputed nature of the area before reversing its position in a few weeks. Chinese maps continued to show the Sino-Indian border along the foothills and had the whole of Aksai Chin in China. China expected to discuss the boundary before confirming the alignment. But New Delhi suspected the rational approach as an alarm that China was to advance territorial claims, and the distrust soon became resentful hostility. In December 1958, Nehru wrote Chou En-lai a friendly letter expressing that India had been "under the impression that there were no border disputes" during Chou's visit in 1956.

Chou En-lai replied with equal affability stating that "the Sino-Indian boundary has never been formally delimited" and that "historically no treaty or agreement on the Sino-Indian boundary has ever been concluded" between the Chinese and Indians Governments. Chou En-lai stated that there were border disputes and suggested settling by mutual consultation and joint survey. As Nehru was categorical about the entire boundary, Chou was categorical about Aksai Chin as it "has always been under Chinese jurisdiction" and that the Chinese guards have continually patrolled it. Chou further raised the illegality of the McMahon Line as the product of the British policy of aggression against the Tibetan Region of China, but stated that, in light of the friendly relations China had with India and Burma, China would accept the McMahon alignment as the boundary. Chou En-lai proposed the maintenance of the status quo before the boundary was formally settled. Nehru rejected Chou's proposal and suggested China to evacuate from Aksai Chin and made it an absolute precondition for discussion of the borders. The Indian Government did not take as adamant position as in negotiations with Pakistan over Kashmir.

In 1959, the Tibetan armed uprising failed in Lhasa and the Dalai Lama fled through the old trade route across the McMahon Line to Tawang, where Indian Government took him under the wing. The Dalai Lama later made an issue of the legality of the

McMahon Line, suggesting that if India denied the sovereign status to Tibet, it was also denying the validity of the Simla Convention and the validity of the McMahon Line. There was general sympathy for Tibetans, especially the Dalai Lama in the Indian political class. The latent suspicion of China was revived and the diffidence over China's takeover of Tibet in 1950 sharpened. Peking complained that Kalimpong (the terminus of the trade route to India through the Chumbi Valley), which China declared as the commanding center for the armed rebelling, was a nest of spies and was used as a base to instigate resistance against China. Aside from the activities of émigrés and American and Kuomintang agents, there was evidence that the Indians played a more active role for Tibetan independence. The Chinese National People's Congress made angry references to the "Indian reactionaries" for giving aid and comfort to the rebellious feudal forces, working "in the footsteps of the British imperialists, and harboring expansionist ambitions towards Tibet." The old suspicions were thus revived on both sides.

Like Nehru, the Chinese Government recognized that good relations were in its best long-term interests, and the Chinese Ambassador conveyed the concern to the Indian Foreign Secretary: "China will not be so foolish as to antagonize the United States in the east and again to antagonize India in the west." The Ambassador stated that the outcry of Tibetan rebellion in India overcastted dark clouds over Sino-Indian relations and that it would "speedily disperse." The statements expressed urgency and directness, but were undiplomatic. A week later, the Chinese Ambassador was called to the Ministry and was rebuked for having used "discourteous and unbecoming language." He was told that India treated all countries as friends "in consonance with India's past background and culture and Mahatma Gandhi's teachings."

The diplomatic exchange was coupled with stronger presence of Chinese troops on the McMahon Line to prevent the Tibetan rebels from crossing. On the other side, the Indians also pushed their outposts right up to and over the McMahon Line. The McMahon Line was never demarcated, i.e., marked out on the ground and agreed by both parties, but it followed an unmistakable and inaccessible crest-line. A demarcation must be a joint process, but Indians were unilaterally establishing border posts according to their maps without seeking China's approval. In September 1959, Nehru rejected Chou En-lai's letter in which China complained that the Indians were overstepping the McMahon Line. But Nehru admitted that there was "slight" difference in the Migyitun area with the map, which he justified as modifications "based on definitive topography" in accordance with "established international principles." India insisted that China not only should first formally recognize the McMahon Line, but also should accept the boundary India claimed in the western sector. China protested the Indian forward moves and complained that on August 25, Indian troops intruded south of the Migyitun and fired on Chinese. New Delhi protested the next day that China moved into Indian territory and forced Indians out of Longju, accusing China of "deliberate aggression" and warning that it would "use force on the trespasser if necessary," a bluff threat that was not founded in international law.

China's account of the Longju incident was contrary to India's. China maintained that the Chinese border guards merely returned fire at the unprovoked attack by the Indians. The Indian claims were militated by the fact that China did not attack the other Indian posts set up along McMahon Line. However, in India, there was no doubt that the incident was Chinese aggression. The Chinese were denounced for the "expansionism" and the "cynical contempt" to treat the "noble concepts of friendship, toleration and co-existence." Meanwhile, another collision broke out on the western sector of the McMahon Line. The Indian troops went to establish posts on Lanak Pass, which India regarded as the boundary feature. The patrol of about seventy men came into contact with the Chinese at the Kongka Pass, which China regarded as the boundary feature and had established a post.

On October 20, three Indians were detained by the Chinese; next day nine Indian forces were killed and seven taken prisoner. Chinese suffered casualties, with probably only one killed. The Indians reported to have been ambushed from a hilltop, whereas the Chinese said that the Indians attempted to capture the small Chinese patrol and opened fire. The captured Indians, including the patrol commander, confirmed the Chinese accounts, but after release retracted their statements. However, there was no doubt in India, as the newspaper called "the brutal massacre of an Indian policy party."

In the three following years after the Longju and Kongka pass clashed, the Parliament spent hundreds of hours on the dispute with China. Nehru enjoyed his dominance in the House, which accepted his arrogant authority, but he was also submerged with powerful opposition from the Congress Party. The Defense Minister Menon often became a scapegoat target for the critics of Nehru. In August 1959, the "bluster against China" picked up volume and the opposition criticisms attacked the government's China policy over the boarder dispute. The opposition was not deep and was formed primarily by small upper-class group, whose views were regarded as "public opinion" and expressed in newspapers, especially the English newspapers. The newspapers reported of the Chinese troops crossing the McMahon Line and suggested of Indian government to aid Bhutan, of which Prime Minister promptly declared that Bhutan was not an Indian protectorate. But up to the end of August 1959, Nehru had told Parliament nothing at all about the boundary dispute with China, about the Aksai Chin road, or China's proposal to settle the boundary.

After the Longju incident, word got out and the existence of the Chinese road came to the House. Nehru coolly validated that the road existed "through a corner of our north-eastern Ladakhi territory" and affirmed that the Chinese claimed of "the hundreds of miles of Indian territory" was "totally and manifestly unacceptable" and was not "a matter of discussion." Nehru stated a few days later the importance of the "two miles of territory in the high mountains, where nobody lives" entail "national prestige and dignity." He stressed that China "having accepted broadly the McMahon Line, I am prepared to discuss any interpretation of the McMahon Line" and "to have arbitration of any authority agreed to by the two parties." About the western sector of the border, Nehru was vague: "The point is, there has never been any delimitation there in that area and it has been a challenged area," but he maintained that "Aksai Chin was and had always been the historic frontiers" of India.

Nehru's tentativeness about the western sector soon ended with Dr. Gopal, the director of the Historical Division of the Ministry of External Affairs, who was sent to London to review materials on India's northern borders. Nehru told Gopal to disregard all contemporary political consideration and to make an objective appraisal of the historical evidence. Gopal reported in November 1959 that India's claim to the Aksai Chin area was clearly stronger than China's. Gopal removed the reservations in Nehru, whose Government has long adopted a policy that the McMahon Line must not be submitted to renegotiations and, in 1954, the principle was extended to the rest of the northern borders. Menon and other Cabinet members felt that the amateur historian Nehru and the professional historian Gopal were taking the Government in a wrong course. But they only expressed to Gopal and none stood up to disagree with Nehru.

Chou En-lai replied to Nehru's letter on September 8, 1959, and reaffirmed the basic point that the Sino-Indian boundary had never been delimited, further arguing that the 56,000 square miles between the McMahon Line and the foothills had been Chinese. Chou restated the approach of the Chinese Government: to reach a settlement through friendly negotiations, fair and reasonable to both sides, taking into consideration the historical background and existing actualities, and that in the meantime the status quo should be observed. Chou suggested that China, like India, had been subjected to imperialist aggression, and would like to adopt "an attitude of mutual sympathy, mutual understanding and fairness and reasonableness" to settle the boundary question. Chou raised the issue that India refused to recognize the undelimited state of the boundary and attempted to impose upon China its one-sided claims "militarily, diplomatically and through public opinion." Chou finally asked India to withdraw "trespassing Indian troops and administrative personnel" and suggested that would speedily dispel "the dark clouds hanging over Sino-Indian relations."

The Indian Government read the letter as a veiled claim for the whole NEFA. Chou's previous assurance that China would accept the McMahon Line almost disappeared. China suspected that India provided covert assistance to the Tibetan rebels, allowed them to raid back along the McMahon Line, and let Kuomintang agents operate freely in Kalimpong, smuggling saboteurs, weapons and ammunition into Tibet. There was an outburst of anti-Chinese sentiment and calls for war in India, but Nehru maintained his friendly and calm tone, while publicly giving sympathy to the Dalai Lama. To the boundary question, Nehru not only ruled out a settlement by negotiation, but also advanced to a categorical claim to the segment of the Aksai Chin, the only land route from Sinkiang to Tibet.

He further pushed the Indian forces forward across the McMahon Line and the western sectors. Nehru and his government were in no mood to read between the lines of Chou's letter, which offered the settlement to be reached. They took the letter as proof that they were faced with "a great and powerful nation which is aggressive." Nehru replied to Chou expressing "great surprise and distress" and argued that the boundaries had "always been the historical frontier" and were settled by "history, geography, custom and tradition." Indian government decided that it was dangerously against Indian interest to negotiate a boundary settlement with China, and that the only reasonable ground to refuse negotiation was the argument that the boundary is already delimited. This argument was put forth for the international community, which now started trying to follow the Sino-Indian debate.

The 1899 Macartney-MacDonald line was the only boundary alignment that the British proposed to China, which left the whole of Aksai Chin on the Chinese side. In his letter to Chou in September 1959, Nehru claimed the reverse: that the 1899 line "signified beyond doubt that the whole of Aksai Chin area lay in Indian territory." Nehru further introduced the Indian demand for restoration of the status quo ante, which was a veiled demand for unilateral Chinese withdrawal. The two clashes at Kongka and Longju brought forth a convulsive response in Indian political opinion. Nehru's emphasis on long Sino-Indian friendship was criticized fiercely as "irrelevant," "hypocritical," "fatuous," and "dishonest." The critics proposed to pass a resolution to take immediate action to "throw out" the Chinese. Nehru dismissed these as "utterly wrong and useless," but affirmed that "at no time since our independence, and of course before it, were our defense forces in better condition, in finer fettle, "than they are today." Nehru stressed that "I am quiet confidant that our defense forces are well capable of looking after our security." Nehru's allusions to the possibility of war and assurance of the strong defense force nourished the impression that war with China was a possibility and that it could be won. Thus far, Nehru and his advisers choose the directions toward the war, with no significant public pressure. By 1959, there was aroused political opinion that denounced any compromise with China as appeasement or cowardice.

Evasive Action

After the Kongka incident, Chou En-lai wrote Nehru on November 7, 1959, and described it as unfortunate and unexpected. Chou proposed a summit meeting to settle the entire boundary question through peaceful negotiations and suggested that, in order to avoid further border clashes, the armed forces of both sides should be withdrawn twenty kilometers from the McMahon Line. China recommended that before the settlement, status quo should be maintained which meant "the situation obtaining at present." India used the word jiggling of "maintaining status quo" to mean Indian patrols moving into the Chinese-held territory. Despite that the proposal of summit meeting and demilitarization appeared consistent with the general approaches of India, Nehru rejected the summit meeting with Chou En-lai, a decision almost universally welcomed in India. In face of the Chinese willingness, indeed eagerness, to settle the boundary dispute through negotiation, India instantly rejected the idea of negotiations. The idea was solid that there should be no discussions until China withdrew from Aksai Chin.

The Chinese proposal of mutual military withdraws placed India on the diplomatic defensive. Nehru equivocated that the Chinese proposal was the same as Indian position of total and unilateral Chinese withdrawal from the disputed territory in the western sector. The Indians urged that "no negotiations can take place on the basis of prior acceptance by China of our frontiers and the immediate vacation of territories forcibly occupied by them." Nehru made puzzling statements: "we will negotiate and negotiate and negotiate to the bitter end. I absolutely reject the approach of stopping negotiations at any state," and that "as far as I am concerned, I am prepared to meet any body in the wide world." In fact, Nehru reaffirmed his position that "we will never compromise on our boundaries, but we are prepared to consider minor adjustments to them and to talk to the other side about them." Nehru was to refuse to meet Chou En-lai until China accepted the Indian version of the boundaries, and withdraw behind the Indian claim line.

However, the international community failed to appreciate the ambiguities in Nehru's words and almost universally blamed China, rather than India, for refusing to negotiate a boundary settlement. The confidence of India hardened after Chou En-lai pressed his proposal after the rejection of a summit meeting. In December, Chou reiterated the Chinese position that the joint military withdrawal along the border would not prejudice the claims of either side. Nehru wrote Chou to explain the rejection of the summit meeting that without preliminary agreement "we would lose ourselves in a forest of data." Chou wrote back and emphasized the importance of agreements that may prevent "endless and fruitless debates," and proposed to meet on December 26, nine days after the delivery of the letter. Nehru replied promptly and coldly expressing regret that his "very reasonable proposals" for joint withdrawals had not been accepted, and that it was impossible for him to meet Chou in the next few days.

The Indian refusal of the summit brought the diplomatic game to stalemate, as China continued to treat the McMahon Line as the de facto boundary in the eastern sector and the western sector unchallenged. From the moment India accused China with "aggression" for the Chinese presence in Indian claimed territory, the Indian Government was obliged to take actions, and Nehru had pressed for a military operation against China and expected the Government would comply. India thus far took for granted its international esteem for its persistent advocate of a rational and civilized approach, and negotiating table as a lightning conductor for international quarrels.

This Nehru stated at the end of 1959, "whether it is in the United Nations or whether it is elsewhere, we are respected all over the world," and wondered why "it has been an amazing thing." This was attributed to clever diplomacy, the radiance of

Gandhi, and "that we have spoken with conviction and earnestness and sincerity about peace and our desire for peace and "for tolerance" from deep inside our hearts and deep understanding of the world as it is today." India by then occupied a unique position in the world. It was called to act as referee peacemaker or arbitrator from Gaza to the Congo and Korea, and was listened to with respect and courted for understanding. India was the prime articulator of the concept of non-alignment and accepted spokesman for the non-aligned countries. As personified in Nehru, India contributed much to blunt the conflicts of the cold war.

India's successful foreign policy was demonstrated by its acceptance by both the USA and the USSR, of which presidents made successive visits to New Delhi. The visit of President Eisenhower in December 1959 removed the old disapproval of "immoral neutralism" and replaced it with cordial sympathy. Eisenhower stated that the India "speaks to the other nations of the world with greatness of conviction, and is heard with greatness of respect" and especially appraised India's falling out with China, even before it became a public knowledge. The US economic aid to India multiplied suddenly. It was $1.7 billion in the twelve years to mid-1959, and the amount increased to $4 billion in the next four years. Both the US and Soviet Union took a dispassionate view of the Sino-India dispute from the beginning. As the Longju incident occurred on the eve of Krushchev's visit to the US, both the US and Russians have been carefully neutral and deplored the incident as to "discredit the idea of peaceful co-existence."

Those who could read between the lines, the dispassionate regret of Moscow "in reality condemned China's stand." India took the tacit Russian support as high importance. Western countries would readily accept the Indian version of the dispute, and condemn China with, or even before, New Delhi. But such sympathy and support was not easily forthcoming from the non-aligned and especially of other Asian countries, as they were not prepared to accept uncritically the proposition that China was wholly in the wrong. The Russians had already expressed that negotiations were the only way to resolve the border questions, and the fact that India had twice rejected China's proposal for a summit meeting would make it hard for the Russians to appreciate

Indian approach. India extended an invitation to Krushchev for a visit and expected to clarify the validity of Indian approach to the boundary dispute.

In the meantime, China wrote New Delhi another long note stating that Peking was expected the summit meeting and that the Sino-Indian borders were not delimited but China intended to settle the dispute through friendly negotiations. New Delhi studied the note, felt the desire to end the dispute sincere, and decided that there might be something to be gained by meeting with Chou En-lai. It appeared that the summit meeting would serve Indian interest in showing the watching world that India was consistent with its prescriptions of advocating negotiations in every dispute. However, the reversal of policy by dropping the insistence on Chinese withdrawal as a precondition for a summit meeting, the domestic criticism and increasing suspicion over compromise with China would be intensified. To overcome this, a semantic smoke screen was created by making a distinction between "talks" and "negotiations".

The day after Krushchev arrived in New Delhi, Nehru delivered a cordial, or even warm, invitation letter to Chou En-lai on February 12, 1960, without informing his government. Nehru stated to Parliament: "I see no ground whatever at the present moment, no bridge between the Chinese position and ours," and "that is, the present positions are such that there is no room for negotiations on that basis, and therefore there is nothing to negotiate at present." The smoke screen covered the general expectation that Krushchev's visit would bring about negotiations between China and India, and refusal to negotiate confirmed Parliament that Nehru had no intention of meeting with Chou En-lai. On February 16, the members of Parliament learned of the invitation from the newspapers. The Opposition fumed anger on the "sudden and unwarranted reversal" of policy, and described the invitation as a "national humiliation."

Chou En-lai accepted the invitation with "deep gratitude" and arranged a seven-day visit on April 19. The Indian politicians suspected that Nehru would compromise with China and the opposition declared of a "no-surrender week," arranging demonstrations in New Delhi and other cities during Chou's visit in order to make "things hot" for the Chinese party. Nehru and the Government made a nice compromise by ending the "no-surrender week" the day before Chou arrived and holding no customary public receptions in Chou's honor. The oppositions reiterated their view of having no talks without "Chinese vacation of aggression" and put out slogans "invaders, quit India," "no surrender of Indian territory," and "down with Chinese imperialism."

The oppositions found further international reason for refusing to negotiate with China that ill-effects of compromise would "shatter the morale of all" the rest of Asian countries "who are aspiring to build themselves up independently and in a democratic way." The editorial placed on the eve of Chou's arrival that, if the talks succeeded, "China's prestige and power will be enhanced in the eyes of the smaller Asian countries, for India's action will be construed as acquiescence in and compliance with China's attitude." If talks broke down, "India will be held up as unreasonable, (but better) to be held up temporarily as unreasonable than to be dismissed as weak and pusillanimous." The pressure not to settle was further increased by the dispute with Pakistan. One month before Chou's arrival, the Indian Supreme Court reinforced the inflexible approach on the northern boundaries and challenged the compromise that Nehru made with small patch of disputed territory of several square miles with Pakistan.

On April 19, 1960, Chou En-lai arrived in New Delhi, accompanied by Marshall Chen Yi, the Foreign Minister, and a large party. The cheer of "Hindee Chinee bhai-bhai" of yesteryear was replaced with only a polite patter of applause from the diplomats. Both sides exchanged speeches of greeting. Nehru recalled the good will between China and India, and said "unfortunately other events have taken place since then which have put a great strain on the bond of friendship and given a great shock to all our people." Chou replied: "Both of us need peace, both of us need friends," "there is no reason why any question between us cannot be settled reasonably through friendly consultations in accordance with those principles" of Panch Sheel, and concluded that "I have come with the sincere desire to settle questions." In the following days of visit, the Indian Government maintained adamant and immovable position: there could be no general boundary negotiations; the boundaries were already delimited and ran just where India said they did; and China must withdraw before there could be any of the discussions on "minor rectifications" that were all India would agree to. Chou En-lai reiterated that the Sino-Indian boundary question had been left over from history, and not created by either of the two Governments: it was "only an issue of a limited and temporary nature" and it was "entirely possible to achieve a fair and reasonable overall settlement." China was proposing "reciprocal acceptance of present actualities in both sectors and constitution of a boundary commission."

China would accept the McMahon alignment in the western sector, while India would accepted the positions then obtaining in the west. There would be no physical withdrawals involved, as the forward posts on both sides were far apart, but India would drop the claim to Aksai Chin. Chou En-lai maintained the position that he took since his the first meeting with Nehru, that although the McMahon Line was not fair, Chinese Government would accept it because of its friendly relations with Burma and India. After India expressed its claim to Aksai Chin in the note of October 18, 1958, China consistently treated the Indian presence in the territory south of the McMahon Line the same as the Chinese presence in Aksai Chin. China made it clear in the summit meeting that China would accept the McMahon alignment provided that India accept the Chinese control line in the west. However, India insisted on the sin qua non of a boundary settlement that China must concede that Aksai Chin was Indian territory as well as accepting the McMahon Line. The conference had failed from the outset, but the summit meeting continued for the remaining five more days, neither side wished it to break down.

A press conference was held prior to Chou's departure. Chou concisely reiterated the Chinese position: that the boundary had never been delimited, that the question could be settled through friendly consultations, and that, pending settlement, "both sides should maintain the present state of the boundary and not change it by unilateral action, let along by force." In the meantime the friendship between China and India should not, and could not, be jeopardized by the boundary question. Chou stated that Chinese government, like those before it, could never recognize the McMahon Line because it was "illegally delineated through an exchange of secret notes by British imperialism with the Tibetan local authorities." Nevertheless, he said, China was observing the Line as the boundary, and had not put forward territorial claims as pre-conditions in the negotiations.

The press conference displeased the Indians. Nehru waited only until the Chinese were airborne and dwindling in the eastern sky on their way to Katmandu before attacking the Chinese Government as aggressors. He said that Chou En-lai "came here because something important had happened, the important thing being that according to us they had entered our territory "which we considered aggression." After learning Nehru's word, Chou later was not amused but was "very much distressed by such an attitude, particularly as we respect Prime Minister Nehru." The summit meeting thus failed on the unyielding refusal of India to give up, modify or hold over its claim to the Aksai Chin territory. With Burma, China accepted the McMahon alignment as the basis of the boundary, and with Nepal, "adjustments were made in accordance with the principles of equality, mutual benefit, friendship and mutual accommodation."

The Chinese maps showed Mount Everest within China, but China accepted the Nepali (and general) view that the peak itself marked the boundary. Both sides agreed to keep their armed personnel out of a forty-kilometer zone along the boundary. Chou En-lai maintained that the summit had not failed, but the summit cleared the way for a worsening of the situation on the borders. As Chou En-lai faced the American and Indian correspondents who questioned with hostility and suspicion, Chen Yi broke in: "I want to call your attention to the fact that China is a country which is being wronged. I want to stress, China is a country which is being wronged."

The Forward Policy

The Indians had no doubt about their inherent position that Aksai Chin had been incontrovertibly Indian territory and that the Chinese claim was factitious and concocted to camouflage illegal and clandestine seizure. By describing the Chinese presence as an act or aggression, the Indian Government obliged itself to take actions, even to use force if diplomatic methods failed. It was decided that India "must assert its rights by dispatching properly equipped patrols into the areas currently occupied by the Chinese, since any prolonged failure to do so will imply a tacit acceptance of Chinese occupation, and "Indian patrols penetrate into disputed areas of Ladakh."

By the time Chou En-lai left, Indian Government had started implementing a "forward policy," by sending patrols to probe the Chinese-occupied areas and penetrating the spaces between the Chinese positions without attacking them. The objectives were to block potential lines of further Chinese advance and to establish an Indian presence in Aksai China, ultimately undermine Chinese control of the disputed areas by the interposition of Indian posts and patrols between Chinese positions, thus cutting the Chinese supply lines and forcing them to withdraw.

The forward policy sprang from the conclusion that there was nothing else India could do. It was based on the fundamental premise that the Chinese would not physically interfere no matter how many Indians posts and patrols were set up, provided that the Indians did not attack any Chinese positions.

As soon as the dispute started in 1954, the advance of the Indian boundary posts in the middle sectors intended to threaten with force against the Chinese who maintained their positions, but Nehru and his colleagues had absolute faith that the Chinese would not act likewise.

The confidence in the moral unassailability was embedded in the belief that the British were reluctant to use force and if the Chinese did attack, it would rebound against them. It reflected Nehru's perception that the unique position of India in the world, with the reputation and depth of its pacific instincts, would go with the Indian patrols into Aksai Chin like a moral armor. Nehru and his colleagues held this belief, that the Chinese would stand idly while India gradually and laboriously built up positions of strength, until the brutal disabuse took place in October 1962.

The Oppositions and critics in India began to cherish the phrase "police action," that "to defend your own territory is not to wage war" and "that if you throw out bandits "is just police action on your own territory." "We as a peaceful nation who are members of the UN do not believe in war as any remedy" therefore "the only way is to have a police action whereby we can push the Chinese out of our territory" after that have a basis for negotiation." Others argued that war was not the ultimate catastrophe or even an unmixed evil. It was believed that small and local wars could not always be avoided, and "when such wars are fought "the wisdom of the world" would localize them and would find a workable solution later. "So we need not scare ourselves that any resistance to Chinese aggression will lead to a world war and a destruction of humanity.

The world will see to it that this does not happen." The opposition emphasized that "it is conflict that brings out the best in a country, that brings about unity," and that the danger would be turned to good effect "to achieve national cohesion and spur national endeavor." However, Nehru consistently stressed the dangers of war, that "war between India and China would be one of the major disasters of the world "for it will mean world war" which will be indefinite. We would not be able to limit it in time, because it will not be possible for China to defeat us and it will be impossible for us to march up to Peking across Tibet." In the rhetoric allusions to the ultimate possibility of war, the conceived context was that India was going to war for its territory after exhausting its patience and gaining a position of strength. It never occurred to New Delhi that war might arise from Chinese reaction to or anticipation of Indian moves. Nehru and his colleagues were unwavering in their faith that whatever India did along the borders, China would not attack. This basic assumption was the basis of the forward policy, a military challenge to a militarily far superior neighbor.

The Indian armed forces had been neglected in the 1950s. Nehru and Indian Congress ruled out possible threats to India one by one, and concluded that "no danger threatens India from any direction, and even if there is any danger we shall be able to cope with it." As for China, the Himalayas made "an effective barrier and not even air fleets could come that way." It was believed that its size, its geo-strategic position and the interest of the great powers would keep India immune from any significant external attacks. "If any power was covetous enough to make the attempt" to acquiring the commanding position, "all the others would combine to trounce the intruder. This mutual rivalry would in itself be the surest guarantee against an attack on India."

Nehru held this rational and pragmatic view of external threats to India after independence and until the main Chinese assault in November 1962. The Indian Government stressed on development to come first. Military aid from abroad was considered unacceptable since it would impair India's non-alignment and be unreliable.

The positively pacific, almost pacifist approach to international relations, the emphasis on development, and insistence on non-alignment, all reinforced the Gandhian disapproval of men of war as part of the Indian Congress attitude. The civilian leadership thus placed the soldiers into disadvantaged position. After Menon became the Defense Minister in 1957, he was warmly welcomed for being energetic and politically relevant. The military had misgivings about Menon's interference in steadily promoting officer Kaul, who played a central and disastrous role in the border war. Following its conception in the beginning of 1960, the total lack of military means made the Army resist the implementation of the forward policy until the end of 1961.

While the Sino-Indian border dispute halted, China proceeded to negotiate boundary settlements with other neighbors. Since 1954, the US equipped and trained Pakistan's armed forces and it became no longer easy for India to defeat Pakistan. From 1960, the Indian Government tried to tutor Pakistan to adopt the Indian approach and the same attitude in dealing with China over the northern frontier. Instead, Pakistan agreed with China that the boundary had never been delimited and negotiated with China on October 13, 1962. By December 26, 1962, the two Governments jointed announced to have reached "complete agreement in principle," in which China followed for the great part what the British had proposed to China in 1899 and ceded some 750 square miles of territory to Pakistan.

With Burmese Prime Minister, U Nu, China sought a settlement since 1956. U Nu found that after having emphatically repudiated all past boundary agreements with the British, China was prepared to open negotiations on the basis of what the British proposed. China found the "unequal treaties" imposed by Britain as unacceptable, but not the alignment that the British proposed. China offered Burma the whole Sino-Burmese boundary along McMahon Line, an agreement converted to a treaty in October 1960. China settled the boundaries with other neighbors equably and equitably shaded an adverse light on India's position, but brought more sharply the deadlock between India and China. India reiterated its boundary could not be a matter of negotiation, and denied "the necessity of further or formal delimitation." China replied that "refusing to negotiate and trying to impose a unilaterally claimed alignment on China is in actuality refusal to settle the boundary questions," and warned that while India maintained the position, China would "absolutely not retreat an inch."

By the spring of 1961, Nehru found the Chinese position unchanged. China was still ready, indeed eager, to negotiate a boundary settlement with India, while indicating that China would agree to the McMahon Line. In the fall of 1961, Nehru Government gave categorical orders for immediate implementation of the forward policy. China protested about forward moves already made from Demchok that "the Chinese Government has been following with great anxiety the Indian troops" pressing forward on China's borders in "gross violations of China's territory and sovereignty," which would have serious consequences had it not been orders to avoid conflicts. India asserted that the Indian patrols were moving into their own territory and rejected the Chinese protest as unwarranted interference in their internal affairs, as they viewed that "according to our thinking our trouble at the border is not a dispute at all."

The Goa incident further reinforced India's readiness to take unilateral and forceful action in territorial question. Goa had been a Portuguese colony on the west coast since the beginning of the sixteenth century. The Portuguese stayed on after the British left the subcontinent in 1947, but never thought of giving the Goans independence. In 1955, India attempted to force Portugal to cede Goa through nonviolent demonstrations, but Portuguese police opened fire, killing several and wounding many. India severed diplomatic ties with Portugal, but the Portuguese stayed on in Goa. In the end of 1961, the Indian government decided to give its resolve military demonstration to China by invading Goa.

With minimal resistance, India seized Goa, but it became more of a scandal and an irritant to India, especially to Nehru, in face of their persistent advocacy of the doctrine never to justify the use of force as a means of settling international disputes. India insisted that the military operation did not breach the prescription, and few came to criticize Indian action. President Kennedy wrote to Nehru: "All countries, including the USA, have a great capacity for convincing themselves of the full righteousness of their particular cause." The Indian press supported: "Why is it that something that thrills our people should be condemned in the strongest language?" A political journal summed up the Indian view of the seizure of Goa: "No aggression has been committed, because we have regarded Goa ever since 1947 as our rightful territory "To drive out an intruder who is in illegal occupation of part of our territory is not aggression."

The Goa incident reflected the amorphous and subjective processes within which the Indian Government operated. Neither the seizure of Goa nor the forward policy was decided upon in Cabinet. It showed the dualities of India's attitude toward the use of force: reprehensible in the abstract and in the service of others, but justifiable both politically and morally when employed by India in disputes. Some politicians were intoxicated by the Goa victory as talks began of driving Pakistan out of Kashmir and forcing China out of Aksai Chin. The Home Minister, Shastri, paralleled the Goa incident with China: "If the Chinese will not vacate the areas "India will have to repeat what she did in Goa."

The president of the Congress Party announced that India was "determined to get Pakistani and Chinese aggression on its soil vacated before long" and that Pakistan-occupied Kashmir must be "liberated." However, the military operation in Goa did not test the capabilities of the troops or their commanders, as the Portuguese put up no organized resistance against the overwhelmingly superior Indian forces. The Army had been experiencing chronic shortage of boots, and half of one battalion went through the operation in canvas gym shoes. Although this was discussed widely in the Army, little came out in India, which called the operation "our finest hour."

The easy victory over the Portuguese encouraged the hope of similar success against the Chinese. Nehru had repeatedly assured Parliament and public that the Army and other services were stronger than they have been, and were ready to defeat any challenges to the integrity of India. The Indian army would quickly teach the Chinese a lesson in the event of a conflict. Nehru said that the boundary dispute with China was more important to India than a hundred Goas. Although India now had rejected the Chinese proposal for a joint twenty-kilometer withdrawal, China had unilaterally stopped patrolling within twenty-kilometers of the bounder. India refused to open negotiations, and steadily pushed forward, first in the middle and eastern sectors and now in the west.

China warned that India's action "is most dangerous and may lead to grave consequences," but "so far as the Chinese is concerned the door for negotiation is always open." India insisted that the Sino-Indian boundary had long been settled and justified the forward policy as "the legitimate right, indeed the duty, of the Government of India to take all necessary measures to safeguard the territorial integrity of India." The forward policy continued as small Indian posts were being established overlooking Chinese positions and sometimes astride the tracks or roads behind them. The theory was that interruption of the communication lines would ultimately force the Chinese to withdraw from their posts. Nehru dismissed the increasingly emphatic Chinese warnings of "grave consequences," and explained to Parliament that the Chinese became "rather annoyed" as the Indian posts were set up behind their own. Nehru reassured the doubtful members who though Chinese tone dangerous: "There is nothing to be alarmed at, although the (Chinese) note threatens all kinds of steps," and that "if they do take those steps we shall be ready for them."

As Nehru assured Parliament that the position in the western sector was "more advantageous to India," the forwarding Indians in the Ladakh were outnumbered by the Chinese by more than five to one. The strength disparity was beyond the numbers. The Chinese were concentrated where the Indians were scattered; the Chinese were able to move in trucks where the Indians trekked on foot; and the Chinese had all regular supports arms for the troops while the Indian Brigade had nothing beyond one platoon of medium machine-guns. The Chinese ranged heavy mortars and recoilless guns on the Indian posts, and infantry equipped with automatic rifles. The Indians had nothing heavier than three-inch mortars and most posts even lacked those, their troops equipped with rifles last seen in action before the First World War. In early 1961, the Chinese began to react vigorously on the ground.

As the Indians set up a post overlooking a Chinese position, the Chinese promptly took up more positions around it. Since April 1959, the Chinese also resumed the suspended patrol in the western sectors and warned to resume patrolling everywhere if Indians continued the forward movement. China also warned that the continued Indian "pressing on the Chinese post and carrying out provocation" would compel the Chinese troops to defend themselves, and that India would be responsible for the consequences. The Indian Government dismissed the warnings as bluff and the threatening Chinese moves as bluster. In the Chip Chap valley, the Chinese formed in assault formation and gave every indication to wipe out the Indian post. Western Command requested permission to withdraw the post, but Nehru believed that the Chinese were making a show of force to test India's resolution and ordered to reinforce the post. The Chinese later did not follow up on the threats, and the Indian Government and Army concluded the judgement and nerve of the Prime Minister, further confirming the basic premise of the forward policy, which was further validated by the subsequent Galwan incident.

The Indian Amy map showed Galwan valley as one of the best routes to move into Chinese-held territory, which was one of Kaul's orders to establish a post in November 1961. The terrain in the valley was extremely difficult and the Chinese had already had a post there since at least 1959. After the winter pasted, Western Command decided that any move to threaten the well-established Chinese post would certainly evoke a violent reaction, and concluded that no Indian post could be established. But Kaul overruled the command. After over a month of trekking, the Indians emerged on the upper reaches of the Galwan River, and took positions, on July 5, 1962 to cut off a Chinese outpost and also hold up a small Chinese supply party. On July 8, the Chinese first made diplomatically "strongest protest" asking for immediate withdrawal of the Indian troops and warning that China would not "give up its right to self-defense when unwarrantedly attacked."

India replied that India has "regularly been patrolling the Galwan valley" and has "never encountered any Chinese infiltrators" there, and lodged "an emphatic protest" against the Chinese "unwarranted aggressive activity" on the ground. India warned China to be entirely responsible for any untoward incident if China did not "stop the incessant intrusions deep inside Indian territory and ceaseless provocative activities against Indian border guards." The Chinese reacted on the ground advancing on the Indian post with a company in assault formation and quickly building up to battalion strength. In response, the External Affairs Ministry called the Chinese Ambassador and warned that the garrison would open fire if the Chinese troops pressed any closer to the Galwan post, and that India would retaliate against Chinese positions if the post were attacked. In a few days, the Chinese pulled back a little while continuing to surround the post in relatively great strength, cutting off the ground supply. Western Command requested for air supply since any land approach would provoke a clash. India decided that, since China blinked in the confrontation that now relaxed, the moral initiative must be maintained. A small force was dispatched to reinforce Galwan. It was turned back under the Chinese guns, which warned to fire if it advanced any farther. The Galwan post was supplied by air until it was wiped out on October 20.

The news of the Galwan incident appeared in India on July 11, as a new and provocative Chinese advance into Indian territory. When the Chinese did not follow up on their physical and diplomatic threats, a wave of triumph swept the press and the politicians. It was believed that the incident raised the morale of the whole nation, and the Chinese withdrew "in the face of the determined stand of the small Indian garrison." The orders given to the Indian garrison were extended to all Indian troops in the western sectors, and the "fire only if fired upon" changed to "fire if the Chinese press dangerously close to your positions."

Nehru further decided that the military moves had to be coupled with diplomatic pressure. Nehru assured the Indian Parliament with a proposal that would withdraw very large Chinese and very small Indian withdrawal. It was hoped that, with the establishment of Indian posts in Chinese-claimed territory, China would accept what the Indians considered to be the best way of saving face, the complete withdrawal, and that the few Indian posts already established might have brought China to that position. China rejected the proposal as "unilaterally imposed submissive terms" and questioned: "Why should China need to ask India's permission for using its own road on its own territory?" New Delhi concluded that the forward policy had not yet presented enough pressure and decided that it must be pursued until China accepted to withdraw.

The Indian troops pressed hard in the western sector, acting as if they were the vanguard of a powerful army rather than the stake in a wild political gamble. Meanwhile the domestic critics demanded stronger and quicker action against China. To defend itself, the Government drew lines to connect the new forward Indian posts on maps and calculated the enclosed area. One journalist praised the Prime Minister for "a general advance over a wide front of 2,500 square miles" and complimented Nehru as "a unique triumph for audacious Napoleonic planning." Only sporadic report was made on the real situation that the Chinese had a ten-to-one superiority in the western sector and also all the advantages of terrain and communications. Most reported on the superior strength and better equipment of the Indians over Chinese, the latter as garrison troops of poor fighting quality.

The Opposition in India further pushed for yet stronger measures to expel the Chinese. It was claimed that "The bogey of Chinese superiority" should not worry our military experts" and that "two hundred Indian soldiers are equal to two thousand of the Chinese," and asked "Why should we be afraid of them? Why are we not able to hurl them back?" When the Indian Ambassador (Nehru's cousin) in Washington expressed the truth that the Indian defense forces were so badly equipped that they could not ensure the security of the country, he was ignored. Nehru repeatedly assured Parliament that the Army was capable of defending the frontiers, and suggested disciplining the Ambassador for an indiscretion.

Saner voices in the Government suggested that India should give China the same pledge as it gave to Pakistan with respect to the Pakistan-held and Indian-claimed part of Kashmir, and a daily newspaper also urged the Government to negotiate. However, the overwhelmingly dominant attitudes in Parliament were not to negotiate. After Kongka Pass incident on July 21, 1962, China protested. "China is not willing to fight with India, and the Sino-Indian boundary question can be settled only through routine negotiations." China had exercised self-restraint, but could not stand idle while the "frontier guards are being encircled and annihilated by aggressors "If India should ignore the warning and persist in its own way India must bear full responsibility for all the consequences."

India replied on July 26, reminding China that under certain conditions India was prepared to "enter into further discussions" on the boundary question. But India was firm in its position that before any negotiations, China must withdraw all personnel from the India-claimed territory, and when the evacuation was complete, India would meet China at the conference table to discuss minor modifications of the boundary India claimed. In response, China reciprocated the reasonable and positive tone, but rejected the condition of "one-sided withdrawal from large tracts of its own territory," while accepting the proposal for discussion. "The Chinese Government approves of the suggestion put forth by the Indian Government for further discussion" As a matter of fact, if only the Indian side stop advancing into Chinese territory, a relaxation of the border situation will be affected at once.

"The Chinese Government proposes that such discussions be held as soon as possible..." India considered the discussions with China served no purpose since China explicitly rejected the "one-sided withdrawal," which India considered as the only acceptable settlement. India had all the advantages of world opinions, as the newsstands were packed with supporters. The press and governments of the Western world cheered India as it stood against what they believed to be the expansionist China. The historical and documentary arguments about the boundary were too obscure except for the specialists, to whom the archives that might show which side was nearer the truth were closed. Although the invasion of Goa injured India's reputation, there was generally no hesitation in the West to take the Indian side. As Felix Green explained the American reaction: "So solidly built into our consciousness is the concept that China is conducting a rapacious and belligerent foreign policy that whenever a dispute arises in which China is involved, she is instantly assumed to have provoked it. All commentaries, "news reports," and scholarly interpretations are written on the basis of this assumption.

The cumulative effect of this only further reinforces the original hypothesis so that it is used again next time with even greater effect." The Americans viewed the conflict as a race between China and India for the economic and political leadership in Asia. In 1959, then Senator JF Kennedy said: "We want India to win that race with China "if China succeeds and India fails the economic-development balance of power will shift against us." Kennedy's estimation lowered sharply when the Prime Minister visited Washington in November 1961.

The president later described it as "the worst head-of-state visit" ever, and his conversations with Nehru as "like trying to grab something in your hand only to have it turn out to be just fog." The British Government's support for India was as solid as that of the US except for a division of opinion. Some officials in the Foreign Office pointed out that India's account of the historical argument for the boundaries was inflated and recommended less than categorical British support for the Indian claims. But as British viewed that its interest was concerned, it gave wholehearted and unqualified support for India.

In contrast to the committed support of the Western world, the Afro-Asian countries clung to the question of negotiation as the ground to decide their position in the diplomatic-historical argument between China and India. It seemed that China wanted India to negotiate a settlement, while India was refusing. But India proclaimed that in fact it was the other way around.

To avoid the risk of too blunt refusing the negotiation, Nehru made a statement on August 13, reaffirming that there could be no discussion without Chinese withdrawal. "The Government of India is prepared to discuss" not about the alignment of the boundaries, but about the steps by which Chinese withdrew from India-claimed territory. The surrender had to be unconditional, but the Chinese were welcome to discuss the details of the surrender ceremony. In the same speech, Nehru quoted Chen Yi's statement in Geneva that "to wish that Chinese troops would withdraw from their own territory is impossible." Nehru accused China of "laying down preconditions which make it impossible for us to carry on discussions and negotiations." The Indian argument was that the discussions prior to Chinese withdrawal would be "pre-judging or acceptance of the Chinese claim," whereas the Chinese withdrawal before discussion would be "prejudging or acceptance of the Indian claim."

In the meantime, the new "great games" on the borders were reaching climax. At the beginning of September, in the Chip Chap valley, the Indians put into effect of the orders they had been given since the Galwan confrontation, firing into and killing several Chinese who advanced close to one of the Indian posts. By the end of August, the Indians had placed nearly forty posts in Chinese-claimed territory, most staffed between a dozen to thirty and fifty men. They were more than vulnerable, in fact helpless, as they were outnumbered and outgunned. The question was not how long they could resist, if they were attacked, but was how many Chinese they could kill before being wiped out. They were the hostages of the Indian conviction, civilian and military, that China would never attack, as Kaul reported: "I am convinced that the Chinese will not attack any of our positions even if they are relatively weaker than theirs." The Chinese protests became more threatening as August passed into September. "If the Indian side should insist on threatening by armed force the Chinese border defense forces". and thereby rouse their resistance, it must bear the responsibility for all the consequences arising therefrom." Meanwhile, two Russian lumber freighters were among ships delivering arms to Cuba, of which significance was to be recognized later by the U.S. Government.

The View from Peking

Two distinct and divergent strains governed China's attitude toward India. One placed India in historical and dialectical context of the Marxist-Leninist framework, and the other as a neighbor and fellow Asian power. In late 1940s, India appeared to be on the anti-revolutionary path as the US shifted support to India after the bitter ending of supporting Chiang Kai-shek. In 1949, a Shanghai journal accused Nehru and Indian Government's pursuance of British policy as serving "the Anglo-American imperialist designs for the annexation of Tibet" and of nourishing imperialist intentions. In December 1949, India was second country to recognize the People's Republic of China, only after Burma, and actively advocated presenting the new Peking Government as the representative of China in the United Nations. Subsequently, India played an important role in the ceasefire negotiations in Korea and also in prisoner-of-war repatriation. During the years of Hindee Chinee bhai-bhai in the middle 1950s, there was muted resentment. Chou En-lai commented in 1965 of Nehru's "arrogance" and told some visiting Ceylonese politicians that "I have never met a more arrogant man than Nehru." However, the general attitudes toward India were genuinely friendly while a little patronizing. The Indian perception was that India and China were like twins in standing, with Indian seniority, and that it had been largely through India's effort that "Communist China acquired a measure of respectability throughout Asia."

In 1958, as Nehru was constant in his support for China's rightful seat in the UN, the People's Daily summed Nehru as "a friend to China and an opponent to the imperialist policy of war and aggression." Thus far Nehru's polices were consistent with Leninist scheme of a progressive nationalism, in which a temporary but valid alliance formed between the bourgeoisie and part o the exploited classes in the first stage of struggle against imperialism. In 1959, as the Dalai Lama fled to India, Chinese had no objections, as Chou En-lai said that it was normal international practice to grant the Dalai Lama sanctuary, although they complained of the impressive welcome extended to the Dalai Lama. Later Indian Government did not keep up its promise that the Dalai Lama would not be allowed to engage in political activities against

China while he was in India. China also complained of the Kuomintang and American agents who were actively supporting the Tibetan émigrés in Kalimpong, channeling anti-Chinese propaganda, weapons and agents across the still very open border. China denounced the rebellion in Tibet as counter-revolution and an attempt to sustain the "dark, cruel and barbarous serf system" by the class that benefited from it. As the US started developing designs on India's non-aligned virtue, especially the emergence of the Indian approach to the boundary questions, China began to watch Indian attitudes and policy for signs that India entered the imperialists" camp. China regarded seriously India's unilateral and unannounced modification of the McMahon Line and the establishment of posts. In the Longju incident, the Indians fired first. In Kongka Pass incident, a large Indian patrol attempted to move into Chinese-occupied territory and set up post there. This was more ominous as it concerned an area of thousands of square miles, with high strategic importance to China.

China viewed the Indian's insistence for China to accept the unilateral Indian definition of boundary what "British imperialism had fabricated covertly but never dared to put forward." India claimed Aksai Chin in which it did not have any material interests, and China regarded this as "India's "demand that China get out of her only traffic route to Western Tibet, a road India has no use for, was "seeking injury to China without benefit to India." India's attempt for rough disdain for Chinese national sensibilities was nothing new to China. The Chinese history was replete with boundaries unilaterally imposed by stronger countries and with foreign arrogance and power. But now, "the days when the Chinese people could be bossed around are gone for ever." Chen Yi said mildly that by imposing the McMahon Line on China, India had not "given the slightest consideration to the sense of national pride and self-respect of the Chinese people." In spite of China's reasonable approach, India took a path that led to an intractable dispute and "created tensions in relations" with China.

China submitted the Indian actions and attributed the root cause of the boundary dispute to the prisms of Marxist-Leninist analysis in the "ever-sharpening class contradictions and social contradictions and the deepening political crisis facing the Nehru

Government." By the beginning of 1960, the Indian Government substituted reactionary nationalism for anti-imperialist and anti-feudal revolution, and inclined itself closer to the imperialist and feudal forces. China considered Nehru as a captive of the forces of reaction and that he may free himself to bring forth a progressive influence on Indian policy. The People's Daily wrote that Nehru was "respected in China" and regretted that Nehru had "let himself be drawn into the whirlpool of anti-Chinese agitation in India." The Chinese attitude to Nehru changed after the summit talks of April 1960. Chou En-lai was shocked by Nehru's intransigence and described Nehru as impossible to negotiate with, "being both unreliable and impenetrable." Chou resented that "he did not say it face to face, but as soon as we had left he attacked the Chinese Government as aggressors." China did not openly denounce Nehru until late in 1962, but from 1960 regarded Nehru as "the loyal representative of the big bourgeoisie and big landlords of India" and stooge of China's international enemies.

The Indian Government also fulfilled China's ideological expectations as the American assistance doubled in four years, as compared to previous twelve years, after Eisenhower's visit in 1959. The conclusion was obvious: "The more anti-Chinese India is, the greater is the increase in US aid," which had increased "in direct proportion to the extent to which the Nehru Government has served United States imperialism and opposed China." In the Chinese analysis of the Indian politico-economic polices after independence, India continued as a colonial economy, with its foreign investment increasing 150 per cent by 1960, in which the British share doubled and American multiplied, as India became more dependent on foreign aid. A conservative Indian journal, Capital, pointed out in 1960 that "almost he entire third plan depends on (foreign aid): if the foreign aid does not come, the plan will have to be scrapped, since India "sown foreign exchange reserves are already below the minimum." In 1962, an independent journal, United Asia, concluded on the pervasive and profound dependence of Indian economy, that "any drastic cuts in, or cessation, of foreign aid would immediately engender a major economic crisis in India, accompanied by the closing down of large numbers of companies, reduced productions, unemployment and uncontrollable inflation." China noted later: "Whenever imperialist "aid" appears, genuine economic sovereignty and economic independence vanish for all practical purposes."

In the beginning of 1960s, China saw the frequent use of force by Indian Government as the armory of repressive measures inherited from the British. Chinese found another passage from Nehru's own Marxist phase to describe the political processes in India: "So long as capitalism can use the machinery of democratic institutions to hold down and keep down labor, democracy is allowed to flourish, but when this is not possible than capitalism discards democracy and adopts the open fascist methods of violence and terror." China viewed that the Indian Government has made itself "the pawn of the international anti-China campaign," and concluded that "is the root cause and background of the Sino-Indian boundary dispute," which was created as a pretext for domestic and international propaganda. The Chinese policy toward other governments springs from how they act towards China, not from the political characters, as stated in a motto: "It's not what you are, it's the way that you act."

This was illustrated in the Chinese attitudes towards Pakistan, which pursued an unfriendly policy towards China through the 1950s, but changed course at the end of 1959. The settlement of the Sino-Pakistani boundary lead to cordial and civil relations with China, and ultimately a tacit alliance against India. China did not make the full ideological denunciation of Nehru and his Government until very late in the border dispute, and anathematized Nehru in October 1962, while continuing to stress Sino-Indian friendship and that China would never close the door to a negotiated settlement. China repeatedly reiterated that "there is no conflict of fundamental interests between China and India," and that the boundary question was essentially one of small and temporary importance.

The Longju incident had a destructive impact for Sino-Soviet relations. The incident was reported without question in the Indian version that it was an instance of deliberate and unprovoked aggression by China. The Chinese account of the clash was ignored and subsequent Nehru's admission that the boundary was "varied" by India "because it was not considered a good line" completely missed. Western observers were so convinced already that China was a bellicose and bullying power that the incident was interpreted accordingly, confirming their preconception. On September 6, Chinese informed the Soviet Union the background of the incident that it occurred on the Chinese side of the McMahon Line and the Indians fired at the Chinese frontier guards first.

But the explanation carried no conviction with the Russians, who were to release a statement three days later. China handed a letter of Chou En-lai that was written to Nehru on September 8 in a sharply worded statement that the "trespassing and provocations by Indian troops" caused the armed clash at Longju. China urged Russia not to release the statement, but it was circulated that night, which indicated the agreement of the "leading circles" of Soviet Union regretting the incident. Soviet Union deplored that the two largest Asian countries discredited the idea of peaceful coexistence, and expressed confidence that "both Governments will settle the misunderstanding that has arisen." While Nehru viewed the position as "a more or less dispassionate view of the situation," China reacted violently to the Russian Government for "assuming a façade of neutrality" and "making no distinction between right and wrong," which by implication favored India and condemned China.

China was faced with double difficulty that was to beset and damage China in dealing with India. There was a credibility gap in which the universal tendency of people to accept the Indian version as the truth, and also the general readiness to conclude that Indians got the worst of the battle and they could not have possibly have provoked it. A conflict of doctrines emerged between China and India. Krushchev flatly denounced the war as an instrument of policy, for he believed that "force" must absolutely not be used against he capitalist world, no matter how strong the Communists might be." Krushchev placed his denunciation of the "Left revisionists" in Peking in handling the dispute with India. Krushchev rejected Chinese complaint that the Soviet Union had let them down by refusing to take side against India. In contrast he blamed China for having let down the cause of socialism and, by quarrelling with India, China failed to cooperate with the Soviet Union in encouraging India to move toward socialism. China was advised to take heart of Lenin's denunciation of great-nation chauvinism, and accused China for having made Nehru a national hero in India, which was exactly what the imperialists wanted.

The Soviet Union approached its boundary problems responsibly. Had it acted like China, it would have declared war on Iran more than once, after repeated clashes on the Russian-Iranian frontier and with casualties. The Russian position, ironically, was precisely the same as China's, as Pravda put it: "We have always believed, and continue to believe, that there were no reasons for the border conflict between India and China" There is no doubt that had the two sides sat down at a conference table and discussed their mutual charges calmly, soberly and without bias, the conflict would have been settled long ago" Although this was consistent with Chinese argument again and again urging India in an attempt to convince India that the boundaries must be settled by negotiation, the Soviet Union appeared to have concluded that the Chinese were lying in their accounts and hypocritical in their proposals of negotiation. They could not believe that as week a country as India would actually challenge China. The demonstrative neutrality of Soviet Union encouraged India to persist in its approach to the boundary questions, and the Russian aircraft enabled the Indians to implement the forward policy, thereby helping India on the way to disaster.

The Sino-Russian borders were the products of the Imperial Russian's drive for territory and China's weakness during the nineteenth century. In the middle of nineteenth century, Russians annexed all of China's territory north of the Amur River, and was grinding into China in central Asia, pushing back the frontier of Chinese Tukestan (Sinkiang). In 1911, at the establishment of the Republic of China, the Chinese nationalists began demanding the abrogation of the "unequal treaties" and restoration of former frontiers. In 1917, Commissar for Foreign Affairs declared that the Soviet Government repudiated all unequal treaties. The Karakhan manifesto confirmed in 1920 that "The Government of the "Soviet Republic declares as void all the treaties concluded by the former Government of Russia with China, renounces all the annexations of Chinese territory, all the concessions in China and returns to China free of charge and forever all that was ravenously taken from her by the Tsar's Government and by the Russian bourgeoisie." But the Soviet Government very soon came to the view that, unequal treaties or not, the Sino-Russian boundaries should stay where they were. The Chinese were prepared to accept the boundaries and to regard the lost territories as gone for good, despite of bitter resentment of the injustice over the "unequal treaties" and national humiliations. In 1960, the Chinese Government proposed to Moscow to negotiate the boundary settlements.

In 1964, when the negotiations began, the Soviet Union adopted exactly the same approach to the boundary question as had India: "There is nothing to discuss except what we agree to discuss," and was as unacceptable as the Indian approach. Like Nehru, the Russian were willing, indeed eager, to settle with China on minor boundary rectifications, but refused to enter into general boundary negotiations. As the Chinese made explicitly clear that they were prepared to accept the old treaties, the Russians played deaf as did the Indians. It was probable that the Russian and Indian perceived the Chinese insistence on equality at the negotiation table as a challenge.

As the Sino-Soviet quarrel intensified through 1960, the Russian support of India became a key charge in China's ideological denunciation of Krushchev's "revisionism." China viewed the Tibetan revolt marked Nehru's swerve to the Right. Now the national bourgeois Government of India entered second phase, in which the workers, peasants, and intellectuals began their struggle against the bourgeoisie, Nehru Government manufactured a frontier dispute with China in order to postpone the day of reckoning.

In the autumn of 1960, Russia opened a new and deeply provocative chapter by providing a major military assistance to India, including Anthnov-12 heavy transport aircraft and then "Hound" helicopter suited to operate at 16-17,000 feet altitudes in Ladakh. Against vigorous protests of the British and American Governments, the Indians purchased MiG jet fighters from Russia.

In the autumn of 1961, when the Indian military activity increased in the western sector as purposeful and coordinated, China recognized the Indian "attempt to realize territorial claims unilaterally and by force." In the middle of 1962, the People's Daily warned that it would be "very erroneous and dangerous should the Indian Government take China's attitude of restraint and tolerance as an expression of weakness." The Indians "mistook China's long forbearance as a sign that China was weak and could be bullied.

They thought that with the backing of the imperialists and support of the Soviet leaders they had nothing to fear, and that as soon as they took action China would be forced to retreat and their territorial claims would be realized." The alternative became clear. China could either agree to withdraw from the disputed territory and surrender to India's diplomatic and military pressure at the cost of national pride and prestige as well as strategic position in the Tibet-Sinkiang region, or China could take up the Indian challenge and fight.

Like the Russians, China wished to avoid major, especially nuclear, wars, but they could not truckle to the imperialists. As Mao Tse-tung put it, the "US imperialism and the Chiang Kai-shek clique" must not be overestimated as they were "rotten to the core and had no future," and therefore can be slighted in the strategic context. "But in regard to any particular situation or specific struggle "we must never slight the enemy: on the contrary, we can win victory only when we take full account of him and devote all our energies to the fight." In 1929, after a dispute over the Chinese Eastern Railway, the Kuomintang Government of China attacked the Russian border. The Soviet Union invaded Manchuria, destroyed a Kuomintang army, and withdrew to its own territory. China now considered this, "compelled to act in self-defense," a perfectly right thing to do.

The resolute Russian counterblow defended the national interests of the Soviet Union, and also "accorded with the interests of the Chinese people and of the revolutionary people of the world." With this thinking, China warned in September 1962, as the Indians determinedly pressed forward: "If the Indian side should insist on threatening by armed force the Chinese defense forces who are duty-bound to defend their territory, and thereby arouse their resistance, it must bear the responsibility for all the consequences arising therefrom."

The Border War

The Ridge and the River

In the summer of 1962, the public attention in India was focused on the western sector of the borders. The Indian Government reversed the actuality and propagated the belief that it was China that was deliberately pushing forward in order to expand. While pursuing a policy of utmost recklessness, the Government successfully obscured the facts to the outside world as well as to the Indian mass that increasingly complained of the inability to challenge China with boldness and determination. Nehru had deprived himself of all options, as suspending the forward policy would be construed as surrender and betrayal of the national cause. Since Nehru had misled the nation into the belief that the Indian Army was strong enough to handle the Chinese, he had no choice but to rely on the military force to counteract the Chinese. While the forward policy was being implemented in the western sector, the border war was triggered by a marginal Indian move forward in the eastern sector, where the Chinese observed the McMahon Line as the de facto boundary.

After the Longju incident in August 1959, the eastern sector had been quiet as Nehru and Chou En-lai agreed to suspend patrol along the McMahon Line on both sides. The forward policy reversed the orders and made the McMahon Line a live border again. In December 1961, Eastern Command was ordered to move forward to the closest practicable posts to the McMahon Line. To reach the Line, it took weeks of trekking, and supplying became an acute problem, often placing the remote garrisons in real danger of starvation. As the senior officers pointed out the impracticability of posting troops, unlike the western sector, their representations were brushed aside. In February 1962, General Kaul went to Assam to personally deal with the protests, and in the first half of 1962, the Army set up twenty-four posts along the McMahon Line.

On the eastern sector, the Chinese did not counteract so long as the Indians kept to their own side of the McMahon Line. As the exact alignment of Longju was disputed, the Indians did not reoccupy it in 1962. However, the Indians set off the border war by establishing a new post at the disputed territory at the western extremity of the McMahon Line. The Line terminated on the boundary with Bhutan at the latitude of 27o44'30"N on the map signed by the British and the Tibetans in New Delhi on March 24, 1914. When the Line was transported to the coordinates to the ground, it did not lie along the highest ridge in the vicinity, which in fact lied three to four miles north of where McMahon drew the line, at Thag La ridge.

Since August of 1959, the Indians set up a post north of the McMahon Line at Khinzemane, by which Indians claimed to and moved into an area of about twenty-five square miles north of the map-marked McMahon Line. This brought instant Chinese reaction. About two hundred Chinese came, as Nehru said later, "physically pushing back" the ten or twelve men of the Assam Rifles a couple of miles in the direction where they came from. But two days later, the Indians returned to Khinzemane and said they would resist to the Chinese who tried to push they back again. The Chinese acquiesced. New Delhi protested to Peking on August 11, claiming that Khinzemane was in Indian territory and that Thag La ridge was the boundary "traditionally as well as by treaty map." India referred "tradition" to the seasonal grazing practiced by the herdsmen from a southern village, but the villagers from the north used the area the same way. The claim of the treaty map was false as neither Thag La ridge nor Khinzemane was identified on the map.

China protested too, claiming that Khinzemane was "undoubtedly part of Chinese territory" and that India made "serious encroachments upon China's sovereignty and territorial integrity," warning India of serious consequences if the Indians post were not withdrawn. India modified a proposal requesting China to leave the status quo at Khinzemane undisturbed, while India would undertake no further change, "pending further discussions." China did not follow up the threat of "serious consequences," and the Indian post at Khinzemane was unmolested for the next three years, until India broke its implicit undertaking by setting up another post in the area.

In May 1962, the ban on patrolling to the west of Khinzemane was lifted and XXXIII Corps was ordered to set up several posts, including one at the trijunction of India, China and Bhutan. The platoon patrol of Assam Rifles, which were under control of the civilian arm through the governor of Assam, disregarded the McMahon Line and treated the Thag La ridge as the boundary. They set up a post there on June 4, overlooking the sizeable Tibetan village of Le, but there was no sign of the Chinese who still observed the 1959 no patrol agreement. Then the Corps recommended to establish Dhola Post in the Khinzemane area, which the Ministry of External Affairs approved and marked the point of no return.

The eastern sector remained quiet until September 8, when the Chinese treated Dhola Post the same as they did to the Indian forward posts in the west. About sixty Chinese suddenly appeared down Thag La ridge and pressed close to the post. The Indian commander in the post exaggerated the number to six hundred, with the hope of bringing the Army to his assistance, calculating that if he reported a realistic figure, his own small force would be left to handle the situation. But the Chinese did not surround or attack Dhola Post. They settled into nearby positions and dominated the post. On September 16, China followed diplomatic protest that Indians were intruding further and "reveal how ambitious the Indian side's aggressive designs are "also show that the Indian side is actively extending the tension to the entire Sino-Indian boundary," warning that India would be responsible for all the consequences.

In the Anglo-Tibetan agreement of March 1914, there were no verbal descriptions of the boundary and the location of the line, which was to be determined only by reading off and transposing the longitude and latitude from the original treaty map to the ground. This would plainly leave Dhola Post and Thag La ridge, like Khinzemane, north of the McMahon Line and in Chinese territory. However, the Indian Government insisted that McMahon intended to run the boundary along the lines of high ridges and, since Thag La ridge was the dominant feature, the boundary must lie along Thag La ridge. In Indian views, Thag La ridge had become a definitive and absolute boundary, and Dhola Post belonged to India as indisputably as New Delhi to itself. Based on its clear logic, India pushed the forward policy one explosive stage further. It was first thought that Indian patrols would infiltrate into Chinese-occupied territory and China would not retaliate. Then the Indian posts would cut off Chinese posts and force them to withdraw, and China would not retaliate. And now Indians would attack and force the Chinese back and China would not attack. The Indian Government built up the public confidence and expectation such that any marginal incursions by the Chinese on the McMahon Line, which was clearly and absolutely the boundary, would not be tolerated. It was further believed that the disadvantages were all on China's side and the Indian Army was well placed to defend the border, while the truth was reverse.

The road construction made movement relatively easy for the Chinese, whose troops had been stationed in Tibet for years, physically attuned and acclimatized to the high altitude as well as suitably clothed and equipped. On the Indian side, lateral movement was extremely difficult as the valleys lay north to south and the constant landslides and washouts during the monsoon made it unaffordable to cut roads. The Indians were disadvantaged throughout NEFA.

As the Chinese road led to a point three hours, it took six days' march for the Indians to reach Tawang. By the time Indian troops reached Tawang, they were exhausted and often sick with pulmonary edema, due to lack of acclimatization to and sudden exertion at high altitude. By as late as October 1962, Nehru still informed the journalists that the advantage lay with India in NEFA, and by September 1962, the belief had become an accepted truth in India.

Despite of public pressure, the Indian Government did not have to be pushed into actions. On September 9, a meeting was held in the Defense Ministry, which decided that the Chinese must be evicted immediately. As Nehru left for a Commonwealth Prime Ministers' conference in London the day before, the meeting was conducted by Menon, who like other ministers, followed Nehru's style of decision making without consulting the Cabinet. Although Menon initially did not favor the forward policy and inclined towards a negotiated boundary settlement with China, after failing to convince Nehru, now he took a strong and public line to eject the Chinese from Thag La ridge.

The officers at the Defense Ministry meeting raised the issue that Dhola Post was in Chinese territory in their own maps, but they were told to disregard the maps and treat the crest of Thag La ridge as the boundary. General Thapar accepted the eviction order, which was code-named Leghorn, and XXXIII Corps was to move to Dhola Post immediately, without considering the difficulties in supplying the troops in an extremely difficult and little-known country. The military and civilian leadership, the latter with overriding command over the former, took unprofessional, overoptimistic and even irrational view of the military possibilities. On September 12, General Singh, of XXXIII Corps assured his superior officers of his determination to take actions, but suggested that Dhola Post should simply be withdrawn because of the limitations of his troops.

The Chinese could quickly build up to divisional strength north of Tawang, and would outbid any Indian reinforcements in Thag La ridge. The Indian troops would have to rely on air supply, and also need heavy winter clothing and tents. General Sen of the Eastern Command personally went to Singh and other officers repeating the order to throw back the Chinese over Thag La ridge. On September 14, 9 Punjab battalion marched out for Dhola Post, with about four hundred rifles, half of the full complement of eight hundred. The second battalion of the brigade was ordered to move within forty-eight hours to Dhola Post, which was also at half strength.

By September 14, Army Head Quarter (H.Q.) learned the actual number of Chinese below Thag La ridge was only fifty or sixty, the true information that would unlikely have brought forth so drastic of reaction. But Army H.Q. did not call off the eviction move, but ordered the Punjabis to capture Thag La by September 19, but the order did not reached the Punjabis until September 19 itself. The Punjabis reached the Namka Chu early on September 15, still two full days of march away from Dhola Post, moving on hard scale rations and pouch ammunitions aside from heavy weapons and mortar ammunition.

The Punjabis encountered the Chinese in company strength on both sides of the river that was forced by the monsoon rains. The Chinese reportedly "shouted in Hindi that the Indians should withdraw from the Namka Chu area as it was Chinese territory. They said that the Indian and Chinese peoples had an unbreakable friendship and this friendship should not be marred by petty border incidents. "They asked (the Indians) to send (their) local civil officers to discuss the exact location of the border." In response, the Indian political officer was ordered not to have discussions with the Chinese. The commanding officer of the Punjabis spread the battalion out along the Namka Chu in order to relieve Dhola Post, reopen the supply route and prevent Chinese incursion. Since September 13, Brigadier Dalvi, who was a forty-two-year-old graduate of the Indian Military Academy, had been ordered to move from Tawang to the Namka Chu. As the Indians laboriously built up force on the Namka Chu, the Chinese on the other side of the river kept pace with them effortlessly.

The Indian military intelligence (M.I.) declined during the last days of the British. There were no Indians in M.I. after 1947, and the civilian Intelligence Bureau (I.B.) replaced its role. Policy officers staffed the I.B., and a former officer Malik headed the Bureau and had an important place in the innermost counsels of the government. By 1960s Malik was widely accepted in domestic politics, especially his predictions about Chinese behavior. The forward policy was based on the rock solid faith established upon his appreciation, or rather divination, that the Chinese would not retaliate, even if India used force against the Chinese. Malik relied on extra-sensory perceptions, and helped to close the ears of Nehru and his official advisers, despite of mounting reports of increasing Chinese troops behind the McMahon Line. Nehru and his colleagues wished to believe that Chinese could be forced back without trouble. When a news agency reported of this on September 10, the Government tried to persuade the agency to withdraw it and then report that it was unfounded.

When spokesman confirmed on September 13 that "some Chinese forces have appeared in the area of the Bhutan trijunction" there was unwillingness to say squarely that Chinese troops deliberately crossed the McMahon Line. The spokesman simply said on September 14, "A Chinese group appears to be on our side." The Government leaked news constantly and most secret decisions appear in the press at extraordinary speed. The official attempt to suppress reports of Thag La ridge was thus unsuccessful, and the domestic critics obliged the Government to expel the Chinese instantly even if single Chinese crossed the McMahon Line, let alone Chinese forced across the line. The public, including the Congress, was outraged at the universally believed new Chinese aggression, unprovoked and insolent. The Swatantra Party called for Nehru's resignation for the "utter failure to protect India's borders," and the demands increased over the Government to issue an ultimatum to China, as impatience grew with the Government's countermeasures.

General Singh at XXXIII Corps were reluctant to put troops where they could not be supplied and to launch an operation that was militarily impossible. The Chief of General Staff, General Thapar, expressed in a meeting in the Defense Ministry on September 22 that China would retaliate in the western sector and perhaps against all forward Indians posts east of the Chinese claim line. But a stock civilian reassurance overrode the concern. The Defense Ministry and External Affairs calculated to give a hard and demonstrative blow at the Chinese beneath Thag La ridge so that Chinese would retreat there but also would take a much more acquiescent line elsewhere. This was derived from reading the mood and character of the Chinese Government and confirmed by Malik's estimations that no one would risk to assault a country as identified as India with the cause of peace.

General Thapar's warning was thus rejected in the Defense Ministry and the order for the Army was confirmed to evict the Chinese. General Thapar requested the order be put in writing, which came from a junior official who consulted through telephone call to the Defense Minister Menon in New York without consulting the Cabinet Defense Committee. The order overruled General Thapar's professional judgment that his force was incapable of handling the Chinese reaction to the eviction operation. Three years before, Thapar's predecessor Thimayya submitted resignation after having had a clash with Menon, and was humiliated and humbled under the name of "civil supremacy." This marked a point of no return in the Indian Army, and Thapar failed to offer his resignation. Brigadier Dalvi, much lower in rank, finally submitted resignation in protest and wrote later: "Resignation is the last constitutional resort of a service chief in a democratic set up "this is the only safeguard against incompetent, unscrupulous or ambitious politicians."

With the confirmation and passing down of the order, implementation was faced with daunting problems. The Indians were under far more strongly armed Chinese troops who outnumbered them by five or ten to one. The Namka Chu was still difficult to access and supply the troops. Rations of thirty days had to be air-dropped and stocked as well as field guns and ammunition. By the end of September, the politicians in New Delhi, including those in the Government, Congress Party and Opposition, were getting impatient with the Army "to take the steps necessary to clear the Chinese from Indian territory across Thag la ridge."

The news media and official comments expressed confidence and optimism to achieve the Indian objectives without difficulty. In contrast to the impatience, the Namka Chu was quiet in the first part of September, as the Chinese offered cigarettes to the tobacco-less Indians and even handled over parachuted Indian supplies that landed on their side. On September 17, the Chinese reported that: "While two Chinese frontier guards were on sentry duty "more than sixty Indian soldiers closed in on them from three direction. The two Chinese soldiers immediately shouted to the Indian soldiers to halt. But the Indian troops pressed forward even faster. Several of the Indian troops gathered round them at a distance of about ten meters and some came as close as three meters to one of the guards, aiming their British-made rifles and Canadian-made sub-machine-guns and howling out at the top of their voices in wanton provocation."

On September 20, the first shooting occurred, leaving two Chinese dead and five Indians wounded. Peking protested and demanded that "the Indian side immediately stop its attack and withdraw," warning that the Chinese would fire back in defense. The People's Daily wrote: "the situation is most critical and the consequences will be serious. Let the Indian authorities not say that warning has not been served in advance." The Indians counter protested in almost the same language, calling China to "cease aggressive activities on Indian territory" and withdraw or "be responsible for all the consequences." Both sides were saber-rattling, but India's scabbard was empty.

The official Indian accounts of exchanges of fire below Thag La ridge blamed the Chinese for having provoked them. This pressed the journalists and politicians to blame the field commanders as sluggish, and specifically pointed the blame on General Singh. When General Singh went to Eastern Command on September 29, General Sen refused to accept Singh's requirement as impossible to meet. Singh wrote to protest both the impracticability of the operation that he was ordered to launch and the impropriety of Sen's handling of the situation. Sen presented the written protest as an example of uncooperativeness and on October 2, both Thapar and Sen asked Menon to remove Singh from commanding XXXIII Corps, to which Menon agreed. The difficulties in finding a replacement made them decide to not simply remove Singh but to form XXXIII Corps into another corps to take over operations on the northwestern border.

On October 3, it was decided that the new IV Corps should be headed by Kaul and would be made responsible for immediate launching of Operation Leghorn. Despite that Kaul had never commanded troops in combat, Nehru and Menon regarded Kaul as savior and were convinced that China would not strike back and the operation would be a straightforward one. The delusion was fused such that the operation would speedily succeed only if the right man commanded the troops. When Thapar repeated the possibility of Chinese counterblows, according to Kaul, Nehru replied that he had "good reason to believe that the Chinese would not take any strong action against us." As Kaul went to see Nehru prior to his appointment to command IV Corps, Nehru expressed that "the Chinese would see reason and withdraw from Dhola but in case they did not, we would have no option but to expel them from our territory. If we failed to take such action, Government would forfeit public confidence completely."

While the tension was building up on the border, the last rally of diplomatic exchanges was played out. In August the Indians expressed to China that they would be glad to discuss joint withdrawal from the disputed territory in the western sector. By "joint withdrawal", the Indians meant that China withdrew from all of the territory India claimed and India withdrew only the forward posts recently established in the western sector. After the completion of those withdrawals, India would proceed to talks with only minor adjustments of the "international boundaries," i.e., the Indian claimed lines. China replied on September 13, and accused India of seeking "excuses for rejecting discussions," pointing to the continuing Indians military activities in the western sector as "sham negotiations and real fighting."

China would welcome seriously intended negotiations, but would "resist whenever attacked." China then reiterated the proposal put forward by Chou En-lai in November 1959 that the armed forces each withdraw twenty kilometers and urged further discussions first in Peking on October 15 and then in Delhi alternatively. On September 19, New Delhi agreed to talks in Peking as proposed but only based on Indian demands. "The Government of India are prepared to hold further discussions at the appropriate level to define measures to restore the status quo in the Western Sector which has been altered by force in the last few years and to remove the current tensions in that area." India would arrange talks with Peking on October 15 when China had indicated acceptance of that Indian formulation. By this time India refused to discuss the eastern sector at all, having the Punjabis set up along the Namka Chu.

China replied on October 3, when the situation along the Namka Chu had become as tense as that in the western sector. Peking dismissed the Indian demand as absolutely unacceptable that "China must withdraw from vast tracts of her territory before discussions on the Sino-Indian boundary question can start." The Chinese expressed that they were against any preconditions set up to talks, and proposed that the October 15 talk proceed in Peking to discuss any aspect of the boundary question. But India replied on October 6, explicitly and categorically refusing to discuss while blaming China for preventing the talks. India retracted its earlier agreement to open discussions, and declared that it would "not enter into any talks and discussion under duress or continued threat of force."

India insisted that it would talk only after China withdraw from Thag La and explicitly acknowledged that the talks concern only mutual withdraw in the western sector. China described this as "finally categorically shut(ting) the door to negotiations." As usual, most onlookers accepted the Indian accusation of China that "it is the Government of China who are not only refusing to undertake talks and discussions but are creating further tension and conflict in the eastern sector." Nehru had also to the last maintained that "I shall always be prepared for talks, whatever may happen, provided that the other side is decent, and it is self-respecting for us. I have never refused to talk to anyone."

As Kaul left, the newspapers in New Delhi reported with headlines "special task force created to oust Chinese" and "Gen. Kaul leaves for NEFA to assume command" as the "Indian Army poised for all-out effort." The Times of India described Kaul as "a soldier of extraordinary courage and drive" to lead the "task force," ignoring that the news of his appointment and the formation of new corps should be of highest military secret. The Defense Ministry did nothing to diminish the optimistic expectations that the Army would soon drive the Chinese out of NEFA. On October 4, General Sen met Kaul and his handpicked officers at Tezpur airport. Although Sen was formally superior, but since Nehru charged Kaul himself, Kaul was the Supreme and he notified the Army H.Q. that he was taking command. Kaul's task was to command 7 Brigade, complete the operation, and return to his job in New Delhi. After flying to visit military stations, Kaul reported on October 6 to Army H.Q. of heavy Chinese build-up below Thag La ridge, with artillery, heavy mortars, and medium machine-guns, "apart from other dangerous weapons they possess such as recoilless guns and automatic rifles." The Operation Leghorn was to be launched on October 10, and Kaul was "taking every possible step to outwit the enemy and capture our objective." After warning the possibility that the Chinese might overrun the Indian forces, Kaul proposed that Air Force should be alerted to be quickly deployed and to retrieve the situation.

Kaul reached Dhola Post on the afternoon of October 7, and spent the rest of the day studying the ground, which presented discouraging difficulties on the Indians side with deep and fast-flowing Namka Chu. The Chinese dominated the Indian positions and lines of communications, and had prepared strong bunks and cleared timbers with infantry and equipment, taunting the Indian troops who tried to cut logs with entrenching tools and shovels. On the evening, Kaul sent another message to New Delhi, bypassing the regular channel through Army H.Q., in an immensely lengthy report, which were chatty and descriptive, more like a letter to a fond uncle at home than military signals. It took eight hours to transmit the lengthy message which described the difficulties confronting the Indian forces, including the strength of the Chinese, desperate supply position, lack of ammunition and rations, and lack of winter clothing as two of the three battalions were still in summer uniforms.

"I must point out" the Chinese are bound to put in a strong counterattack "to dislodge us from the positions we capture. I have no resources with which to meet this threat and therefore recommend "all military and air resources are marshaled now for restoration of position in our favor." Kaul's faith that the Chinese would fight back came under great strain and could no longer take the strength of the Chinese positions, the power of their weapons, and their easy reinforcements as exaggerated report by officers who did not have stomach for battle. "Despite all these difficulties," Kaul decided to proceed with Operation Leghorn and to order the more heavily armed 7 Brigade into an attack.

On October 7, Kaul received a report from Army H.Q. that was sent from the Indian Consul General in Lhasa. The report informed, without comment, that heavy mortars and artillery in divisional strength were concentrating on the Chinese side of the McMahon Line behind Thag La, and that the troops talked of an attack on Tawang. On October 8, Kaul began the opening moves in Operation Leghorn, and on October 9, he disclosed his intentions to officers that there was no option but to carryout the operation on October 10 as it was the last acceptable date to the Cabinet. He then ordered the Rajputs to move next day to Yumtso La pass at 16,000 feet on the west of Thag La, who were to take up positions behind and dominate the Chinese. This order came as unbelievable to the officers as they all knew the conditions of the Indian troops and the great strength of the Chinese positions.

The Chinese were bound to respond violently to the move as they have warned repeatedly that they would not allow any

Indians across the river. Kaul dismissed the demurrals of Brigadier Dalvi and General Prasad who pointed out that the Indian troops could not survive at 16,000 feet without winter clothing and could not be supplied, and that they could be slaughtered on the way without covering artillery. Instead, he ordered a patrol of some fifty Punjabis who crossed the river on October 9 and reached Tseng-jong before dusk, without being interfered or attacked by the Chinese. This put Kaul on high spirit, who had just received a signal from Thapar affirming the Government's faith in him and those who warned of the Chinese reaction felt like "bloody fools" as Prasad put it. Kaul sent another long signal describing the manifold disadvantages of his forces and reporting that his "bold and speedy tactics" took the enemy by surprise and had in fact already occupied the crest.

As the Rajputs grouped and moved towards the Yumtso La pass on October 10, Kaul kept to deadline. But the Chinese reacted, shattering the eviction plan and the premise upon which the forward policy was constructed and border dispute was handled. Kaul described "when I was getting ready and my batman was boiling water for tea". I heard considerable fire from across the river." A full battalion of Chinese quickly moved down the ridge and formed up for an attack on Tseng-jong, where the Indian position came under heavy mortar fire. The Chinese troops outnumbered the Indians by nearly twenty to one, with the smashing mortar barrage, Dalvi exclaimed to Kaul: "Oh my God, you're right, they mean business."

Kaul handed control over to Dalvi and decided to personally apprise Nehru of the situation and set off down the Namka Chu for New Delhi. Meanwhile he ordered that the eviction operation should be suspended and the brigade should hold its positions along the Namka Chu and at Tsangle. The first Chinese assault on the Indians at Tseng-jong were beaten off. The Chinese came under enfilade fire and suffered heavy casualties, being unaware of the section covering the Tseng-jong position from the flank. The Punjabis commander asked for covering fire from the mortars and machine-guns. Dalvi refused, unable to risk the whole force to be wiped out. Dalvi ordered the Punjabis to disengage and retreat to the river. The Chinese held their fires and let the Indian survivors to cross the bridge to the south bank. Indian casualties were seven killed, seven missing, and eleven wounded, whereas the Chinese reported thirty-three killed and wounded. The Chinese buried the Indian dead with full military honors as watched by their comrades across the river line.

Kaul reported to New Delhi of the grave situation and requested permission to return to give firsthand account of the "new and sudden development" before Nehru left for Ceylon on October 12. The little battle of Tseng-jong, in which the Chinese fought with massive force and determination, was grave for the Indians as it belied the conviction that was at the heart of the forward policy, that the Chinese would never deliberately and determinedly attack Indians. Kaul was now, like many of the troops, suffering from a pulmonary disorder as a result of lack of acclimatization to high altitude. As he return to New Delhi on October 11, a fullest conference on the border crisis was held. But despite of the dangerous crisis that India faced, Nehru still did not bring the Cabinet or the Cabinet Defense Committee for consultation. Kaul opened the meeting, reporting the battle in all graphic and subjective accounts.

When asked for recommendation, Kaul did not urge to withdraw 7 Brigade, but proposed to seek speedy and copious military assistance from the United States, which Nehru dismissed with some irritation. Kaul then suggested postponing the eviction operation and then pulling 7 Brigade back to better tactical positions, but other participants contradicted.

A consensus appeared that eviction operation had to be postponed, but no clear instructions were issued. Thapar and Sen intended to keep their troops at the present position, while Kaul planned to cancel the attack order but keeping the brigade on the river line. Operation Leghorn committed too many reputations in civilian and service sides now to be demonstratively abandoned. Nehru announced that it was a decision that soldiers need to make and asked that their views and advice be given to the Government. Nehru's military advisers gave him what he wished to hear, with assurance, that China would not "do anything big". The mutual delusion led the October 11 meeting to decide that 7 Brigade should stay at its present location.

The next morning, as Nehru left for the three-day visit to Ceylon, he gave his usually accessible briefing to the press prior to boarding the plane. During the past month, as the Government gave orders to force the Chinese out of the McMahon Line, there were always suggestions that Indian troops were beating off Chinese attacks. When asked what orders were given to the troops in NEFA, Nehru replied that "our instructions are to free our territory" and, when asked for a timeline, "I cannot fix a date, that is entirely for the Army." He then "pointed out that wintry conditions had set in already in the (Thag La) region, and the Chinese were strongly positioned because they were in large numbers and were situated on higher ground." When the correspondents sought assurances that the Government had no intention of having talks, Nehru said: "As long as this particular aggression lasts, there appears to be no chance of talks."

After the debacle, Nehru was criticized for deliberately misleading the country with this public confirmation of the eviction order, which had been suspended because the operation was beyond the capability of the Indian troops. Nehru later defended himself: "It was the viewpoint of the military people too, they wanted to do it, otherwise I would not have dared to say anything like that." Nehru emphasized that he tried to give warnings about wintry conditions and the Chinese advantages. However, if Nehru intended to warn the public, the public was not listening. Official spokesmen had long been giving assurances that everything in NEFA was under control, and even Nehru himself was convinced that the physical advantages were all on India's side in NEFA. The press was enthusiastic of Nehru's statement in the airport. "Mr. Nehru has told the country, clearly and firmly, what it has been waiting to hear, that the armed forces have been ordered to throw the Chinese aggressors out of NEFA and that until Indian territory in that area is cleared of them there can be no talks with China."

Encouraged by the Goa operation, the public was so confident in the prowess and invincibility of the Army that it demanded for hasty actions. A New Delhi editor with good official contacts revealed that the Chinese below Thag La ridge were "third-rate garrison troops" who would present no problems once the attack began. This information was presumed to originate in Malik's crystal ball in the Intelligence Bureau. Dalvi said of his first contact with the Chinese: "I must admit I was impressed with the Chinese soldiers. Those were no scruffy Frontier Guards; they appeared to be healthy, well-clad, well-armed and determined troops." However, the universal impression in India was that the Indian troops were strong, properly equipped and confident task force who was held back from surging over the inferior Chinese force only by the excessive forbearance or timidity of the Indian Government.

Nehru's airport statement slipped the least leash and the Indian public began to await victorious news from their troops in Thag La. China also draw a similar conclusion, as the People's Daily wrote: "Prime Minister Nehru has openly and formally authorized the Indian military to attack China's Tibet region at any time," and "a massive invasion of Chinese territory by Indian troops in the eastern sector of the Chinese boundary seems imminent." The Chinese then advised Nehru: "Pull back from the brink of the precipice, and don't use the lives of Indian troops as stakes in your gamble."

The Chinese looked down from strong bunkers on Thag La ridge, in their comfortable thick padded uniforms and confidence in their numbers and weapons, at the unfortunate hungry and cold Indian troops on the river line. China had no reason whatsoever to fear an Indian attack, but had every reason to expect it. Chinese intelligence learned of October 10 Operation Leghorn, and on October 8 the Soviet informed the Foreign Ministry in Peking that India was on the point of launching a major attack. Krushchev told the Chinese Ambassador in Moscow later that it was natural for China to fight back if it were attacked. The Chinese remarked that the Russian helicopters and transport aircraft that helped India to prepare the offensive did not help the Sino-Russian goodwill among the Chinese frontier guards. For months, India ignored all China's warnings of retaliation, but probed forward in the western sector and applied exactly the same tactics to take over territory north of the McMahon Line.

After heavy Chinese casualties on the first Indian attempt at Tseng-jong on October 10, the Indians had learned no lesson but intended to mount further attacks as soon as they were ready.

Nehru's words were not bluff and confirmed that Indian troops at Namka Chu were deployed for assault and indeed were being reinforced. China did not have many options. China could continue trying to persuade India to settle the boundary through negotiation and to convince other governments that the Chinese position was reasonable and that if conflict broke out on the boundaries, it was the result of India's behavior. But by now this policy did not seem worth while. Enjoying its higher credibility, India continued skirmishing along the Sino-Indian boundaries while accusing China of provoking clashes and committing aggression. The Western countries were solidly with India, the Soviet Union was in sympathy with India as were most of the fraternal parties, and many afro-Asian countries also leaned toward India's side. Prolongation of the situation on the boundary was militarily injurious to China as well. It would require troops to be in a state of readiness for battle, and also complicating the problem of pacifying Tibet. By October 1962, the alternative was clear: meet the Indian challenge with a counterblow so powerful and resolute as to end it.

The political objective of the Chinese military action was to bring India to the negotiating table, and to demonstrate to India and to the world the fallacy of their assumptions. The western formulations, especially popular in the U.S. was that China was going to "humble India and to seize the leadership of Asia," or to "put a brake on India's development by forcing her to build up militarily." These assumptions were uncharacteristic and unlikely, as the Chinese leaders would never for a moment have supposed that any country but China could ever aspire to the leadership of Asia, and that India, with its capitalist system and national bourgeois government, could challenge China in a race to development.

This idea must have been absurd to Peking's Communist purists even in 1962 when China had economic difficulties after the Great Leap Forward failed. But Indians, especially Nehru, who thought of China as equal of China or superior, suggested that war between India and China would shake the world, but neither would "knock the other flat." Furthermore, the Sino-Indian dispute contributed much to China's great falling-out with the

Soviet Union. A blow at India would expose the covert Indian alliance with the Americans and the ideological error of Moscow's support for India. Such a blow must be on a grand scale, as wiping out the forty or some small Indian posts might achieve nothing but bringing in continued disturbances from the Indians when they felt able and start moving forward again. The real provocation for China was in the west, but the military and political opportunity for demonstrative and destructive retaliation was in the east in a strong move into the disputed territory beneath the McMahon Line. From the beginning of October, the Chinese Army was concentrating behind the McMahon Line, and by October 17, the Chinese troops on Thag La ridge began active preparations for the actual assault.

The meeting on October 11 left no definite decision and created confusions and contradictions that followed. Kaul returned to his headquarters on October 13 and informed his subordinates that he failed to persuade the Government and that the eviction order must be carried out. General Thapar though appeared to have understood that Leghorn was to be postponed. Argument and uncertainty followed the next nine days. Menon, Kaul, and the General Staff still hoped that the Chinese could be thrown back and were determined not to withdraw from the Namka Chu. On October 14, Menon made his commitment to evict the Chinese more clearer than Nehru, by declaring that it was "the policy of the Government of India to eject the Chinese from NEFA, whether it takes one day, a hundred days or a thousand days," and to fight it out in Ladakh "to the last man, the last gun."

All were aware that withdrawal from the Namka Chu would instantly become public knowledge and Menon would be the first to take the public disappointment. Thus those in the back were crying "Forward!" and those in the front were crying "Back!" Brigadier Dalvi and General Prasad were reinforced on the Namka Chu with another battalion between October 12 and 14, who were as unacclimatized and exhausted and with poor equipment as the others battalions. The Indians had about 3,000 men, about 2,500 of them troops. As the first snow fell on October 17, winter clothing and tends were only available to two or three hundred, and the rest still wore cotton summer uniforms and made shelters with branches or parachute material. The gunners who were brought over to march on 16,000-foot route suffered fatal casualties due to lack of acclimatization and cold. Since October 9, the troops had been on hard rations, of which reserve now was down to two days, with no sugar, salt or matches. Many airdrops were lost or smashed as the parachutes failed to open. To conserve foreign exchange, the Army had for years been returning used parachutes for repair and repacking in India. Only thirty percent of the loads dropped were being retrieved.

It has become a political ploy, not a war. It was absurd or criminal to pit troops in such circumstances against an enemy superior in every aspect of military strength. To leave them through a winter of heavy snow would lead them to illness and starvation. On October 12, 7 Brigade received a signal from Kaul confirming the troops to stay where they were. On the same day Nehru confirmed on a radio broadcast that they were to clear the Chinese off Thag La ridge. On October 16, the Defense Minister told Dalvi that November 1 was the last date acceptable to the Cabinet to complete the operation. The key staff officers at IV Corps extended emphatic support for the field officers to pull back the bulk of the brigade. Brigadier Singh suggested that the force on the Namka Chu should be formed to one battalion and should concentrate in tactical positions to support Dhola Post, a suggestion almost exactly the same as what General Singh recommended six weeks before. In the debate, Tsangle became a central question, which was marked by a herdsman's hut at the source of Namka Chu in a small lake.

The Army map marked it as two to three miles from Dhola Post but in fact it was two days' march away. Survey maps placed it within Bhutan, but the Indian Army was ordered to disregard that boundary, as it did to the McMahon Line. Tsangle provided a tactical position from which a flank attack can be made against the Chinese position beneath Thag La, and Brigadier Dalvi had planned to advance to Tseng-jong through Tsangle. General Singh backed Dalvi and urged not to move to Tsangle before the operation actually began in order to take advantage of surprise attack. General Sen overruled their suggestion and ordered a company to occupy the position at the beginning of October, and the Chinese promptly dispatched troops to cover that approach. Before leaving the Namka Chu to report to Nehru, Kaul ordered that the Tsangle position must be held unless pressured by the Chinese, in which case General Prasad could withdraw it. But a few days later, Kaul ordered that Tsangle be held at all costs. As Dalvi, Brigadier Singh, and Prasad all urged that it should be evacuated because of the difficulties in maintaining and supplying "due to impassable bluffs," Kaul was adamant. Menon, the officials and Army H.Q. all came to attach high political and strategic importance to holding the Tsangle position, an order reaffirmed in a conference on October 17.

Another company was ordered to reinforce the company already there, thus stretching the supply effort of 7 Brigadier to breaking point and the force on the river line depleted in a hopelessly vulnerable situation. Meanwhile, Kaul's pulmonary trouble worsened on October 17 with difficulty breathing and discomfort. The medical officer at IV Corps diagnosed him as bronchial allergy exacerbated by respiratory infection, stress and exertion. On October 18, the officer judged his condition so serious that he was flown to New Delhi immediately for treatment. Kaul returned to New Delhi but went straight to his house, indicating that his condition was not as serious as suggested. Spreading the map on his bed and telephone at hand, Kaul continued to issue detailed orders for the movements of troops on the Namka Chu. On the night of October 18, two more companies were ordered to strengthen Tsangle, to which Dalvi angrily protested. General Prasad passed on the protest to Kaul, who repeated that the build-up at Tsangle must be carried out and that commanding officers who defaulted in executing the order would be removed.

On October 18, the Chinese activity intensified on the southern face of Thag La ridge. On October 19, a force of two thousand moved at Tseng-jong, who prepared for a night advance with no effort to conceal their intentions. Dalvi suggested that the brigade was not able to hold off a Chinese assault and requested to pull in the Tsangle force for support. General Prasad passed on the categorical order from Kaul that Tsangle must be held at all costs. Dalvi told Prasad that "rather than stand by and see the troops massacred," he would put in his resignation, saying, "it was time someone took a firm stand." Dalvi's words were noted and he was promised that Kaul would be contacted in New Delhi. On the night of October 19-20, the Chinese troops deployed for assault. They lit fires to keep warn while waiting and were confident that the Indians would not open fire.

At 05.00 on October 20, on the signal of two Very lights, Chinese heavy mortars and artillery opened heavy barrage on the central Indian position of Thag La ridge. Dalvi recalled: "As the first salvoes crashed overhead there were a few minutes of petrifying shock," in impressive contrast to "the tranquillity that had obtained hitherto." The weight of the Chinese attack was thrown in the center of the river line against the Gorkhas and the Rajputs, whose positions were overrun one after another and met the final Chinese assault with the bayonet. By 09.00, the Gorkhas and Rajputs were finished, and the Chinese then brought Tsangdhar under attack, who fought on until the crews were wiped out. The Chinese plan of breaking through in the center and seizing Tsangdhar and Hathung La worked out perfectly. 7 Brigade ceased to exist. On October 22, Brigadier Dalvi was taken prisoner. General Prasad trekked back to Tawang reaching there on the evening of October 22. The Chinese ignored Tsangle, which was given high political and strategic importance by the Indians, as it probably showed in Bhutan on the Chinese maps as it did on the Indian maps. The Chinese attacked simultaneously in the western sector, in the Chip Chap River valley, on the Galwan, and in the Pangong Lake area. After reporting that the Chinese began to shell, the Galwan post was not heard again. The posts fought their bests, but were soon overwhelmed and the little garrisons were either killed or captured. Western Command withdrew some of the smallest and most isolated posts. The fate of the forward policy and Operation Leghorn ended just as real soldiers foresaw from the beginning.

Between Two Passes

When the Chinese began preparing for the assault on the night of October 18, there was a riot outside the Prime Minister's residence in New Delhi, not related to the border, but a protest against the Government's "apathy towards the grievances and demands of the poor." As late as October 1962, the mounting tensions on the border was not the subject of extensive reporting in the Indian press, which often mentioned nothing of the border other than occasional front-page news or inside the papers. As the demonstrators attempted to break through the police, about twenty people were injured including women and police. In mid-October, a headline in the Hindu read "Unprovoked Attack on India" referring to an incident in Nepal in which Nehru had been burned in effigy. As for the borders the political public in India expected a victorious Indian attack on Thag La until the very last. On October 19, a published interview reported Menon's reaffirmation that the Government was determined to "throw the Chinese back until Indian territory is cleared of all aggression."

He admitted that in Namka Chu the Chinese outnumbered the Indians and their supply base was closer, but the Indians had beaten back again and again the Chinese attempts to develop a bridgehead on the river. On the same day, another paper carried the headline "Unconfirmed Report of Big Indian Push" reporting a leak form the Defense Ministry that Indians advanced two miles below Thag La. The next day the paper issued an official denial, and a few hours later, the news of the disasters on the Namka Chu began to reach New Delhi.

A shaken Menon told the reporter when asked where the advancing Chinese could be stopped: "The way they are going there is not any limit to where they will go." All the past assurances of the Indian advantages were reversed to become the excuses for defeat. In the evening, Menon explained that India "had not conditioned her reserves for war purposes." The Indian soldiers were fighting at high altitudes and had to be air supplied, whereas the Chinese could be easily supplied from the Tibetan tableland. The Prime Minister was for once inaccessible to the press. In the first shock, Nehru was not blamed for the defeat, but had received instinctive sympathy and trust as the embodiment of an injured and resolute India. Menon served as a surrogate target, and was to be brought down three days after the Chinese attack. On October 23, the Congress charged Menon for having misled Nehru, Parliament and the country. On October 31, Nehru took over the Defense portfolio as Menon continued in a new post in the Cabinet as a Minister for Defense Production.

This change was mooted years before and dismissed, but it was a typical political style of Nehru to flout Menon's critics by having Menon relinquishing the Defense portfolio. Suspicious that the change meant nothing but a title, the following day the political correspondents quoted Menon as saying "nothing has changed" in the working of the Defense Ministry. On November 7, Nehru played his last card to defend Menon in front of the Congress Parliamentary Party. He suggested that complaint against Menon should be leveled at the entire Government and that if resignations were wanted he might have to proffer his own. A leading Congressman replied: "Yes, if you continue to follow Menon's policies we may have to live without you too." Next day Menon's resignation was announced. For the first time the Congress Party openly defied Nehru, and Nehru's threat of resignation was exposed as a bluff. Menon's resignation became a necessary sacrifice for his own survival.

Nehru chose Chavan, the Chief Minister of Maharashtra, to replace Menon. Chavan accepted with great reluctance and arrived in the capital the day the border war ended. Profound changes took place in the political balance in New Delhi. Nehru's nearly absolute moral authority waned fast, as the Congress Parliamentary Party began to assert itself.

The world outside also underwent marked shifts. In the West, the Chinese attack was seen as an assault on the chief Asian democracy. The Daily Telegraph called it "the first round of struggle for the Asian mind between the Communist and non-Communist giants of the continent." UN intervention, as in Korea, was called. The Times printed an apologetic of Nehru's: "We were getting out of touch with reality in the modern world and living in an artificial atmosphere of our own creation."

But under the leadership of the British and American Governments, the Western world extended quick and unquestioning sympathy and support for India. President Kennedy wrote to Nehru: "Our sympathy in the situation is wholeheartedly with you. You have displayed an impressive degree of forbearance and patience in dealing with the Chinese. You have put into practice what all great religious leaders have urged, and so few of their followers have been able to do."

Then he appraised the spirituality of Indian policies with an offer of material assistance. Professor Galbraith, the American Ambassador, took great satisfaction from and encouraged the emotional gratification of the Indian opinion towards the U.S. He issued a statement that his Government recognized the McMahon Line as the international border "sanctioned by modern usage." He overcame the previous reluctance and lack of commitment of the American Government to endorse the McMahon Line, and immediately received approval from the State Department, which at once brought forth "frantic protest" from the Nationalists. The British Government promptly extended expressions of sympathy and condemnation of China, while offering help.

As the Western world was solidly with India, the non-alignment countries whose leadership India aspired were reserved and wary. An Indian correspondent in the Middle East reported: "Not a single expression of sympathy for India has come from any Arab Government, any political party or newspaper, or public personality even a week after the invasion." Another in Africa reported that Kenyatta and other leaders were non-committal while Nkrumah of Ghana went farther by rebuking Britain for its offers of military assistance to India. He wrote to the British Prime Minister, Macmillan: "Whatever the rights and wrongs of the present struggle between India and China, I am sure that we can all serve the cause of peace best by refraining from any action that may aggravate the situation."

Since Nehru just visited Ghana, Nkrumah's attitude was more offensive to India. Ethiopia and Cyprus were the only countries among those that attended the 1961 Belgrade Conference of Non-aligned governments to openly support India. Others showed more interests in urging restraint and patience on both sides while volunteering to act as mediators, the role often played by India so far. When Parliament reassembled, Nehru expressed his resentment at India's friends, the "well-intentioned countries" who tried to bring about a ceasefire. "People advise us to be good and peaceful as if we are inclined to war. In fact, if we are anything, as the House well knows, we do not possess the war-like mentality and that is why for the purpose of war there is weakness "So, people talking to us to be good boys and make it up has no particular meaning, unless they come to grips with the issues involved." Nehru said that the "so-called non-aligned countries" (unexpected phrasing from Nehru) were confused and a little frightened of China, so "it is no good our getting angry with them (because) they do not stand forthright in our defense, in support of our position."

The non-aligned countries did less damaging to India's interests when compared with the position of Moscow, which now clearly sided to China. The first intimation of the shift came to New Delhi on October 20, a few hours after the Chinese attack, in a letter from Krushchev to Nehru warning India that to take up arms to settle boundary dispute with China was "very dangerous path." The Indians had made no secret of their intention to use force against China, as Menon met the Russian Ambassador twice while preparing for Operation Leghorn. Menon told him about the plan and hoped that Moscow may pass Peking the word that India meant business and persuade the Chinese that discretion was better part of diplomacy. In the letter Krushchev urged Nehru to accept the Chinese proposal for talks. On October 24, Peking renewed the proposal for disengagement and talks. The next day Pravda commended the Chinese move as sincere and constructive, providing an acceptable basis for the talks.

The editorial said: "The question of the China-India frontier is a heritage from those days when British colonialists "who drew and re-drew the map of Asia at their own will" ruled on the territory of India. The notorious "McMahon Line," which was never recognized by China, was foisted on the Chinese and Indian peoples. Imperialist circles have done everything in their power to provoke an armed clash by speculating on the border conflicts connected with this Line. The imperialists are dreaming day and night of setting these great powers at loggerheads, as well as undermining the Soviet Union's friendship with fraternal China and friendly India." Pravda went on to note that "reactionary circles inside India" were fanning the conflict, and warned that "even some progressively-minded people" might yield to chauvinistic influences in the heart of the moment.

The critical implications and pro-China attitude of the Russians came as a blow to the Indian Government. A political correspondent of the Hindu put it: "It was thought that at best the Russians would continue to adopt a neutralist attitude. All these hopes were dashed to the ground when Pravda came out with an editorial wholeheartedly endorsing the Chinese stand "Mr. Krushchev's letter to Mr. Nehru runs on exactly the same lines "The reaction in the capital, not only in official and non-official circles but also among a section of the Indian Communists, is one of dismay, and the Soviet attitude is regarded not only as unkind but even as offensive."

The Russians further intimated to the Indian Embassy in Moscow that they would not be able to supply India with MiG fighters. At the same moment, Washington detected the first evidence of Russian missiles in Cuba on October 14. After keeping the discovery secret for a week, on October 22, President Kennedy announced that America would put the island under a selective blockade, and next day the American Ambassador in India left a copy of the statement to the Indian Government. In the confrontation with the U.S., it was plainly of high importance for Krushchev to repair the rift between Moscow and Peking, and to come out on China's side in the dispute with India. As disappointed as he was, Nehru quickly saw the point and said to an American television interviewer at the end of October: "I should imagine that developments (in) Cuba, et cetera, probably made it necessary for them not to fall out with China." He said that he hoped that the missile problem was "out of the way" and that the Soviet Union would return to its former position. Krushchev agreed on October 28 to withdraw the missiles, and Russia soon did just what Nehru hoped for.

For the retreating forces, the most important decision was where to make a stand. General Thapar and General Sen intended to hold Tawang, where two infantry battalions and some artillery were stationed. Sen flew to Tawang on a helicopter on October 22 and ordered the troops to hold Tawang at all cots, and said that two more brigades were to reinforce them. Next Morning Sen held meeting with General Prasad, during which each implied the other lost nerve. But both in Army H.Q. and at IV Corps, the cooler heads argued strongly that it would be disastrous to hold Tawang. Meanwhile, the Chinese had developed a three-pronged attack and on October 23 were advancing toward Tawang, which had no natural defense and the troops standing there were as easily overcome as on the Namka Chu. In New Delhi, the Director of Military Operations, Brigadier Palit, strongly urged on Thapar that Tawang must be evacuated.

Thapar consulted Nehru, who told him to make the military decisions themselves. Kaul was out of picture again. He was persuaded to hang up his telephones and relinquish command of IV Corps on the morning that the Chinese attacked. On October 23, IV Corps ordered the force at Tawang to withdraw sixty miles back to Bomdi La, calculating that it was the farthest point to the north where the Indians could build up more quickly than the Chinese. But at Army H.Q. Brigadier Palit urged strongly that the troops should be ordered to hold at Se La, a high pass only about fifteen miles behind Tawang, believing Se La an impregnable natural position that had to be held. Later on October 23, Sen countermanded the order to pull back to Bomdi La and ordered that Se La must be held. Brigadier Singh urged to inform New Delhi that it was logistically impossible to build sufficient defense at Se La. Sen replied that the Cabinet had decided that Se La should be held and the Government's orders must be implemented.

The decision was crucial and disastrous. Se La was 14,600 feet high, flanked by peaks a thousand feet higher. The 5,000-foot climb from Tawang valley was very steep and was a strong defensive position, but it was a trap for the Indians. It was too far away from the plains, and the road could take only one-ton vehicles on a grueling trip of several days from the foothills to Se La. It was also too high for the defense force who lacked acclimatization. Air supply was possible but the terrain and weather made it wholly unreliable. Se La was also too close to Tawang and the Chinese could mount assault with minimum regrouping and without having to move their bases forward. The decision to hold Se La committed the Indians to holding a very deep area from Se La to Bomdi La separated by difficult and unreliable road through broken country.

The Government ruled out the tactical air support with bombers or ground-attack aircraft for fear of Chinese retaliation against Indian cities, especially Calcutta. During the Second World

War, some random Japanese bombs fell there and swept the city with so huge panic that the Government resolved not to risk a repetition. Considering the terrain in NEFA and the limitations of the Indian Air Force, it was doubtful that it could have played an effective tactical role. Tawang was evacuated on October 23, with hundreds of civilians, including lamas from monastery, going with the troops. On October 25, the Chinese occupied Tawang without opposition. On the night of October 24, one battalion, 4 Garhwal, panicked and broke to trickle back. They were intercepted and braced back in the line. Later this battalion cleared its record by beating off repeated Chinese attacks from its positions flanking Se La.

Meanwhile in the western sector, the Chinese moved south and concentrated on the Indian forward posts. On October 21, they overran the posts on the north side of Pangong Lake after severe fighting, the Gorkha garrison fighting almost to the last man. On October 27, they attacked the posts around Demchok with similar results. Western Command ordered to evacuate some posts before the Chinese assault. General Singh of Western Command methodically and rapidly pulled out troops out of Kashmir to build up strength. By the first week of November, a Divisional H.Q. was established at Leh, with an additional brigade of four infantry battalions, and was reinforced by another brigade by November 17. On the eastern side, there was no such decisive dispatch. IV Corps got a new commander on October 24, Lieutenant-General Harvaksh Singh, who was stationed in Simla. Sen removed General Prasad from the command of 4 Division, replacing him with a soldier with a good combat record. These kinds of command changes occupied much of Eastern Command's energies.

This time Peking used verbal smoke screen to obscure the reality on the ground. On October 20, the Chinese Defense Ministry issued a statement that at 07.00 hours that morning the Indian troops had launched large-scale attacks on the Namka Chu and in the Chip Chap and Galwan valleys in the western sector. "In self-defense, the Chinese frontier guards were compelled to strike back resolutely, and cleared away some aggressive strong points set up by the Indian troops in China's territory." The Chinese took the tactic of "turning truth on his head" so often used by Indians and accused India. The Chinese played into New Delhi's hands by obscuring the truth. The Indian intention of attacking the Chinese below Thag La ridge was by then known everywhere, and Nehru's airport statement on October 12 confirmed of Operation Leghorn. However, the Chinese charge that the Indians had "launched massive attacks" rebounded from the general skepticism about Indian strength, and was almost immediately belied by Peking's own announcement that the Chinese "frontier guards" were carrying out the defensive actions.

It appeared that Chou En-lai did not at first subscribe to the false statement that the Indians had attacked on October 20. In his letter to Nehru on November 4, Chou said only that the Indian troops on the Namka Chu had "made active dispositions for a massive military attack," which was precisely true as a brigade attack with four battalions could be described as massive. However, in a letter to the Afro-Asian Governments ten days later, Chou wrote that India had "launched massive attacks all along the line." Following the military and diplomatic measures, China made another diplomatic move adroit in both timing and content.

On October 24, Peking released a statement precisely recapitulating the course of the dispute with India, and reminding that three times in the past three months India had rejected China's proposals for talks without preconditions, and that Nehru had then publicly ordered the Indian army to "free Indian territory." The statement pointed to the impossibility of settling the boundary question by force, and the need to reopen peaceful negotiations. Three proposals were set forth:

(1) That both sides affirm that the dispute must be settled peacefully; agree to respect the line of actual control; and withdraw their armed forces twenty kilometers from that line.

(2) If India agreed to that, Chinese forces would be withdrawn to the north of the McMahon Line.

(3) The Prime Ministers should meet again, In Peking or New Delhi, to seek friendly settlement. Chou wrote Nehru the same day urging that "we should look ahead" and appealing to Nehru to respond positively.

The Chinese proposal had nothing new in detail, and was the same as Chou put forward originally in his letter to Nehru of November 7, 1959. The proposal would have created a ceasefire line along the "line of actual control," the term that Peking had used to describe the situation from the beginning in 1959. The Chinese would pull back over the McMahon Line, and Indian troops in the remaining forward posts in the western sector would withdraw to the line before the forward policy of 1961. Pulling the armed forces twenty kilometers back on both sides would create a demilitarized zone, while leaving civil personnel alone. The proposal had no ambiguities, but did not state in precise locational detail. The phrase "the line of actual control" had throughout been used by Peking to describe the situation in November 1959, when the Chinese were nowhere south of the McMahon Line or even south of Thag La ridge. The Chinese described the proposal as equal, mutually accommodatory and based on mutual respect, which objectively merit the description, but India could not see them objectively.

The Indians viewed that the Chinese had simply added a new and more violent aggression and now seeking to confirm their criminal gains through diplomacy. New Delhi rejected instantly the Chinese proposal, in fact without waiting to receive them officially; they would get the contents from the news agencies' account. In its reply, the Indian Government released a statement on October 24, first claiming that it was "wedded to peace and peaceful methods (and had) always sought to resolve differences by talks and discussions with China," but "India cannot and will not accept a position under which Chinese forces continue to commit aggression into Indian territory, occupy substantial Indian territories and use these as a bargaining counter to force a settlement on their own terms." The statement proceeded to confuse the Chinese proposal: "There is no sense or meaning in the Chinese offer to withdraw twenty kilometers from what they call "line of actual control". What is this "ine of control"? Is this the line they have created by aggression since the beginning of September? Advancing forty or sixty kilometers by blatant military aggression and offering to withdraw twenty kilometers provided both sides do this is a deceptive device which can fool nobody."

It was most improbable that the officials in the External Affairs Ministry in New Delhi were really uncertain about the meaning of the Chinese proposal. Peking had used "the line of actual control" in clear and consistent meaning. But the Chinese left an opening by not going into more detail, and the Indians exploited it. Asking for clarification is a classic diplomatic way of playing for time. A counter-proposal followed: "If the Chinese professions of peace and peaceful settlement of differences are really genuine, let them go back at least to the position where they were all along the boundary prior to 8th September, 1962.

India will then be prepared to undertake talks and discussions, at any level mutually agreed, to arrive at agreed measures which should be taken for the easing of tension and correction of the situation created by unilateral forcible alteration of the status quo along the India-China boundary." The proposal concluded that if China accepted it, India would welcome Chou En-lai in New Delhi. The Indian proposal was as consistent as that of China. It was precisely the same as New Delhi put forward on October 6, which would have the Chinese drawing back over Thag La ridge and relinquishing the posts in the western sector so that the Indians could return to the positions at Dhola Post, on the Namka Chu, and at Khinzemane. Once China accepted and implemented that, India would be prepared to talk, but only about Chinese withdrawal from Aksai Chin. Nehru sent the statement with proposal to Chou En-lai on October 27, in a letter with civil tone, which was remarkable since Nehru called "a Chinese invasion of India."

On November 4, Chou En-lai replied that the "line of actual control" was referred to the same line that he had proposed in 1959. He explained: "The fact that the Chinese Government's proposal has taken as its basis the 1959 line of actual control and not the present line of actual contact between the armed forces of the two sides is full proof that the Chinese side has not tried to force any unilateral demand on the Indian side on account of the advances gained in the recent counterattack in self-defense." The Indian counter-proposal would have Indian troops return to their dispositions for attack on the Namka Chu and to the forward posts in the western sector. Chou asked: "How can the Chinese

Government agree to revert to such a position?" Chou appealed to Nehru to reconsider the Chinese proposal.

Nehru's next letter sharply changed the tone. He described the Chinese attacks as "cold-blood(ed) "massive aggression" and declared that for India to accept the Chinese proposal "would mean mere existence at the mercy of an aggressive, arrogant and expansionist neighbor." He reiterated that the Indian troops must go back to the positions they had occupied all along the boundaries on September 8, and suggested that China could demonstrate its bona fides by withdrawing its forces to the 1959 positions. The effect of that was that the Indians would reestablish in all their forward posts, while the Chinese would stay well back from their positions set up to counter India's forward policy.

The diplomatic exchange during the Chinese occupation of Tawang showed that New Delhi's approach to the boundary dispute only hardened. The Indians were as adamant as ever that they would not negotiate a boundary settlement, and their insistence on return to their forward posts showed that the assumptions of forward policy remained unchanged. Peking gained nothing after smashing the puny threats that India built up below Thag La and wiping out half the forward Indian posts in the western sector. The Indians were more confident than ever and the political atmosphere in India had now become almost unanimously bellicose. But the Chinese conception had only begun to be put into effect. Before the attacks on October 20, a senior minister in Peking said that China was going to have to advance well to the south of the points and then withdraw.

Like a jab of a boxer that seemingly jolts the opponent, the first attacks only set up for the knockout. The political side was also working out as planned. The defeat on the Namka Chu and belief that India was at war with China swept away Nehru's resistance to accepting military aid. Only a few weeks before, he had rejected the suggestion that India might seek arms aid, saying it meant becoming "somebody else's dependent" by "joining some military bloc," and declared that he would never agree to this, "even if disaster comes to us on the frontier." But on October 29, when the American Ambassador called, Nehru instantly accepted the offer of military equipment. The writer reported to The Times:

"The decision to accept American military assistance, reversing policies that India had cherished since she became a nation, was taken formally at a Cabinet meeting today." Lists of India's military needs were prepared and handed to the Americans, with the Embassy in New Delhi expressing dismay at the scope of the Indian requests and the disorganization and confusions. The Pentagon used its new computerized stock-keeping record and quickly flew first supplies from West Germany in jet freighters, which began landing in India five days later.

Chou En-lai wrote to the heads of the Afro-Asian Governments: "The Indian Government has openly begged military aid from the United States." The People's Daily described the "development of historic significance:" India's acceptance of American military aid "points to the fact that Nehru Government has finally shed its cloak of non-alignment policy "The more Nehru depends on U.S. imperialism, the greater the need is there for him to meet the needs of U.S. imperialism and persist in opposing China. And the more he persists in opposing China, the greater the need for him to depend on U.S. imperialism. Thus he is caught in a vicious circle. His gradual shedding of his policy of "non-alignment" is precisely the inevitable result of his sell-out to U.S. imperialism."

This statement confirmed Peking's analysis of the nature of Nehru government, making a key point in the argument with Moscow, and also underlined to Peking the importance of not letting the fighting drag on. A Chinese official "disgustedly" told a Western correspondent early in November that "as long as the Indians go on attacking us they will get anything they want out of the United States. They're making millions of dollars out of these skirmishes, they'll probably go on for ever." As the Afro-Asian Governments declined to come out clearly on Indian side, it may have indicated to the Chinese that India's version of events now at last being met with skepticism. In mid-November, Chou En-lai wrote the heads of Asian and African governments thanking them for their "fair-minded endeavors to promote direct negotiations between China and India" and affirming that China wanted only a peaceful settlement with India.

As the Cuba crisis relaxed, Moscow's sudden objectivity about the dispute died, as Nehru expected. Early in November, Moscow called on both sides for a ceasefire and negotiations, ignoring the fact that India had just refused negotiations once more. In Peking's view, the Cuba confrontation was brought on by Krushchev's "adventurism" in deploying Russian missiles, and compounded by his "capitulationism" in backing down and removing them under American pressure. The completion of the Chinese operation against India would show the world that threats and vaunts of the imperialists and their creatures could be ignored with impunity, thus underlining the pusillanimity and incompetence of Krushchev and his "revisionist clique."

The first defeat sent shock waves into India's resolution to war, which grew into optimism, and then was seen and enjoyed as India's hour of greatness, of which fruit was national unity and ultimate triumph. After the initial unfeigned astonishment and outrage over Chinese attack, it was almost forgotten that Indian Army had been about to take offensive action, and that the Government had refused to meet with the Chinese for talks. Nehru now complained that if the Chinese "had any claim they could have discussed it and talked about it and adopted various means of peaceful settlement." Asok Mehta asked later: "Why, in the face of our patience, goodwill and obvious anxiety for settlement, have the Chinese persisted in this aggression?"

Menon commented: "We never went into Chinese territory. And even if it was "disputed" territory in Chinese eyes, did that justify them starting a war? for us, it was not disputed territory. It was ours." The Lok Sabha put formally a resolution, in which it affirmed the "resolve of the Indian people to drive out the aggressor from the sacred soil of India": "This House notes with deep regret that in spite of the uniform gestures of goodwill and fellowship by India towards China "China has betrayed that good-will and friendship" and has committed aggression and initiated a massive invasion of India." It was entirely forgotten in disapproval of China's use of force that India had intended the same, as Nehru pointed out: "We are perfectly justified in pushing them and attacking them." The reaction of the Indian political classes and urban masses was vigorous.

The Chinese were condemned in public meetings, army-recruiting stations were rushed, and students burned effigies of

Mao Tse-tung and Chou En-lai. The shops of Chinese in New Delhi and Calcutta, shoemakers and curio dealers, were mobbed and their owners beaten up. Japanese diplomats plastered their cars with "rising sun" emblems to avoid mistaken identification for Chinese. The Government introduced an ordinance that treated even Indian citizens of Chinese descent as enemy aliens, and several thousand were interned in camps in Rajasthan and were later expelled to China.

The popular commitment to the struggle with China deemed the signs of disunity as "fissiparousness" as superficial, underneath that lay an emotionally integrated nation. The Lok Sabha praised "the wonderful and spontaneous response of the people of India to the emergency "this mighty upsurge amongst all sections of our people." Nehru thanked China more poetically for having "suddenly lifted a veil from the face of India, (giving) a glimpse of the serene face of India, strong and yet calm and determined, an ancient face which is ever young and vibrant." An Opposition Socialist invoked "the blood of our martyred jawans, (which) is becoming the seed of a new, virile nation that is being born in our country."

Ignoring the obvious gusto of the response toward war, Nehru insisted on the inherent and unshakable pacifism of Indians. He said, in contrast to the Chinese who were conditioned to war and seemed to "think that war was a natural state of affairs," the Indians were "disliking it, excessively disliking the idea of war" emotionally disliking it, apart from not liking its consequences." He invoked Gandhi and reminded parliament that "basically we are a gentle people" and expressed fear that war would change it. "It alarms me that we should become, because of the exigencies of war, brutalized, a brutal nation. I think that would mean the whole soul and spirit of India being demoralized, and that is a terribly harmful thing. Certainly I hope that all of us will remember this." Nehru had made central the belief in the inherent and peculiar pacifism and gentleness of the Indian people in the course of the dispute with China, in domestic utterances, letters to Chou En-lai, and diplomatic notes to Peking. Nehru's belief in this myth derived perhaps from his closeness to Gandhi. But the truth lies somewhere between Nehru's view of "a gentle people" and Nirad

Chaudhur's, that "few human communities have been more warlike and fond of bloodshed (than the Indians)."

A cartoon in the Time of India epitomized the intense gratification with public response heard in almost every comment. Captioned as "War with China," Nehru and his Cabinet colleagues labeled a wall of graphs with "Emotional Integration, Industrial Peace, People's Faith in Government." Nehru commented: "We never had it so good," and pointed out elegantly: "This challenge may be converted into opportunity for us to grow and to change the dark cloud that envelops our frontiers into the bright sun not only of freedom but of welfare in this country." For the Indian political classes, war was remote, romantic and therapeutic. For the urban masses it was circus, an open opportunity to join a parade and shout slogans. For the villagers, it was remote but vaguely alarming threat to the village, rather than the nation, which was a concept beyond the interest of the village mass in India. In contrast to the excitement and commitment in India, in China the fighting was consistently played down and the conflict minimized.

A Western correspondent in Peking reported that "newspaper coverage is more political than military and even Chinese successes have constantly been played down. There has been no attempt to make the reader keenly war-conscious. Rare and laconic situation reports are printed in the guarded words of the New China News Agency." On the other hand, the Indian government treated the border fighting as an undeclared war. Nehru explained: "We may not be technically at war, but the fact is that we are at war, though we have not made any declaration to that effect "it is not necessary at the present moment to do so, I do not know about the future." However, Nehru resisted strong pressure throughout to break off diplomatic relations with Peking and in the UN, India maintained its support for Peking, although no longer taking the lead to press the issue of China's representation.

The Indian Government declared statement of emergency, overriding powers and suspending civil liberties. The shock of the Namka Chu debacle was worn off, and replaced by euphoria of "mafficking in defeat," as it was called. At the end of October, The Times reported: "There has been a palpable growth of confidence in New Delhi that, whatever the Chinese intentions, they can be held and in due course beaten." The newspapers reported "heartening indications that after the initial reverses the Indian troops in NEFA were beginning to consolidate themselves into effective defensive positions, and were even initiating attempts to dislodge the Chinese from Indian territory." As Parliament was called into session ten days early on November 8, Menon took the edge off Parliament's anger. Nehru still had a lot of explaining to do, but he was confident and not at all apologetic. Nehru gave the basic reason for the Indian reverse as they were outnumbered. The only hint of whether 7 Brigade should be pulled back from Namka Chu was: "The only fault we made" if it is a fault, was even to stick (it) out where the military situation was not very favorable. It was not that we told them to stick it out "it is folly for any politician to say so. But our soldiers themselves have a reluctance to go back, and they stuck on at considerable cost to them."

The statement implied that Nehru was never informed about the urgent representations made by the field commanders to speedily withdraw the troops. Kaul, Sen and Thapar must have impressed him that the troops had "a reluctance to go back." Nehru made his long and familiar argument to Parliament in response to the rumors of inadequate equipment and supplies of the troops, which were circulating in the capital by now. Nehru assumed the role of the country's war leader, and snapped at other politicians who questioned him: "It is really extraordinary that many persons here who know nothing about arms talk about arms." Since 1954, when Pakistan began receiving American military aid, and especially after the first boundary clashes with China in 1959, the Indian Government had been urging to accept whatever assistance available and strengthen the armed services. Now Nehru was bitterly criticized for his refusal to follow the suit.

In a previous Parliament session, Nehru said, "taking military help is basically and fundamentally aligned to that country." But now American jet transports were landing in India with eight flights per day, each carrying about twenty tons of equipment including automatic rifles, heavy mortars, recoilless guns, et cetera. The British had been quicker as their first loads of arms aid landed the day Nehru accepted Kennedy's offer of help. It was plain that only the U.S. had the means and the motive to provide the massive assistance India required. The British made their first contributions an outright gift, and the Americans left terms to be negotiated later. The French and others saw no reason to waive the usual commercial requirements, earning certain amount of ill will in New Delhi as a result. India also turned to Israel, which India had refused to open diplomatic relations for fear of losing Arab support for its position about Kashmir.

Now India asked if the weapons Israel agreed to provide could be delivered in ships that did not fly the Israeli flag, thereby allowing India to avail itself of Israel's help without incurring Arab displeasure. But Ben Gurion reportedly replied that "no flag, no weapons," and a shipment of heavy mortars arrived in Bombay in an Israeli ship.

As American weapons were unloaded a few miles away, an independent politician suggested that India should point out to the west that it was fighting a world war on behalf of democracy, echoing Churchill's words: "Give us the tools and we will finish the job." Nehru maintained that because the supplies of armaments were "unconditional and without any strings" they did not affect non-alignment. It was soon to be seen that Britain and the U.S. used their supply of armaments to lever Nehru into reopening negotiations with Pakistan over Kashmir, with the implicit threat to cut the supply. The six days of debate, in which one hundred and sixty-five members spoke, a generalized critique of the Government's policy was mounted, with strong feeling that India had been let down by many countries. One party questioned: "How is it that so large a number of these countries (for whom) we did so much in the many spheres of world politics" were not sympathizing with and supporting India?

The resentment over the failure of the non-aligned and Afro-Asian countries not to repay India's past generosity gave rise to a wave of enthusiasm for the U.S. and the Commonwealth. The Hindustan Times described that "a great fellowship of nations suddenly stirred to a sense of responsibility for the security and freedom of one of its members." In reconsidering its foreign policy, New Delhi changed even its approach to the Nationalist

Government on Formosa. As one newspaper put it: "India should maneuver to spring a second front on the Chinese "This means that we must do everything to activate Formosa's invasion threat on the south China coast" and "to this end liaison with Taipeh and even more so with the Pentagon is called for." The following March, a Nationalist representative came to New Delhi for talks with the Ministry of External Affairs.

The Chinese Nationalists were ready to join India in all expressions of hostility towards the Peking Government, but were careful to point out that there were no differences with the Chinese Communists in their approach to the boundary dispute. The Formosa Government released a formal statement at the end of October: "The so-called McMahon Line is a line unilaterally claimed by the British during their rule over India. The Government of the Republic of China has never accepted this line of demarcation, and is strongly opposed to the British claim."

Parliament also criticized Nehru's harping on the special peaceableness of Indians and the national commitment to non-violence. Now war had come, taking up arms was more meaningful to Indians than that of Gandhi and his non-violence. From the end of October, the general optimism that the worst was over and victories were at hand grew steadily, encouraged by official accounts of what was happening in NEFA. The press proclaimed: "Indians attack under cover of artillery" heartening forward thrust in NEFA." A Congress M.P. who went to the front reported that the morale of the troops was exuberant: "They are simply shouting our Mahatma Gandhi's name and the Prime Minister's name to enthuse themselves." Another told a public meeting on November 12 that "India was now strong enough to repulse the Chinese attackers and was building its military might to drive the invaders from Indian soil." Meanwhile, the Chinese in October and beginning of November continued their methodical elimination of the Indian forward posts in the western sector, softening the Indian positions with intense barrages before overrunning them with infantry. But the continuing defeat in the western sector did not shadow the Indian optimism, of which attention was focused on the Walong front. A big Indian victory was expected, as the headlines read on November 16: "Jawans swing into attack."

The Army H.Q. and down the line of command also shared the belief that the Chinese would not launch further attacks in NEFA and that the worst was over with the debacle on the Namka Chu. The orders to move the troops to NEFA were countermanded when the Chinese stopped their advance, and for three weeks there was little urgency in the Indian build-up around Se La. The contingency plan was based on the assumption that Pakistan would not take advantage of a Chinese attack, but in October 1962 intelligence report of President Ayub's attitude led to second thought in New Delhi. Although American representation to Pakistan and reassurance relieved the Indian anxiety, moving troops to the northeast was delayed. The Chinese were working twenty-four hours a day, and steadily getting nearer to Se La ridge, from which the blasting of explosives could be heard. The road was through by early November and the Chinese trucks moved in Tawang towards Se La. Meanwhile, they patrolled forward towards and around the Indian positions, without the knowledge of Indians, penetrating into NEFA by passes and trails.

General Harbaksh Singh at IV Corps expressed his pride "with abiding faith in our nation and our leaders and in the sacred cause of our motherland," but he was soon replaced by Kaul, who resumed command after having recovered from the "chill and severe attack of bronchitis." General Sen protested to General Thapar against this change, and the latter replied that Kaul was returning to be rehabilitated. Nehru stated in front of Parliament about the rehabilitation of his protege: "I want to mention his name especially because quite extraordinarily unjust things have been said about him." He went on: "Some people say he had not had any experience of fighting. That is not correct. He had the experience of fighting in Burma "I doubt in sheer courage and initiative and hard work, if we can find anybody to beat him." The truth was as General Thimayya put it: "Every sepoy in the Army knows that Kaul has never been a combat soldier, you can't hide that sort of thing in the Army. The officers don't respect Kaul." The troops reacted in tune with Thimayya's view to Kaul's resumed command.

On October 26, just before Kaul resumed command, he described that his tactics had been deliberately "a policy of cheek."

The Tseng-jong battle was only the result of his move to feel out Chinese intentions. He was confident that the Chinese could be held at Se La, and in due course beaten back. On October 29, Kaul returned and resumed control of IV Corps, as the Indians forces were being built up in NEFA. The troops were inducted to NEFA and distributed wildly, not as part of an overall defense plan but according to the Intelligence Bureau's estimates of where the Chinese were likely to move. The troops trekked into the hills with the weapons and ammunitions they could carry to take up positions picked out on maps at headquarters in New Delhi. These deployments were made to engage the Chinese on the McMahon Line and were rationalized with the expectation of no strong Chinese attack. Nehru explained in Parliament why the Army tried to fight below Thag La ridge, "partly because to the last moment we did not expect this invasion in overwhelming numbers, partly from the fact that we disliked "the idea of walking back in our own territory." Five years later Menon conceded that it would be strategically better to "let (the Chinese) come into Indian territory in depth before giving them a fight," admitting that he and his Prime Minister consciously went against the strategic advantage to mollify an uninformed and shallow "public opinion."

In 1962, as the Intelligence Bureau pointed to the Lohit valley as a likely marching line for the Chinese, the Indians built up at Walong, which was one hundred miles, of two-week march, in addition to the enormous difficulties for air supply. The Chinese attacked on October 21 on the two-infantry battalions and some Assam Rifles, and were beaten off with heavy losses on both sides. The Walong sector was initially the responsibility of 5 Infantry Brigade, part of 4 Division. After fall of Tawang, a new divisional headquarters was created to command the whole of NEFA, which was designated as 2 Division under the command of Major-General MS Pathania. By the beginning of November 2 Division had settled down with three infantry battalions and some Assam Rifles platoons at Walong.

General Pathania was convinced and in turn convinced Kaul that with an additional battalion, he could drive the Chinese back to the McMahon Line. The opening attack was planned for November 13 and was to be completed on November 14. The additional battalion began arriving only on November13, but II brigade did not delay its attack. The dates otherwise had no military significance, but November 14 was Nehru's seventy-third birthday. Kaul and Pathania came up to Walong with the thought of giving a present for the Prime Minister, as "our first major success against the enemy." On November 14, two companies of the 6th Kumanon battalion, supported by heavy mortars and field guns, moved into an assault on the hill held by the Chinese, who were believed to be company strength. After six hours of fight, they were still fifty yards away from the crest. At night, a Chinese counterattack cleared the surviving Kumanois off the hill, which was what the Indian newspapers hailed on November 16 that "Jawans swing into attack."

The Chinese followed up the retreating Kumaonis and penetrated the main Indian defense positions. Having fire off all the shells in support of the Kumaonis, the Indian artillery could not engage the main Chinese assault when it came at first light on the 16th. The Indians fought grimly. After ceasefire, the returning Indians found in some posts every man dead. Kaul ordered withdrawal, but some troops did not receive it and fought on until their ammunition ran out or they were killed. Kaul sent a frantically worded signal reporting the defeat at Walong: "It is now my duty to urge that the enemy thrust is now so great and his overall strength is so superior that you should ask the highest authorities to get such foreign armed forces to come to our aid as are willing to do so without which, as I have said before and which I reiterate, it seems beyond the capacity of our armed forces to stem the tide of the superior Chinese forces which he has and will continue to concentrate against us to out disadvantage. This is not a counsel of fear, but facing stark realities." Kaul had the idea of getting allied expeditionary armies for some days. When the Cabinet Secretary called him for ideas, Kaul reportedly "produced from beneath his pillow a paper of recommendation. India should seek help of some foreign powers; Chiang Kai-shek and the South Koreans should be induced to invade China with American help."

As the climax developed in the crucial Se La-Bomdi La sector, the western sector also had endured attacks. Unlike Eastern

Command and IV Corps, Western Command showed more concern for the survival of their troops than ordering isolated units to "fight it out" in useless and sacrificial gestures. In the eastern sector, the troops often fought to the last round or the last man to hold tactically insignificant and indefensible positions. Western Command continued an urgent and heavy build-up withdrawing troops from Kashmir, and despite arduous conditions, strength was built up in Ladakh by November 17. On November 18, the Chinese artillery bombardment began on the Indian outposts, airfield and brigade positions. Heavy mortars, recoilless guns and rockets softened the shallow Indian entrenchment. Of one company of another Kumaonis battalion, three wounded reached Battalion H.Q. in the valley, five were taken prisoner, and the rest of the company were found, three months later, frozen as they died with weapons in their hand. Only the Chinese bodies were removed, and evidence showed that there had been many. Five hours after, the Chinese launched assault on the hill positions, but stopped at their claim line and no attack was made on Chushul.

In the Se La-Bomdi La sector of NEFA, the Indian build-up was relatively sluggish, spreading in three main locations the 4 Division with a full complement of infantry, ten battalions, and supporting arms of field artillery, heavy mortars and a dozen light tanks. General Pathania ordered 4 Division to hold Se La to block the Chinese entry through NEFA to the plains. In the beginning of November, Pathania dispatched troops taken from the Bomdi La garrison to block what he saw as likely routes for Chinese outflanking moves. On the night of November 16, the Bomdi La garrison was reduced from three battalions (twelve companies) to six companies, about a third of the strength required to defend the position. On the midday of November 17, the Chinese attacked the Guards who fought for three hours until they ran out of ammunition, and withdrew to Bomdi La.

After disintegrating the Guards, the Chinese had cut the road between Bomdi La and Dirang Dzong. The Chinese also attacked a battalion deployed several miles north of Se La. By early afternoon, Pathania asked IV Corps at Tezpur for permission to pull his headquarters out of Dirang Dzong. Pathania realized that the Chinese had cut the road meant that Se La would be wholly dependent upon air supply, and that the garrisons would be wiped out as they ran out of supplies. On the evening of the 17th, Pathania telephone IV Corps again and asked for permission to pull the troops off Se La. Kaul still had not returned from helicoptering around the rear of the lost battle in Walong, but Generals Thapar and Sen, who were superiors to Kaul, declined to give Pathania any orders. Kaul returned to headquarters in the evening and, with Thapar and Sen, drafted a signal to 4 Division, in what was a masterpiece of military buck-passing.

It could be read in two ways. Pathania was given authority to fight if he decided to do so. The signals said: "You will hold on to your present positions to the best of your ability. Your only course is to fight it out as best you can." However, if he decided to withdraw, the signal authorized him to withdraw, as the signal said: "When any position becomes untenable I delegate the authority to you to withdraw to any alternative position you can hold." The signal was phrased to shift responsibility for the decision back to Pathania. For the Commander 48 Brigade at Bomdi La, Kaul ordered "to attack this enemy force tonight speedily and resolutely and keep this road clear at all costs." Brigadier Hoshiar Singh protested pointing out that he was left with only six rifle companies. Kaul agreed to suspend the order until next morning when two battalions of reinforcements were expected to reach Bomdi La. Next morning Pathania received the ambiguous signal and decided to withdraw in the following night.

The Chinese moved at nights, without firing, and followed up the withdrawing Indians closely and occupied the positions. When the Chinese opened fire, troops of one battalion began to break and move back. At dawn of the 18, the Chinese assaulted the last Indian troops in territory claimed by Peking in the western sector. The Chinese found the Indian forces emptying on Se La, their heavy weapons, artillery and stores left where they stood. Among these were American automatic rifles still in crates. The Chinese moved into the deserted positions around the pass and opened fire on the retreating Indians beneath them. At five in the morning, at Dirang Dzong there was "a complete absence of war-like atmosphere" with quietness and officers sleeping in their huts. As a company Pathania dispatched came to cover Dirang

Dzong, the Chinese opened light small-arms fire on Divisional H.Q. from a thousand yards away. Pathania gave hurried oral orders to the cavalrymen to fight through to Bomdi La, and if they could not, abandon their tanks and head for the plains. Pathania then left Dirang Dzong with fellow officers and a few troops headed toward Bomdi La and, after finding out it had fallen, made for the plains.

No one took command at Dirang Dzong in Pathania's place. The forces there, including two battalions of infantry, a squadron of light tanks, a battery of field guns, and hundreds of personnel from Divisional and Brigade H.Q., went to a sauve qui peut in the morning of November 18. One of the battalions reached the plains as a unit, the rest struggled through in small parties. Chinese ambushes took a toll, so did the wild country and the winter. Divisional H.Q. did not inform anyone that it was quitting the field. The commands at Se La and Bomdi la were left quiet in the dark, as was IV Corps at Tezpur. Brigadier Hoshiar Singh attempted to knock out the Chinese machine-guns, which fired on the withdrawing troops from Se La, but the attempt failed. With the road impassable, the Chinese fire took heavy casualties, and the brigade disintegrated into small parties, making for the plains individually.

Many of the parties were ambushed and killed or captured in the following days, and Brigadier Hoshiar Singh was shot dead at Phutang on November 27. By mid-morning on November 18, 48 Brigade at Bomdi La was the only organized Indian formation left in NEFA. The brigade had six rifle companies, and was awaiting the Chinese attack in prepared positions supported by field guns, heavy mortars, and the guns of four light tanks. At about 11.00 a.m., Kaul ordered 48 Brigade to send out a mobile column to relieve Dirang Dzong (not knowing it was empty by then). Brigadier Gurbax Singh protested again, Kaul angrily and categorically ordered him to get the mobile column on the road within half an hour irrespective of the consequences to Bomdi La. Ten minutes after, as two infantry companies with two tanks and tow mountain guns were pulled out towards Dirang Dzong, the first shock of the Chinese assault came and was beaten off. But Indian counterattack against the next major Chinese attack failed.

Gurbax Singh ordered a withdrawal of eight miles south to Rupa, where they began to organize a defense on the night of 18th.

But IV Corps ordered them to pull back to Foothills, a village just above the plains. As troops moved accordingly, Kaul ordered them to stand at Rupa. The troops turned back to Rupa, and came under fire from the Chinese who had already taken up dominating positions in the hills around. The brigade, now about one battalion in strength, marched back through November 19 and reached Chaku just after dark. But the Chinese struck at Chaku from three sides soon after midnight, ambushing a column that was bringing up supplies and ammunition. The surviving troops made for the plains in small parties. By November 20, no organized Indian military force was left in NEFA or in the territory claimed by China in the western sector. Militarily the Chinese victory was complete, the Indian defeat absolute. However, the retreat continued, as Kaul returned to Corps H.Q. in Tezpur late on the night of November 19, he ordered the Corps H.Q. to move immediately to Gauhati, nearly a hundred miles to the west and on the other side of the Brahmaputra. Next day Kaul helicoptered over the trails and gave Pathania and some wounded men a lift to Tezpur.

The news of the fall of Walong, released in New Delhi only on November 18, sent a greater shock than the debacle at Thag La ridge. There the public believed that Indian troops were taken by surprise by the Chinese attack as an infantry Pearl Harbor. But in Walong, the Indian Army had three weeks to prepare itself and was in fact on the offensive. In the evening briefing to the press, it was announced that the Chinese had attacked Se La and fighting was going on there. After a glow of optimism and expectation of an Indian victory at Walong, now the Prime Minister not only confirmed in the morning newspaper reports on the fall of Walong, but also said that Se La had fallen too. After the House heard Nehru's short statement in dead silence, there was uproar of angry questioning and expostulation. Nehru sat silent, with his dominance of the House gone for good. Nehru addressed himself to the people of Assam: "Now what has happened is very serious and very saddening to us "We shall not be content till the invader goes out of India or is pushed out. We shall not accept any terms that he may offer because he may think that we are a little frightened by some setbacks"

On November 20, the American Ambassador noted "ultimate panic in Delhi, the first time I have ever witnessed the disintegration of public morale." Fear was in the air, and rumors were spreading that the Chinese were about to take Tezpur, even land paratroops in the capital, and that General Kaul was taken prisoner. Late that night Nehru made an urgent and open appeal for the intervention of the United States with bombers and fighters squadrons to go into action against the Chinese. Nehru requested fifteen squadrons and appealed American aircraft to undertake strikes against Chinese troops on Indian territory and to provide cover for Indian cities. In response, an American aircraft carrier was dispatched from the Pacific towards Indian waters, but the crisis passed twenty-four hours after Nehru made this appeal, and the aircraft carrier turned back. That appeal was not the only step taken in the shock of the debacle. Nehru had been emphasizing from the beginning that India was not fighting Communism because it was fighting China. The distinction was necessary not only to the posture of non-alignment, but to cushion India's relations with the USSR. But on November 20, orders went out to arrest several hundred leading members of the Communist Party. The intention was to arrest only those belonged to the left wing, but a muddle in the Home Ministry resulted in arresting many of the party's centrists and some of its pro-Moscow wing. Nehru complained to the Home Minister that it would give India a bad name in the Communist countries. But simply to let them all out again would compound the embarrassment, so it was decided to release the mistakenly imprisoned ones one by one in order not to make it look like a confession of error.

As the Home Minister was looking to the country's security, some politicians were worried about the political stability. Some in the Opposition and Congress suggested to President Radhakrishnan of suspending Parliament and making the Cabinet an advisory committee to the president, which was wooly and short of a coup, to which the Radhakrishnan gave no encouragement. In Tezpur, it was feared that the invaders would reach the town in a few hours. On November 18, the civil administration ceased to function, with the loudspeaker warning the townspeople that the authorities could no longer be responsible for their safety. Great crowds, including released convicts and inmates of the local asylum, gathered at the ferry, which carried up to a thousand pcople a trip, rather than their safe load of three or four hundred, across the Brahmaputra River. Those who stayed at the State Bank tried to burn some £300,000 worth of currency, including the coin; they first tried to get rid of coin by throwing it in a lake but people began diving for it.

The disorganization at Tezpur was later blamed on the state Government and local administration, but at least part of the responsibility can be traced to the Home Ministry in New Delhi, which instructed selective evacuation of the town and destruction of currency. Kaul had personally briefed two ministers of the state government on the morning of the 20th that the Chinese were coming, with a possible paratroop landing at Misamari and air raid on Tezpur likely. General Thapar returned to New Delhi late on November 19 and submitted his resignation to the Prime Minister. Even now Nehru's first thought was that Kaul should succeed Thapar as Chief of Army Staff. After discussing with the Radhakrishnan, as there was still no Defense Minister, the idea was dismissed as absurd and instead suggested General Chaudhuri as the new Army Chief. On the morning of November 21, as the Home Minister's party prepared to fly to Assam, they noticed a crowd and an air of excitement around the newsstand. One of them went to buy a paper and learned the headline announcement that China was going to unilaterally stop the fighting and then withdraw from NEFA. They immediately went to the Prime Minister's residence, where Nehru gave the impression that he had not heard the Chinese announcement, although the news had reached the newspapers several hours before. Thus the Government learned that China had been engaged not on an invasion of India, but on a giant punitive expedition.

Ceasefire

When the world learned on November 21, 1962, the border war in the Himalayas was to be ended by China's unilateral ceasefire and withdrawal. The Times expressed the universal reaction: "Astonishment almost blots out relief at the sudden Chinese decision." Chou En-lai called the Indian chargé d affaires to his residence and told him in detail of China's intentions: "1) Beginning from 00.00 on November 21, 1962, the Chinese frontier guards will cease fire along the entire Sino-Indian border. 2) Beginning from December 1, 1962, the Chinese frontier guards will withdraw to positions 20 kilometers behind the line of actual control which existed between China and India on November 7, 1959." The proposal further spelled out clearly that "in the eastern sector" the Chinese frontier guards "withdraw" to north of the line of actual control, that is, north of the illegal McMahon Line, and to withdraw twenty kilometers back from that line" and that "in the middle and western sectors, the Chinese frontier guards will withdraw twenty kilometers from the line of actual control."

The Indians would be expected to keep their armed forces twenty kilometers away from the line of actual control too, and China "reserved the right to strike back" if they did not do so. This proposal was the same when Chou En-lai first made it to Nehru in his letter of November 7, 1959, and was reiterated after the Namka Chu battle. India rejected the repeated and consistent Chinese insistence of it as the only possible way to defuse the border, most recently and brusquely on October 24 after the first Chinese attack. Now, at the point of smoking gun, a victorious China imposed not a victor's terms but what she had proposed all along.

The Indian Army had no doubt about the response to the ceasefire. The new Chief of Army Staff, General Chaudhuri, reported that his forces were in no condition to do anything but reciprocate the Chinese move. However, the story was different for the politicians, as usual, whose most frequent use of the word was "humiliation." While the soldiers were relieved, the civilians took the unilateral Chinese ceasefire as rubbing salt in the wounds. There was nearly unanimous opinion to reject Peking's "offer" out of hand. Nehru played for time, simply saying that no official message about a ceasefire had been received from Peking. As for negotiations, "our position" continues to be "that the position as it existed prior to September 8, 1962, shall be restored." The Opposition members denounced "a typical piece of calculated

Chinese trickery" and demanded assurances that the Government would ignore the ceasefire and continue to refuse negotiations. One politician cried: "Decency, dignity and self-respect require that we negotiate only after the barbarians are driven out."

As some called the Chinese move "fraudulent," others saw it as an ultimatum. All the Opposition Parties except the Communists issued a joint statement: "The Chinese offer of a unilateral ceasefire is only another of their notorious maneuvers, calculated to cause confusion and disruption in our national front, gain time for consolidation and build up for another infamous offensive and prevent us from mobilizing resources from inside and outside and create doubts in the minds of our friend in world democracy." The statement continued that the Prime Minister must not allow himself to be taken in, and the Government should reassure the nation that it would stand firmly by the policy of determined resistance and no negotiations.

When it was announced that the Chinese declaration was received that night, the spokesman refused to comment: "Let us wait and see." Neither then nor later would officials confirm that the troops had been ordered to observe the ceasefire, for that would be taken as admission that India had surrendered. In contrary, the Government strove to give the impression that India had just started to fight. Nehru fondly reassured a gathering of school-children: "The war with China will be long-drawn-out affair, it may take years it may take so long that some of you will be fit and ready to fight it." In the following days, the Chinese diplomats were called to the Ministry of External Affairs for clarifications on the meaning of "line of actual control," and if the Chinese withdrew twenty kilometers, "where will that be?"

Peking described these questioning as meaningless. These were clearly spelled out in the ceasefire statement and restated by the diplomats, but the Indian Government complained that it was still vague and would require further elaboration "before the Chinese ceasefire proposals can be fully considered." What China intended, of course, fell short of what the Indians desired. The Indians wanted to restore the positions they had held prior to September 18 and to resume the positions inside the Chinese claim line in the west and north of the map-marked McMahon

Line in the Thag La area. It was not enough for the Chinese to withdraw their troops. The Indians wanted all Chinese personnel to withdraw so that the Indians would return to their forward positions.

A week after the ceasefire, Chou En-lai wrote to Nehru again and appealed for Indian reciprocation of the Chinese measures. He urged that the Chinese proposals had given "full consideration to the decency, dignity and self-respect of both sides," and argued that their implementation would not involve gain or loss of territory for either side. But he warned that Chinese withdrawal could not by itself be expected to prevent clashes, and that Indian refusal to cooperate would jeopardize the ceasefire. A sharply worded Chinese note of December 8 accused India of "deliberate haggling and evading an answer."

Peking put three blunt questions: "Does the Indian Government agree, or does it not agree, to a ceasefire? Does the Indian Government agree, or does it not agree, that the armed forces of the two sides should disengage and withdraw each twenty kilometers from the November 7, 1959, line of actual control? Does the Indian Government agree, or does it not agree, that officials of the two sides should meet?" The Indian position to these questions was: "Yes and No." For domestic and international effect, Nehru and his colleagues were saying that the struggle with China would continue, and that the deceitful Chinese proposals must be rejected. But in fact the Indian Army was ordered to preserve the ceasefire and to avoid any provocation to the Chinese. It had no intention of moving right up to the McMahon Line again. The forward policy was dead, with the two or three thousand Indian soldiers lost in the fighting, but the fundamental position of the Indian Government had only been confirmed with no negotiations at their stand.

But as from the beginning, the Indian reputation for a pacific approach was so high and the general opinion of China was so low that it was not difficult for India to clock the unyielding and unchanging refusal to negotiate and to shift the onus for preventing settlement to China. The border war was almost universally reported as an unprovoked Chinese invasion of India, which only confirmed the general impression that Peking pursued a reckless, chauvinistic and belligerent foreign policy. The unilateral Chinese ceasefire and withdrawal was explained as a Russian ultimatum that brought it about, or that the U.S. had cleared its hands of the Cuba and was about to intervene. Others accepted the popular Indian explanation that the Chinese stop was "basically inspired by fear" because their lines of communication were overstretched and they became vulnerable to Indian counterattack. In time it was believed that, as Nehru put it, the Chinese had turned tail rather than face "the unexpected anger of the Indian people when aroused."

In the NEFA front, the ceasefire that came into effect at midnight on November 21 was a formality. Although organized fighting had effectively ended nearly forty-eight hours before, skirmishes continued in NEFA for a week after the ceasefire. The ceasefire was more definitive in the western sector than in the eastern sector. Survivors continued to emerge from the foothills for several weeks. The trek was so arduous that many Indian troops died from exposure or starvation on the way back. In 1965, the Defense Ministry released the figures of Indian losses: 1,383 killed, 1,696 missing, and 3,968 captured. Twenty-six of the Indians died of wounds in captivity, and the remainders were repatriated. About ninety percent of the Indian casualties were suffered in NEFA. The Indian Army later estimated that the Chinese had used three divisions in the NEFA fighting; one normal and one light division for the main thrust through Tawang, Se la and Bomdi La to the foothills, and another division for the Walong action. The Indian forces in NEFA numbered about twenty-five infantry battalions, equivalent to just under three normal infantry divisions. So the Chinese probably had only a narrow numerical superiority. But the Indian forces were so scattered that Mao's teaching could be easily put into effect: "In every battle, concentrate an absolutely superior force "encircle the enemy forces completely and strive to wipe them out thoroughly." Not one Chinese prisoner was taken by the Indians.

The new Chief of Army Staff, Chaudhuri, proposed to transfer the displaced Kaul to a training command in Punjab, but Kaul put in his resignation. Nehru tried to dissuade him and then wrote him a letter: "The events which have led to your retirement are sad and have distressed many of us. I am sure, however, that you were not specially to blame for them. A large number of people and perhaps just the circumstances were responsible for them." Nehru suggested to Kaul later that he might be appointed lieutenant-governor of Himachal Pradesh, but the idea was dropped, and the position was given to Dr Teja, who was later indicted for fraud. General Thapar made Indian Ambassador to Afghanistan. General Sen continued in East Command until he resigned from the Army. General Prasad was reinstated in Western Command. General Pathania resigned soon after the ceasefire. Brigadier Dalvi was repatriated in May 1963, received two substantive promotions and commanded a brigade in the 1965 war with Pakistan, and resigned in 1966 after superseded in promotion to the rank of major-general. Krishna Menon stayed on the Congress until being defeated twice in the 1967 general elections, but returned to the Lok Sabha in 1969.

The Indians and to some extent people abroad held skepticism that China would fulfill the proclaimed intention to withdraw behind the McMahon Line. On November 30 the Chinese Defense Ministry in Peking announced of the punctual withdraw to begin on December 1. The withdrawal was slow as the Chinese had a lot of tidying up to do, and went about the task with meticulous and even fussy care. They made it a matter of principle or pride to hand back the equipment left by the retreating Indians in as good condition as possible. It was collected, sacked, piled or parked; cleaned, polished, and carefully inventoried "small arms, mortars, artillery, trucks, shells and ammunition, clothing, and all the other impedimenta of a defeated army. Among the return equipment were a few American automatic rifles as the first installment of American military assistance captured at Se La, and a Russian helicopter in serviceable condition.

China did not publicize this extraordinary transaction, and said it was simply a gesture "to further demonstrate" sincerity for a peaceful settlement." But although Indians cooperated by formally receiving the returned equipment, they bitterly resented what they perceived as added humiliation and denounced the Chinese gesture as a propaganda maneuver. The Indian Army did not return to NEFA on the heels of the withdrawing Chinese. Civilians took over administration and reached Tawang on January 21, 1963 and many months later the Indian troops moved back into NEFA. New Delhi ignored the Chinese demand that Indian troops be withdrawn twenty kilometers from the line of actual control in the western and middle sectors, and Peking did not press that point. But in the eastern sector, the Indians kept out of the territory between Thag La ridge and the map-marked McMahon Line, and kept well back from the Line.

After the ceasefire, the Afro-Asian countries showed marked inclination to credit Peking for a genuine attempt to return the dispute to the negotiation table. Now New Delhi felt the pressure to accept the Chinese ceasefire proposal and resented it. The official spokesman explained at the end of November: "Those who do not understand the full significance of the deceptive Chinese proposals naturally ask why we cannot accept (them)." Nehru noted with some exasperation that the non-aligned countries were failing to grasp things that were obvious to India. However, President Nasser of the United Arab Republic (UAR) gave no ground to Indian Government for complaint this time.

As he put forward a proposal to convene a conference to discuss the ceasefire and possible bases of bilateral negotiation, the Indians found him "one hundred per cent" behind them. On December 10, the Prime Minister of Ceylon, Mrs. Bandaranaike, agreed to convene the conference in Colombo, where six delegations met, including Ceylon, the UAR, Cambodia, Ghana, Indonesia and Burma. The Governments concerned had previously been carefully briefed by special ministerial missions from New Delhi as to the minimal Indian requirement. It remained the restoration of the positions that Indians obtained on September 8, which would permit the Indians to return to posts set up in the western sector under the forward policy and to Dhola Post in the east. Accordingly the UAR delegation in Colombo presented for full restoration of the September 8th position, but that was plainly unacceptable to China. The Colombo powers proposed that the line of actual control (i.e. the McMahon Line) could serve as the ceasefire line, ignoring the Chinese stipulation that both sides keep armed forces twenty kilometers back from the line.

In the western sector, the Colombo powers proposed that China should carry out the twenty-kilometer withdrawal, but there should be no reciprocation on the Indian side. Then, "pending a final solution of the border dispute, the area vacated by the Chinese military withdrawals will be demilitarized zone to be administered by civilian posts of both sides to be agreed upon, without prejudice to the rights of the previous presence of both India and China in that area." This passage permitted the return of Indians to areas they had infiltrated under the forward policy, but it left ambiguous point that the presence of Indian civilians across the line of actual control in the western sector had "to be agreed upon" by China. When Mrs. Bandaranaike went to New Delhi in January to submit the Colombo proposals, the Indians persuaded her to allow them to remove the ambiguity. The Indian Ministry of External Affairs released the "clarification" of the original passage, by adding that "the number of posts and their composition that there has to be an agreement between the two governments of India and China."

For once it seemed that Nehru and Chou En-lai both informed Mrs. Bandaranaike to have accepted the proposals in principle. But Chou stated "two points of interpretations" which were in fact reservations. As "clarified" by the Indian Government, the proposals looked to China's fulfilling most of the provisions of her ceasefire declaration, but exempted India from any obligations of reciprocity. Chou suggested that India military forces should stay where they were in the east as in the west. He argued that Indians should not be allowed back into the strip in the west where they had infiltrated under the forward policy, either with troops or civilian personnel. Peking maintained that to allow this would be "tantamount to recognizing as legitimate the Indian armed invasion of this area and its setting up of forty-three strong points there between 1959 and 1962." Instead, Chou volunteered that China would pull all her posts out of that area, civilian as well as military. Chou suggested that neither his "points of interpretation" nor reservations on the Indian side should delay the opening of talks. Such differences could be resolved in the talks themselves.

But the Indian Government was as resistant as ever to any kind of direct exchanges with the Chinese. Nehru told the Lok

Sabha: "We cannot have any kind of talks, even preliminary talks, unless we are satisfied that the condition we had laid down "about the 8th September position being restored "is met." Beneath the rhetoric of Opposition in Parliament that pressed Nehru for clearer undertaking, the Indian approach was unchanged. They were seeking a way to avoid meeting the Chinese without seeming to rebuff the attempts of the Colombo powers. Peking's reservations to the Colombo proposals provided them the answer. The Indian Government promptly declared that it accepted the Colombo proposals as clarified by themselves "in toto," and declared that there could be no further step towards talks or discussions until Peking had also accepted the proposals together with the Indian clarifications in toto. Once again, skilful Indian diplomacy had avoided negotiations by making physical concessions by China a precondition, and shifted the onus of obstructing a meeting to China.

In the International Court at The Hague, Nehru's reference strengthened the general impression that it was India who was anxious to explore every avenue for peaceful settlement, and China who was balking. Nehru's stated: "I am prepared when the time comes, provided there is approval of Parliament, even to refer the basic dispute of the claims on the frontier to an international body" The foreign press reported this as a substantive Indian concession, ignoring Nehru's gloss latter on the remark. When members objected Nehru's reference to the International Court, Nehru immediately backed away: "What I said was that if and when the time came of it, if the House agrees, if Parliament agrees, we might perhaps think of it."

By this time it was plain that the Indian Government's determination not to negotiate for a settlement had only been confirmed by the defeat on the borders. Chou En-lai wrote Nehru in April 1963, accusing him of taking a dishonest approach and of having no intention whatever of holding negotiations. He said that India exploited ambiguities in the Colombo proposals to interpret those as conforming with the Indian demand for restoration of the September 8th positions, and was now trying to convert them into an adjudication and force them on China. As for the reference to the International Court, that was "plainly an attempt to cover up the fact that the Indian Government refuse to negotiate." Chou reiterated China's readiness to open negotiations immediately on the basis of the Colombo proposals, which both sides had accepted in principle.

But, he went on, "if the Indian Government, owing to its internal and external political requirements, is not prepared to hold negotiations for the time being, (China) is willing to wait with patience." A year later Nehru said in Parliament that he would be willing to consider opening talks if the Chinese completely evacuated the twenty-kilometer strip in the western sector.

Chou En-lai had proposed exactly that compromise, and when two emissaries of Bertrand Russell put it to the Chinese Government, the Chinese did not rule it out. New Delhi instantly denied that the Nehru entrusted the Russell emissaries and said that only if the Chinese evacuated the western strip "the new situation" might merit considerations." But by this time the Chinese Government had decided that it was useless to open discussions on the borders with India unless there was evidence of a radical change in Indian approach. New Delhi continued to publish the diplomatic exchanges for years, and the Indians continued to present themselves as the aggrieved party, and the Chinese as aggressive and recalcitrant. On the ground the position was reversed. There the boundaries had already been settled by China's crushing victory.

As the dust of battle subsided, most of the internationally conscious class of Indians had to come to terms with a sad new world. That India had preached the world to stopping the fighting in situations of dispute was forgotten, and there was strong resentment towards the non-aligned countries, "these amoral neutralists who have refused to give India the unreserved sympathy and support she has asked for." The Soviet Union also came in for a share of this displeasure. The U.S., Britain and other Western powers stepped forward staunchly in the hour of India's need, denouncing China and offering India weapons and other assistance. America's most active efforts were increasingly in Asia against China. The Soviet Union had serious split with China and soon also moved in the same direction as the U.S. India's falling-out with China fitted in with the emerging new pattern of big-power relationships, with India moving towards a bi-alignment with both Washington and Moscow against Peking.

The substantial American military assistance to India did not put off the Russians, who replied that they understood the Indian needs and requests. In thc immediate aftermath of the border war, India appeared to be moving closer to the U.S. Nehru maintained that non-alignment was alive and unimpaired, but in 1963 the Indian Foreign Secretary expressed the Indian Government's willingness "to work with the United States both politically and militarily in the rest of Asia" for the containment of China.

After receiving Nehru's call for help, President Kennedy dispatched Averell Harriman to India with a team of high-level State Department and Pentagon advisers and General Paul Adams, commander of the mobile strike force for emergency ground action. The Chinese announced their ceasefire before Harriman and others left Washington, but unlike the aircraft carrier, this mission did not turn back. After an eighteen-hour flight, the Americans arrived on the evening of November 22, and found Nehru had constraint in his attitude. One member of the mission wrote later: "His letters to Kennedy asking for help had painted a desperate picture, but face to face Nehru seemed to want to avoid talking about it all," and observed that "it must have been difficult (for him) to greet Americans over the ruins of his long-pursued policy of neutralism." The Harriman mission was paired with one from Britain led by Duncan Sandys, and laid the groundwork for substantial military assistance for India over the next three years. Later in 1963 a joint Anglo-American air exercise was held in India, with long-range fighter aircraft flying in to operate from Indian Air force Bases. Nehru had always explained his earlier resistance to acceptance of military aid, as such dependence would reduce India's independence.

Harriman's mission hinted, "with exquisite delicacy," "at the need for a settlement of the Kashmir dispute and for taking measures for joint defense with Pakistan." But the "delicacy" soon disappeared, with Harriman and Sandys launching all-out effort to use the promise of arms aid to lever India into settlement with Pakistan. That meant compromise by India, involving at least the surrender of a good part of the valley of Kashmir, and there was never a chance that India would agree to that. The British and Americans had been misled by a mirage effect of India's mood of "nothing matters but repelling the Chinese." Indians at all levels were saying that the time had come to settle with Pakistan, but they meant to settle on the status quo in Kashmir. To the Pakistanis, that was no settlement, but rather a refusal to reach one. Harriman and Sandys pressed on, and a week after their arrival, it was announced that Nehru and President Ayub of Pakistan were to meet in an attempt to resolve the Kashmir dispute. The very next day, Nehru assured an alarmed Parliament that his meeting with Ayub was not "negotiations" but "talks."

The Indo-Pakistan exchange broke down after a series of fruitless preliminary meetings, when it became unmistakable that the most India would concede fell unbridgeably short of the least Pakistan would accept. American military aid continued until 1965 when Pakistan attempted to shake Kashmir out of India's grip by force that set off their three-week war. India turned to the Soviet Union for assistance, and thereafter Moscow became India's biggest source of defense equipment. Meanwhile, Pakistan moved into more cordial relations with Peking and began receiving military equipment from China. The Indian role in international affairs after the border war was never the same as before. The debacle brutally exposed Indian weakness and its tacit alliance with the U.S. against China, and India can no longer claim the role of leader of the non-aligned countries. The 1960s were also the beginning of a period of mounting domestic difficulties for India, further diminishing its international role.

The defeat from the border war was not so bitter, after all. The country was united as never before and the Government was so confident that it suspended the committee set up to promote national integration, arguing that the war had done the work for it. The mythmakers were soon at work on the defeat. A week after the ceasefire a journalist wrote: "The planned withdrawal of several thousand Indian jawans (soldiers) and officers from the besieged 14,000-ft Se La region in NEFA will surely be regarded by future historians as a great page in military history." The official explanations of the debacle were accepted, with the blame put on the Chinese rather than on the Indian Government or the military leadership. It was suggested that the Chinese had won because they fought in overwhelming numbers, without regard for casualties, and took the defenders often by surprise.

Much was made of the climatic and logistical difficulties that faced the Indian troops, and few asked why they had been made to engage the Chinese without preparation in such adverse circumstances. The Army was instructed to conduct an inquiry into the reverses in NEFA, but Major-General Brooks and Brigadier Bhagat were ordered not to concern themselves with individual responsibilities for the debacle. Furthermore, they were not allowed to question officers in the General Staff or in other sections of Army H.Q., nor given access to Army H.Q's records.

General Thapar declined to give a statement to the board of inquiry, but offered to record his own comments on the report, a procedure ruled as entirely improper. Kaul submitted two long statements, but along with the report of Brigadier Dalvi, they were not passed on to Brooks. The inquiry was almost closed, and the crucial exchanges between the civilian leadership and Army H.Q. were undisclosed. The report followed the NEFA fighting in detail, and the responsibility of Kaul, Sen and Thapar was made clear although the blame was left tacit. The report could have been but most damaging to Nehru and the Government, and therefore it was classified and kept top secret. Defense Minister, Chavan, merely made a statement to Parliament: "We should never" say or do things which could only give heart to the enemy and demoralize our own men." Chavan explained the "series of reverses" from the Namka Chu to Bomdi La: "These battles were fought on our remotest borders and were at heights not known to the Army and at places which geographically had all the disadvantages for our troops and many advantages to the enemy."

Nehru made no gesture towards resignation, and he and his Government thus survived the disaster, which would surely have overturned any other democratic Cabinet. But Nehru's old moral and political domination in Parliament and the Congress Party was gone, not to be recovered in his remaining eighteen months of life. The inner balance of power in New Delhi shifted with uncertainty and indecision as Nehru remained to be the Prime

Minister. Before the border fighting, when Nehru was in his prime, it might be said that India had a dictator who would not establish a dictatorship. One area of decisive and determined change in the Indian Government was that of defense.

In the next two years, India's defense expenditure was more than doubled. The latest available American and British supplies replaced the obsolete equipment and stores. The political position of the Army was sharply changed, almost reversed by the debacle. There would be no more interference by the civilians in internal Army matter. In a letter to Bertrand Russell in December, Nehru referred to "the danger of the military mentality spreading in India, and the power of the Army increasing." In broader political terms, a marked shift to the Right appeared as a consequence of the border war, which exposed the intrinsic shallowness and weakness of the Indian Left as a national political force. The Left leadership, represented by Kerala and West Bengal, showed avowed sympathy for Peking and refused to denounce China for aggression, and as a result lost popularity. But the influence of the Sino-India dispute on the political balance was far from racial in India, and probably did no more than accelerating trends already in progress.

One of the most marked and saddest consequences of the border was perhaps the personal and political decline of Nehru. Menon said later in 1962: "I think he collapsed; it demoralized him completely because everything he had built up in his life was going." The remaining youthfulness was stricken from his shoulders, and he was left stooped and unsteady, cherishing a bitter sense of injury against the Chinese, whom he felt had betrayed him and all he had striven for. Much less was heard in India about forcing the Chinese "to vacate their aggression," although in 1970 the opposition Congress tried to commit the Government to doing just that. The forward policy was not revived. The Army build up its strength in Ladakh and opened roads to its forward positions, but they remained outside the Chinese claim line and the dispositions were defensive.

The overall superiority in numbers of the Chinese Army and their advantages in movement on the Tibetan plateau make it likely that the Indians can never hope to mount a successful offensive action anywhere on the northern borders, so long as China's central power is unbroken. As the borders settled into an armed truce, diplomatic relations between China and India were also frozen. Nehru resisted the pressure to break off the diplomatic relations with Peking, but closed the Chinese consulate in Bombay. It was a concession to domestic opinion, but it cost India its consulate in Lhasa, a loss which must have made Lord Curzon turn in his grave. It was years before anyone in India was bold enough to suggest mending relations with China. In 1969, when Mrs. Indira Gandhi, then Prime Minister, made the suggestion, she was criticized in Parliament. The Chinese showed no interest in improving relations with India. Chinese maps continue to ignore the McMahon Line. Presumably Peking's long-standing offer to negotiate a boundary settlement on the basis of the status quo when India is ready to do so still stands. But thus to go back to the beginning would mean India's tacit admission of error, and recantation of the deeply cherished belief that in 1962 she was the innocent victim of unprovoked Chinese aggression. That will never be easy.

6

A Quaker in the Military

My first serious exposure to the "Harmless and Innocent People of God called Quakers" came when I was about 14 years old. At the time, I was living in Lahore, Pakistan, where my doctor father was working for the Ford Foundation on population research. My father, who had been a conscientious objector and ambulance driver during World War II, was invited to attend an international peace conference organized by the Quakers in Dharmsala, India, the new home of the recently arrived Dalai Lama and thousands of Tibetan refugees. As well as meeting the Dalai Lama, an honor I accepted with the casual thoughtlessness of a 14-year-old, I also encountered for the first time the profound dedication of Quakers to the cause of peace, and their particular style of being in the world: meditative, mystical and moral. In the high, clear mountain air of India, I felt an inner response to a spiritual purpose that was larger than any I had encountered before.

Later, while enrolled in a Quaker boarding school in Pennsylvania, I resonated strongly to the spiritual mysticism and the silent meeting for worship, and I loved the absolute rejection of war, slavery, and corporal punishment. From that time I began to identify myself as a Quaker, even though I have since come to accept that traditional Quaker morality is not free from ethical problems.

There is an old joke about Quaker pacifism in action. It seems there was once a Quaker farmer who could not get his mule to move, no matter how he cajoled, pushed, or pulled. Finally, he looked the mule straight in the eye and addressed him by name. "Josiah," he said, "Thee knows I shall never curse thee, and thee knows I shall never strike thee; but if thee doesn't start moving this very instant, I shall sell thee to a Baptist who will!" Of course, the mule began moving immediately, being an animal of great wit and sagacity.

Like all good jokes, this one works because it contains a germ of truth. Quaker pacifism is founded on a bedrock of personal nonviolence, but Quakers live in a society that uses both violence and threats of violence as means of social regulation. It is simply impossible to live in a human society and not to participate in its violence. For centuries, we Quakers have papered over this ethical dilemma in three ways: by personally refusing to be violent, by being a witness for any and all acts of violence and oppression, and by working tirelessly with the victims of violence.

In Pakistan we lived literally around the corner from a refugee camp. From the older people in the community, I frequently heard stories of the War of Partition, when violence between Hindus and Muslims drove some ten million people from their homes. Entire trains filled with Muslim refugees arrived in Lahore station with only the engineer left alive, trailing unspeakable carnage behind him, and similar atrocities occurred to Hindu refugees traveling the other way across the new border between India and Pakistan. These stories and countless others like them demonstrated to me that violence and warfare were always just under the surface, barely under control, constantly threatening to break out into the open.

As a young adult I too started out in the Quaker way, becoming a conscientious objector during the Vietnam War; but I wondered whether some critical element might be missing. As a political tactic, the Quaker approach is only occasionally successful; as a method of social change, it is generally a failure; and from an ethical point of view, it has unfortunate elements of hypocrisy. I hoped it might be possible to find a better way, but at the time I had no idea what that might be.

I began to get an inkling when, later in life, I picked up the teachings of Mahatma Gandhi, once more returning in my mind to the complex atmosphere of the subcontinent. In contrast to the stark black-and-white thinking of Quakers on the subject of nonviolence, Gandhi had a subtle and nuanced approach.

"Nonviolence of the strong" was his lifelong theme, and by strength he was thinking of several things: spiritual development, psychological fortitude, and political strength. He was certainly not thinking of military strength, but one can extend his ideas into this area.

For example, he wrote, "Man for man, the strength of non-violence is in exact proportion to the ability, not the will, of the non-violent person to inflict violence." This is a remarkable statement for any pacifist to make, and it bears close study. On the surface, he meant that the political impact of nonviolence is greatest when practiced by those who could be very violent if they chose. At a deeper level, I think he believed that any movement which gathers political strength, psychological fortitude, and spiritual development simultaneously develops the ability to act powerfully, in either a violent or nonviolent mode. The essential question is how to tip the balance in favor of the more difficult choice: nonviolence.

For Gandhi, the key to this conundrum was spiritual development. Many times he wrote that when oppressed people lack spiritual development, they may use violence to free themselves. In fact (and surprisingly to me when I first read it), he was scathing in his criticism of passive or subservient nonviolence as a response to oppression, which he found unacceptable at any time. He said, "It is better to be violent, if there is violence in our hearts, than to put on the cloak of non-violence to cover impotence. Violence is any day preferable to impotence. There is hope for a violent man to become non-violent. There is no such hope for the impotent." In Gandhi's view, every person and every nation should use active methods appropriate to their level of spiritual development. He hoped that his beloved India would become the first example of a nation to free itself from a foreign oppressor entirely without violence, drawing upon his spiritual doctrine of ahimsa, or nonviolent action. As we know, India did succeed in this sixty-year effort, ridding itself of British colonial rule without warfare - although Gandhi, who died in 1948, sadly considered that he had failed when more than a million people were killed immediately after the partition of India and Pakistan.

A Personal Journey

About 20 years ago, after I was well established in a professional career as an applied mathematician in a medical school, a very strange thing happened. A mathematical paper of mine mentioned an application in nonlinear social change, and this attracted the attention of someone in, of all places, the CIA. One of that exotic tribe of analysts in suits appeared in my office, took me out to a slightly surreal lunch, and offered me a job in their analysis wing-the non-covert branch of the agency, I hasten to add, very different from the undercover espionage operations.

I quite happily turned them down, only to be approached next by the U.S. Office of the Joint Staff for help with a project in Europe. NATO had been running computer simulations of a Soviet invasion through the Fulda Gap in Germany, and every one of their projections ended in worldwide nuclear holocaust. Analysts at SHAPE (Supreme Headquarters Allied Powers Europe) wanted an explanation for this ultimate disaster, and they wanted me to help analyze their data. For a mere college professor with exactly zero prior military experience, this was heady stuff, and best of all it seemed to provide a way to contribute materially to the cause of peace. I accepted the job.

It soon became clear to me that my nonlinear mathematical models could not help us to understand the nuclear holocaust problem, and I told them so. The root cause lay elsewhere; it turned out that the use of tactical nuclear weapons was destabilizing the battlefield and leading to an unstoppable "tit-for-tat" escalation. In the end, my only contribution was merely to help validate a theory they already had, but my honesty apparently impressed them. I began to receive a steady stream of military research contracts, all dealing with the dynamics of war and peace, and with the instabilities of conflict and social development.

Eventually this led to full-time work developing mathematical simulations of UN peacekeeping and disaster relief missions, a topic that has led me ever more deeply into the heart and soul of the military, and to a personal confrontation with the same ethical dilemma that has plagued so many Quaker pacifists for so many centuries.

In 1994 I was asked to work with U.S. Southern Command, the somewhat notorious American military organization responsible for Latin American and the Caribbean. They were developing a new series of multinational military exercises in UN peacekeeping operations.

My role was to support these exercises with a simulation of the fictional society in which the operation would take place. This meant writing the software which predicts the social consequences of actions taken by all parties: massive refugee flows, political and ethnic polarization, civil unrest and violence, epidemics, economic collapse, etc. In effect, I and my computer program were acting as the role player for the entire population and society of the fictional country in which the operation was taking place.

A lifelong pacifist, I now found myself part of a military team, interacting with mid- and high-ranking military officers from all over the hemisphere, and an alphabet soup of UN agencies and civilian nongovernmental organizations. Although the purpose of the exercises was training in "military operations other than war," or MOOTW as the military insists on calling it, I still felt somewhat uncomfortable working so closely with warriors. I remember the disbelief that I saw in the faces of members of the Albuquerque Friends Meeting when I first described what I was doing in my professional life. Quakers find it easy to forgive an individual who enlists as a soldier to defend his country, but in a time of peace to help US Southern Command? The Pentagon? NATO? Unthinkable! Needless to say, I have a different view.

From the very first exercise, it was apparent that one of the greatest problems was, and still is, communication between military and civilians. Even when two people speak the same language (not always the case in these trilingual exercises), each has enormous difficulties in understanding the other across the military divide.

I quickly found myself becoming an informal liaison officer, right in the middle of that intense three-way nexus between the military command staff, the UN leadership, and the civilian NGOs. In the process, I learned a great deal about how the great international institutions of the modern world work - and how they fail to work.

During this time, I also became aware of a different form of pacifism - one that I never knew existed. This is "military pacifism," a phenomenon that sometimes occurs among officers who have experienced combat and know the price of war. It turns out, to my surprise, that a significant minority of American military officers are absolutely passionate about peace and nonviolent conflict resolution, even while serving an institution designed for war. Their politics and personal ethics differ from mine, and they are clearly prepared to obey all legal orders, but it would be the height of foolishness to discount them. The military "pacifists" that I have met are informed and intelligent people, whose unusual views are seldom expressed in print. They form a fascinating but hidden military subculture, and led me even more to feel that strict black-and-white thinking about war vs. peace can blind us to the subtleties of understanding and communication that are necessary to finally achieve an end to war.

The Causes of War

I have come to believe that war has causes on three levels: personal, psychological, and institutional.

The "personal" level is the level of personal choice, in which every citizen chooses his or her own degree of involvement in acts of war. Quaker pacifism is focused like a laser on this level. It is vital and necessary work, but spiritually incomplete and utterly inadequate for the task of eliminating war, since as long as there is a majority, or even a substantial minority who opt to fight, pacifists are left standing on the sidelines with limited influence.

Secondly, there is the deep psychological level, where transgenerational epidemics of child abuse and domestic violence lead to powerful unconscious urges towards violence, war, and genocide. Ironically, centuries-old Quaker efforts to eliminate slavery and domestic violence, and to establish the rights of women and children, may have done far more to eliminate the causes of war at this level than any Quakerly effort to inspire pacifism. This work affects the deepest psychological levels of a society, freeing the next generations from the hidden but deeply damaging effects of early childhood trauma and neglect. The more that parents can understand the effects of trauma and violence on children, instead of denying and belittling these insights as many still do, the better will be our chances for a peaceful future.

Nevertheless, the immediate cause of the outbreak of war is most often an institutional failure, a breakdown that occurs within the institutions responsible for conflict resolution. In the world of today, these institutions include the United Nations, regional organizations such as the Organization of American States and Association of Southeast Asian Nations, the World Court, the World Trade Organization, the World Bank, the International Committee of the Red Cross, and many more. In civil wars the breakdown occurs within national institutions for conflict resolution. The American Civil War, for example, was triggered by a disastrous decision of the Supreme Court in the Dred Scott case, and the subsequent failure of Congress to resolve the constitutional issues.

At the institutional level, pacifists are conspicuous by their absence. All too many peace-oriented organizations work well with the victims of oppression, but very poorly with their institutional perpetrators. I prefer to concentrate on the institutions that cause the problems in the first place: court systems, legislatures, civil services, armed forces, police, unions, political parties, and education systems. This work could perhaps be called nation-healing. The Hebrew phrase tikkun olam, "repairing the world," comes closer to the intended sense, because it includes the idea of institutional as well as individual healing.

I believe that there is a powerful connection between spirituality and nation-healing. Institutional decisions are made by individuals who must act in the interests of the institution or face expulsion, loss of power, and even death. This is the institutional imperative - the force which, in a sick institution, coerces individuals into acting in ways that are contrary to their personal ethical standards. There are only two ways of overcoming the institutional imperative of a corrupt organization: legal pressure from an external system of justice, or internal spiritual strength. The essence of nonviolent action as taught by Gandhi is the creation of revealing situations that allow spiritual values to gain ascendancy over the institutional imperative. For example, a well-timed hunger strike by a single respected person can halt an entire nation in its tracks by virtue of the moral force of the act and the spiritual dilemma that it reveals. Similarly, a single investigative article, published in a free press, can shame authorities into actions that are contrary to their institutional imperatives, and which then permit structural reforms of the system itself. Gandhi entitled his autobiography "The Story of My Experiments with Truth" because his career was, in fact, a long series of spiritual experiments that he hoped would reveal profound truths to authorities and people alike, and thus initiate irreversible institutional reform.

I often wonder what Gandhi would have thought about modern United Nations military peacekeeping operations. This is a use of military force that he never saw and probably never imagined. When hostile armed forces in a civil war are separated by lightly armed UN troops, whose presence has been approved by representatives of all nations, does this operation fall within ahimsa or not? Quite likely it does, based on the premise that if the United Nations is not sufficiently developed spiritually to be able to go into such a situation unarmed, then it is better to go in lightly armed. But what about heavily armed "peace enforcement" operations, taken under Chapter VII of the Charter of the United Nations, by order of the Security Council? This is quite another matter! I am not at all sure what Gandhi would have said, but I am certain that psychological and spiritual development is still the key.

As the world community matures spiritually and heals psychologically from centuries of war trauma, it will require less and less military force to resolve conflicts. Perhaps we can then allow the resources currently spent on military might to diminish as the institutions of global society strengthen - the very institutions whose present weaknesses are the direct and immediate cause of outbreaks of war. This means that the international system of justice could gradually grow to include binding arbitration between nations, and deliberative bodies like the Security Council could gradually shoulder the responsibility for enforcing decisions taken by majority vote.

Referring to India, Gandhi once said, "Our non-violent revolution is not a program of seizure of power. It is a program of transformation of relationships, ending in a peaceful transfer of power." The world has changed enormously since that time. In our world today, ahimsa is a program of transformation of institutional relationships, ending in a peace made durable by a system of checks and balances between the democratic organs of government and society.

The Road to Peace

Many nations today are trapped in states of poverty by multiple vicious cycles that involve their critical institutions. Corruption weakens the institutions of government, which are then less able to suppress organized crime in all its many forms. Organized criminal industries directly foster corruption, and the cycle repeats. Similarly, a weak government cannot take the steps necessary to reduce poverty, and poverty itself breeds corruption. These two vicious cycles reinforce each other, and, taken together, form the core of the poverty trap.

Through many years of international work, I have come to realize that a surprising number of national governments of poor countries are little more than organized criminal operations, in which the government as a whole is effectively "owned and operated" by a small group of elite citizens for their own financial benefit. Around the world today, there may be as many as fifty such national governments, in addition to a small collection of collapsed and dysfunctional states like Somalia and Haiti. Is there a greater threat to the collective security of the people of this planet? I don't think so. Not even nuclear or biological weapons pose as great a danger, in my opinion. Wars are fought and millions of people suffer and die every year because of governmental corruption and institutional weakness.

At the same time, momentum is gathering for an international reform movement. The so-called "civil society" of international NGOs is gathering strength and moving in this direction, while the individual agencies of the UN are acting more like a world government with every passing year. We have several international courts in operation, now capable of prosecuting government leaders who engage in genocide and other international crimes. We have seen the harbingers of an international police force in three areas: the emergence of an international civilian police organization for use in peacekeeping operations, the rapid growth of cooperation between national police forces, and coordination between national intelligence agencies in the fight against terrorism. Finally, as the war in Iraq showed, it has become the norm for international military interventions to require permission and sanction from the Security Council of the United Nations, despite all imperfections of the system.

In my view, all of these developments are merely the latest and most visible steps in a long evolution towards worldwide integration that began during the Napoleonic Wars, about 200 years ago. The world has become smaller as technological development has increased the speed of communication, the volume of transportation, and the lethality of military weapons. Thus, the nations of the world are increasingly enmeshed in each other's business. The consequence is necessarily greater cooperation and integration, with episodes of war declining in frequency and severity. The speed of technological change is actually accelerating, which means that the pressure on governments and institutions will double and redouble in coming years. We can expect extremely dramatic changes.

The next step in this evolution, whose beginnings are already visible, will be a serious international effort to effect institutional reform within nations trapped in the vicious cycle of corruption and poverty. Initially this will be voluntary, in the sense that it will be an international service that governments can request; but ultimately I expect it to become legally sanctioned. Just as individual states of the American union cannot long remain egregiously corrupt without federal intervention, so corrupt or tyrannical national governments that cannot reform themselves will be forced to submit to reform under the supervision of the UN - which itself will undergo major structural reform. To my mind, this will be the single greatest step towards peace that the world will ever have taken.

A Last Word

The last word belongs to Jeff (not his real name, of course), a retired army colonel. Some years ago we met in a bar in Rio de Janeiro, on Copacabana beach. Jeff needed to drink and wanted to talk, so I listened and bought him beer after beer. I heard hair-raising stories of night flights of helicopter gunships into El Salvador, unexpected encounters with massively armed narcotraffickers in Colombia, and psychological warfare against rebels in Perú. The night wore on, and we fended off yet another approach by ladies of the night. I heard about his childhood, when he watched terrified as a man was murdered in his own kitchen. I heard about his struggles with alcohol, his difficult marriages, and the journal that he kept through all the years of pain and trauma.

Long past midnight we went out to walk the beach under the stars, and our conversation turned to the future of the army. Like many military officers he was well read in history, and acutely aware of the changing role of the modern military. "Loren," he said, "The greatest battle of the American military is being fought right now, within the inner rings of the Pentagon, between the 'warfighters' and the 'peacemakers.' The warfighters have the upper hand, but they know they are losing a little more every year. The world is closing in on us; the days of million-man armies surging across Europe arc gone forever. We have already changed so much and so fast, our own public doesn't know what we do or how we do it anymore. We don't even have good words to describe our new missions; we mess around with wretched phrases like 'civil affairs' and 'information ops.' Where are we going with all this? All I know is that war isn't going away, and peace isn't arriving to take its place. They are both changing so fast we can hardly keep up."

7

Civil War Ambulance Wagons

Ambulance wagons, or wagons especially designed for the transport of sick and wounded, had not been in use in the armies of the United States until a year or so before the outbreak of the War of the Rebellion. Transport carts, army wagons, ox teams, in fact anything that could be made available for the purpose, had been employed. In the War of Independence, in April, 1777, the Congress of the United States passed a bill "devising ways and means for preserving the health of the troops" which contained the following paragraph:

"That a suitable number of covered and other wagons, litters, and other necessaries for removing the sick and wounded, shall be supplied by the Quartermaster or Deputy Quartermaster General; and in case of their deficiency, by the Director or Deputy Director General." There is no record that such vehicles were supplied. During the war with Great Britain, in 1812-'14, there were evidently no ambulance wagons in the United States army, as Surgeon James Mann, in his report of that campaign, is found to make the request that, "to facilitate the movement of the hospital department attached to an army, it should be furnished with a number of wagons and teams, so as not to be immediately dependent on the Quartermaster's Department, when requisite either to take the wounded from the field of battle, or transport the sick in case of a retrograde march, or remove invalids after having recovered from wounds to a remote hospital.

The flying machines called volant, drawn by horses (an improvement of Larrey, Chief Surgeon of the French army), are useful in open countries, where a corps is assigned to accompany them on the field of battle, upon Larrey's plan." The same author (loc. cit., p. 126) relates that he transported, in February, 1814, four hundred and fifty sick men from Malone to Plattsburgh and Burlington, a distance of seventy miles, in sleighs, losing six patients by death. In the Florida war, in 1838, ambulance wagons are mentioned by Surgeon R. S. Satterlee, U. S. A., Medical Director south of Withlacoochee, in a report from Fort Brooke, Tampa Bay, dated January 5th: "I found the ambulances very serviceable, but as some of the wounded could not be transported in them, on account of the roughness of the road, between thirty and forty of them were brought a part of the way on litters between two horses." Surgeon Satterlee probably had reference to the ordinary transport wagons used on this occasion for conveying sick and wounded.

In the General Regulations for the Army of the United Sates, Washington, 1847, page 123, paragraph 704, it was ordered that: "For the accommodation of the sick and disabled, a wagon will be attached to the rear guard, when necessary and practicable, and a surgeon will attend to give assistance, and to see that no improper persons are suffered to avail themselves of the accommodation." No ambulance wagons were attached to the American army in Mexico in 1846-'48, or to the expeditions in Indian territories before the outbreak of the war.

In 1858 an ambulance wagon had been proposed by Dr. I. Moses, of New York, and on March 2, 1858, a Board of Officers, consisting of Surgeons R. S. Satterlee, O. H. Laub, and Assistant Surgeon C. H. Crane, had been appointed to examine and report on its merits.

The report of the Board is appended: "The ambulance resembles an omnibus, is entered by two steps in the rear, contains seats for eighteen persons--fourteen inside and four on the front seat. By raising the flaps of the inside seats and supporting them by the uprights attached, and removing the cushions from the backs of the permanent seats, a bed is arranged which will accommodate one, two, or, on an emergency, three men lying down. With one man in a recumbent position, room for twelve men seated remains; with two men lying down, room for eight, and with three men lying down, room for six remains.

A canvas, stretched and suspended by cords from the top, will accommodate two men lying down where the roads are rough. A close-stool is provided in the vehicle. Two seats, separated from the rest, next to the door, are provided for the hospital steward and attendant. Two movable chests are placed under these seats to contain what may be required for daily use. The movable door closing the ambulance may become, by change of position, a table for writing or dispensing medicine. The interior is closed entirely by curtains of prepared canvas, or partly by curtains and Venetian blinds for free ventilation--windows admitting sufficient light when entirely closed. Under the front seat are placed two store chests. Underneath the carriage, on either side of the door, are two five-gallon kegs for water. Under the body of the vehicle are hooks for camp kettles, pails, and cooking utensils.

Two drawers are arranged on each side, between the wheels and under the carriage, which may be used as panniers when necessary. On the hooks surrounding the ambulance, five feet from the ground, canvas is stretched, extending ten feet on each side of the carriage, the front and rear being protected in the same manner, which forms a comfortable and ample tent protection for thirty sick men, and which may be arranged in a few minutes after arriving in camp by one or two men. In more permanent encampments, or in hot weather, this canvas may be fastened to hooks around the top of the ambulance wagon, serving a better purpose by giving more space and freer ventilation.

It is suggested that a light iron railing, about four inches in height, should surround the top of the ambulance, where, by having a suitable canvas cover, blankets and other indispensable articles might be securely carried. A lantern suspended over the front seat may be removed to the rear of the carriage, at will. It will admit of sufficient accommodation in the way of transportation and provide tent shelter for the sick of a regiment on marches. The dimensions are: extreme length, thirteen feet eight inches; height of floor from ground, three feet three inches; height of top from ground, eight feet four inches; height of inside, five feet; width, four feet four inches. Weight, two thousand one hundred and fifteen (2,115) pounds. When loaded with men, medicines, tent canvas, etc., it can be readily drawn by six horses or mules.

The size of the wheels and the track of the same correspond with those of the government wagons. After a close examination of the ambulance, the Board is of the opinion that it is well adapted for field and frontier service, and for the comfortable transportation of sick and wounded men on long marches; that the tent arrangement forms a valuable, useful, and comfortable shelter for hospital patients. On marches it does away with the use of hospital tents, is easily arranged, keeps the hospital separate, and requires no detail of pioneers or extra duty men to pitch and arrange it. In submitting this opinion the members of the Board must also express their views, based upon their own individual experience, that to be made thus available and useful for the comfort and well-being of the sick the ambulance should be the property of the Medical Department, and that the team, harness, etc., should be under the exclusive control and direction of the medical officers under all and every circumstance." No action seems to have followed the recommendations of this Board, and no ambulances were built.

In October, 1859, a Board of Medical Officers, consisting of Surgeon C. A Finley, R. S. Satterlee, C. S. Tripler, J. M. Cuyler, and Assistant Surgeon R. H. Coolidge, had recommended: 1st, that ambulance transportation ought to be furnished for forty men per thou-sand--twenty lying extended and twenty sitting; 2d, that both two and four-wheeled ambulance wagons are necessary for the hospital service; 3d, that a two-wheeled ambulance wagon is the best for the conveyance of dangerously sick or wounded men * * *; that to each company one two-wheeled ambulance wagon, to a battalion of five companies one four-wheeled and five two-wheeled ambulance wagons, and to a regiment two four-wheeled and ten two-wheeled ambulance wagons be allowed; and that for hospital supplies to commands of less than three companies one two-wheeled transport cart, to commands of more than three or less than five, or five companies, two, and to a regiment four two-wheeled transport carts be assigned; and that the transport carts be made after the models of the two-wheeled ambulance wagons (their interior arrangement for the sick excepted).

The same Board selected, from a number of the most approved plans laid before them. the two-wheeled wagons designed by

Surgeon C. A. Finley and Assistant Surgeon R. H. Coolidge. The bottom of the body of the Finley pattern was divided into two compartments, each containing a movable mattress frame or stretcher; four longitudinal pieces either in or upon the framework were grooved on their upper surfaces so as to receive the rollers in the mattress frame. The body of the wagon rested on four elliptical springs fastened upon the shafts, which extended the whole length of the body, crossing, and connected with the axle.

The body of the Coolidge cart was hung on platform springs. The body was seven feet long, four feet wide, and one foot and eight inches deep, covered with a ribbed frame-work five and a half inches above the floor. Upon the relative merits of the two patterns of two-wheeled ambulance carts the Board hesitated to express an opinion, and therefore recommended "that one of each pattern be sent to the respective Military Departments of Texas, New Mexico, Utah, California, and Oregon, and two of each pattern to Fort Leavenworth, and that they be placed in service at the scene of Indian hostilities and on marches across the plains, in order that their practical advantages might be ascertained." The Board considered the two-wheeled cart as the most convenient for the conveyance of dangerously sick and dangerously wounded men. A number of these two-wheeled carts were furnished to the troops in the early part of the war, but experience soon proved them useless; their motion was intolerable and excruciating; wounded men begged to be taken out, wounded officers insisted upon leaving them, and they were supplanted by four-wheeled vehicles, the earliest of which was the Tripler ambulance wagon recommended by the Medical Board of 1859.

It was constructed to carry ten men, four lying at length and six seated, and required four horses. The body of the wagon was ten feet long, four feet wide, and the sides three feet high. Upon the floor were permanently laid four parallel iron rails seven feet long and one-fourth of an inch wide and high, with convex faces. Two spring mattresses were run in upon these rails. Twenty-two inches above the surfaces of these mattresses another set of rails was fitted to the wagon, upon which another set of mattresses was run. In front of the wagon was a chest intended for instruments, dressings, etc., which, when closed, formed a seat for three persons.

At the tail of the carriage was another seat for three persons. All or any part of the interior of

(1) On May 20, 1861, Acting Surgeon General R. C. WOOD wrote to the Secretary of War: "It is highly important that provision be made for the safe and comfortable transportation of the sick and wounded, and in conformity with the recommendations of a Board of Medical Officers convened by the Secretary of War. and their report approved by him in General Orders No. 1, January 19, 1860, I have to recommend that .two hundred of the two-wheeled ambulances be immediately constructed by the Quartermaster's Department. The recommendation was approved by the Secretary of War and the wagons were constructed and sent to the troops."

(2) LONGMORE (T.) (A Treatise on the Transport of Sick and Wounded Troops, London, 1869, page 382) erroneously states that this wagon was constructed to carry eight men, all lying down.

the wagon was arranged so that it could be removed at pleasure, making it available for the transportation of hospital supplies. The cover of the wagon was of heavy duck supported on five hoops. The carriage was hung on platform springs, and underneath the body was suspended a water-butt three feet six inches long and fourteen inches in diameter. This wagon was extensively used and answered the purpose, although it was cumbrous and very heavy.

The Wheeling or Rosecrans ambulance wagon was also used in the early part of the war. It was built in the Government workshops after a design of General W. S. Rosecrans, U. S. A. It was lighter than the Tripler or the Coolidge, could be readily drawn by two horses, and would accommodate eleven or twelve sitting or two recumbent and two or three sitting patients. Two cushioned benches were attached to the two sides of the interior of the wagon, running along its whole length. From the edge of each of these benches, fastened by hinges, depended a cushioned seat the length of the benches. These seats could be readily brought on a level with the benches, and when thus elevated could be securely fixed by iron feet, folded in the suspended seat. For the ends of the iron feet receptacles were fitted in the floor of the wagon. When both seats were raised they met, in the middle of the carriage and made one continuous bed for two patients.

When only one seat was raised it formed a bed for a recumbent patient, while the other bench, with its suspended seat, allowed space for at least four sitting patients. A water-tank, capable of holding five gallons, was stored away under the seats in the rear end of the ambulance wagon; not unfrequently stretchers took the place of one of the water-tanks. In front of the benches a transverse seat, accommodating the driver and two or three patients, was provided. Under the seat was a box for medicines and other articles for field use. Accurate specifications for the building of this ambulance will be found on page 59 of the Report of a Board of Officers to decide upon a pattern of ambulance-wagon above referred to. The body of the wagon rested upon four elliptical springs, two placed, transversely (one on the front and one on rear axle), and two on the rear axle running longitudinally. A frame of light wood, with canvas cover, protected the patients against the inclemencies of the weather, and on the sides curtains of canvas could be closely buttoned to the top and the body. At the rear of the wagon was a step to assist patients and bearers in lifting in the wounded. The weight of the wagon was between seven hundred and eight hundred pounds.

A four-wheeled ambulance wagon. designed by Assistant Surgeon R. H. Coolidge, was very little used. The sills of the wagon were ten feet four inches long, and the body rested between two semi-elliptical springs seven feet nine and three-quarter inches in length. It was intended to accommodate two patients in recumbent and four in sitting postures, two with the driver on the front seat, and two at the end of the wagon, one on each side. The beds for the two prone patients were so arranged that they could be changed into seats, when the wagon would accommodate ten patients and the driver.

Other plans for ambulance wagons were proposed during the war, and for the information of those interested in this subject we will here refer to such as were submitted to boards of medical officers for examination and report. In June, 1863, A. W. Süs (Subject-Matter Index of Patents for Inventions issued by the United

States Patent Office, Washington, 1874, Vol. I, page 14, No. 39,595) exhibited a wagon intended to carry four severely wounded men in a recumbent position. A Medical Board (Medical Inspectors E. P. Vol-lum and W. H. Mussey, and Surgeon J. H. Brinton, U. S. V.) considered an "increase in the carrying capacity advantageous and feasible," but was not prepared to endorse the plan of Mr. Sos in all its details.

The Board was of the opinion that the Wheeling ambulance wagon, then largely in use in the army, could readily be altered to carry four patients in a lying position, as in Mr. Süs's plan. Mr. Süs, in April, 1864, offered an improved plan, which was, by order of Surgeon R. O. Abbott, Medical Director, Department of Washington, inspected by Assistant Surgeon W. E. Waters, U. S. Army, who reported, on June 2, 1864: "These improvements consist in adapting the ambulance for the conveyance of four patients lying down, instead of two, as with the present arrangement, while, at the same time, the carrying capacity for such as can sit up is' not at all interfered with. The improvement is effected by having the seats fastened with hooks to the side of the ambulance so that they can be detached and put upon the floor, thus forming a bed, on which the patient can lie with full as much comfort, as regards position, as with the present arrangement, while they are made more comfortable by the addition of elastic springs within the cushion."

Surgeon Waters' report was approved by Medical Director Abbott, who recommended that ten or twelve ambulances fitted with these improvements be sent to the field for trial. In April, 1864, G. W. Arnold brought to the notice of the Surgeon General an ambulance wagon for which he claimed advantages over the Wheeling ambulance wagon in the arrangements of the seats or beds. The Board to whom the examination of the vehicle was referred reported, on April 5, 1864, that "the only advantages it possessed over the Wheeling model was that its litters could be removed from the wagon, the patient, placed upon them, and then easily returned; but that the capacity for carrying men was diminished, and that the litters accompanying the wagon were too heavy, weighing about seventy pounds each, and would add, with their apparatus for suspension, nearly two hundred pounds to the weight of the ambulance wagon." On October 11, 1864, E. R. McKean patented an ambulance wagon with litters or beds suspended by rubber rings. Surgeons R. O. Abbott, C. Sutherland, and Assistant Surgeon William Thomson inspected the wagon and reported, on March 25, 1865: "The principle of suspending the stretcher upon which the patient lies by rings of India rubber, in lieu of the springs of steel usually placed beneath the body of the wagon, is the main difference between this and the ambulance now in general use. However valuable this principle may be, the mechanical contrivances by which it is obtained in the wagon submitted are, in the opinion of the Board, too complicated, wanting in solidity and durability, and too liable to the loss of detached pieces, to render this ambulance fit for the severe test of field service."

In September, 1865, an India rubber spring ambulance wagon, by Perot & Co., was brought to the attention of the Surgeon General by Brigadier General C. H. Crossman, U. S. Army. Surgeons C. McDougall, John Campbell, and A. K. Smith, and Assistant Surgeon C. H. Alden, appointed a Board to examine the rubber spring wagon, reported, on October 26, 1865: "The Board is very favorably impressed with the plan proposed, and as its peculiarities are best shown by contrast, would state the following as some of the particulars in which it is thought the India rubber spring is superior to the ordinary steel spring. It more perfectly controls the movements of the body of the ambulance in every direction, either upward, downward, or laterally, rendering the motion of those seated or lying within steadier and more equable. It is better adapted to carrying weights in the ambulance, acting with nearly the same effect with a light or heavy load.

It is believed to be more durable. An ambulance built upon this plan was shown to the Board, belonging to the West Philadelphia Fire Company, which had been in use for several years, and which showed but little evidence of wear in the springs. It is easily repairable, as a spare spring can be readily carried in the ambulance wagon, and can be substituted for a broken one with but little delay and trouble. The India rubber springs weigh thirty-five and three-quarter pounds, which at seventy-five cents per pound would amount to $26.81. Steel springs of the same power would weigh about two hundred pounds and cost about $50.00."

The most serviceable ambulance wagon used during the latter part of the war was that designed by Brigadier General D. H. Rucker, and built at the Government repair shops at Washington. It accommodates patients either in the sitting or lying postures. On the floor of the vehicle are two stretchers suitable for carrying one patient each, and each divided by a longitudinal hinge-joint. These stretchers have the usual handles, and run on elastic rollers so as to move readily longitudinally in the bottom of the wagon. When required as seats, the joints of the stretchers are bent and the two parts are made to assume a position at right angles to each other, the half which has the horizontal position being hooked to the sides of the vehicle, the other part forming the support or leg for the front of the seat. When the lower bed or stretcher is thus bent to form a seat, the upper beds are turned down to make backs for the lower seats.

These backs are only joined to the sides of the wagon by hinges at their upper edge, and the lower edge can be raised upward and inward, toward the middle of the carriage. When thus elevated the two backs meet in the middle of the carriage and are there supported by iron supports, which, being hinged to their under surfaces, can be readily lowered for the purpose. In the floor are springs for the reception of the iron supports. A platform is thus built on which two patients, on stretchers, can be laid. These stretchers ordinarily are suspended from the roof of the carriage, each stretcher being slung with one side to the middle of the roof and with the other to the bend of the arched roof.

The space between the upper surface of the lower and the lower surface of the upper stretchers was about twenty-one inches. This space was ventilated by lattice openings on each side of the body of the ambulance wagon. The body rested on platform springs, and the fore wheels were smaller than the hind wheels. The water-cask was under the driver's seat, and the spigot projected slightly through the side of the body. The weight was about one thousand one hundred and twenty pounds, exceeding that of the Wheeling, which only weighed from seven to eight hundred pounds, but the Rucker wagon was somewhat longer and broader. Detailed specifications of this ambulance wagon will be found on page 48 of the Report of a Board of Officers to decide upon a Pattern of Ambulance Wagon for Army Use, Washington, 1878.

In October, 1864, Assistant Surgeon B. Howard, U. S. Army, constructed an ambulance wagon for which he claimed many advantages. A full description, with illustrations, will be found on pages 981-994 of The Sanitary Commission Bulletin, Vol. I, 1866; an extract, omitting some of the minor details, is here reproduced: "To enable the badly wounded to be easily loaded and unloaded, two litters or beds are provided, made of wood, like an ordinary shutter, with sliding handles at each corner. Upon this the patient is easily shifted, and without any disturbance. The litter is slid into the ambulance wagon on rollers. In the same way the patient is removed on arrival at the hospital, and without being disturbed until he reaches his bed.

If part, or all the patients are able to sit up, one or both of the litters can be slid into a compartment provided for that purpose under the floor of the vehicle. There are six permanent seats, each situated transversely, and each a corner seat with back and cushioned seats. This gives a comfortable purchase, secures the patients against much of the usual jolting, and prevents them being driven against each other in going over rough roads. The sides of the ambulance wagon, as also both sides of the back of the driver's seat, and the inside of the upper section of the tail-board, are cushioned, while the middle seats have for a back a leather strap, like that used in stage coaches; thus each seat is rendered very comfortable, and being transverse instead of longitudinal is in every respect easier for the patient. In order to diminish the motion of the body of the wagon and prevent rolling and pitching, so intolerable in the ordinary ambulance wagon, semi-elliptical springs have been substituted for the elliptical ones. In order that the limited motion thus obtained be so modified as to give least jar to patients, internal counterpoise springs are used, the delicacy of which may be modified to any extent desired.

The platform or frame on which the seats and beds rest is as long but not so wide by about two inches as the inside of the body of the wagon. Between the inside of the body and the frame of the platform is an interspace; this is occupied by two lateral semi-elliptical steel springs on either side, fastened at the centre of their arc to the inside of the body of the vehicle, the feet of which-play upon iron plates on the outside of the frame. Opposite the centre of the arc on the frame is fixed a block of soft rubber, so that on the application of much force it should be received by the rubber blocks, which thus act as buffers. The platform or frame on which the seats and beds rest stands upon four iron stanchions, each of which rests on springs like the lateral springs described above, but much stronger, the iron stanchions resting on steel springs, the feet of which play upon iron plates let into the floor of the ambulance wagon. The spring is restrained in its motion upward by an iron staple, and when, by an unusual weight, it is heavily pressed down; the force is received by a block of soft India rubber enclosed within the staple.

An impulse communicated to the floor of the wagon, instead of being propagated to the beds or seats, causes a counteraction downward of the spring, which, if the force be very great, spends itself upon the block of rubber. In this way, both laterally and perpendicularly, a constant poise is preserved, and what would otherwise be a very violent jar is reduced to little more than a vibration. The steadiness of the entire vehicle is preserved by the stout semi-elliptical spring beneath the body, and the delicacy regulated to any degree by the internal counterpoise springs within the body. That the water may be carried securely, immobility of the vessel containing it during transportation is necessary.

This is effected by substituting for the casks in ordinary use a tank, which slides into a grooved bed and is secured by an ordinary fastening. In a military point of view it possesses a great advantage in this: that besides the prescribed articles which may be carried in the driver's box, a large amount of medical supplies may be carried in the body of the ambulance wagon without interfering with the comfort of badly wounded patients. There being but four stanchions, and these being close up to the side of the vehicle, the entire body beneath the platform is free for transportation of supplies. There is an arrangement for suspension of fractures of the lower extremity, which is very grateful to the patients.

Two parallel iron bars are attached to the roof of the ambulance wagon longitudinally over each bed, between which runs a roller with a dependent hook. The fractured limb being placed in a double-inclined plane or other splint, a bandage is passed through terrestra of the box splint and then carried over the hook from which the limb is suspended. In this way, instead of the jolting and jarring so commonly experienced, simple oscillation is substituted, or, if desired, guys of bandage may be so extended to the uprights of the ambulance as to render the limb nearly motionless during transportation."

The weight of the Howard ambulance wagon was twelve hundred and thirty-two pounds. The plan of this wagon, with recommendations of some twenty officers of the Army of the Potomac, was submitted for examination by Surgeon T. A. McParlin, Medical Director of the Fifth Army Corps, to a Board of Medical Officers, consisting of Surgeon J. J. Milhau, U. S. A., Surgeon L. W. Read, U. S. V., and Assistant Surgeon George A. McGill, U. S. A., who reported, on October 6, 1864, that: "the ambulance wagon meets the approbation of the Board as one presenting some decided advantages over that now in use. It is recommended further that at least two to a division be furnished, so that a fair trial can be made of such vehicles."

A number of the old pattern ambulance wagons were thereupon altered according to the plans submitted by Assistant Surgeon B. Howard, U. S. A., at the Government repair shops at Washington. But it seems that after nine months' experience in the field these ambulance wagons failed to meet the expected advantages. In a letter dated Medical Director's Office, Headquarters Fifth Corps, June 29, 1865, Surgeon Charles Page, U. S. A., remarks' "There have been two of the ambulance wagons in each division train of the corps, and for case to the patient the report is universal in their favor. They are apt to get out of order, and being heavy cannot be carried where the other ambulance wagons can go.

For marches I think the Howard ambulance wagon is superior; but for field work, in time of action, I would prefer the present Rucker pattern of ambulance wagon." In a reply to a note of enquiry from the Surgeon Genera dated June 29, 1865, Surgeon

T. R. Spencer, U. S. V., from Headquarters of the Fifth Army Corps, takes a similar view: "So far as I can learn in this corps, it, is not regarded as an improvement upon the old one. It is so heavy as to require four horses, else it rapidly destroys two. It is so complicated as to be continually getting out of order. As now constructed the ambulance wagon does not ride as easy over all roads as the old one. The only advantage it seems to possess is in the greater convenience of loading and unloading; this soon results in the loss of the bed, as officers will not consent to be removed from the bed during transportation. Once lost, or taken from the ambulance wagon, the bed is never returned, and the wagon is henceforth useless."

In the winter of 1864-'65 an ambulance wagon, proposed by Dr. I. Langer, was used at the Fifth Army Corps Depot Hospital before Petersburg. It was arranged to accommodate eight persons, four in sitting and four in recumbent positions, or six in sitting and two in recumbent, or all eight in sitting postures. The advantages claimed were, greater seating capacity, greater facilities for loading and unloading, greater comfort to patients, offering easier access to each single patient, superior ventilation, and that it had apparatus for suspending two patients with compound fractures of the thigh. In April, 1865, a Board was convened, consisting of Colonel R. O. Abbott and Assistant Surgeons J. J. Woodward and William Thomson, U. S. A., to examine and report on this ambulance wagon. The Board considered seriatim the advantages claimed by Dr. Langer, basing its opinions on comparisons with the Wheeling and the Rucker patterns then most generally in use- "The model examined is altered from a Wheeling ambulance wagon; the changes are radical and the additions numerous.

So ingeniously complicated are the appliances, and so multitudinous the objects to be obtained, that the wagon would fail to meet the test of field service. The probable loss of its numerous detached pieces would rob it of all its special advantages, and leave it less useful than the Wheeling and Rucker wagons. In comparison with the former it has some advantages; but it fails to compete in practical usefulness with the ambulance wagon devised by Brigadier General Rucker."

With regard to the apparatus for the purpose of transporting two thigh fractures the Board find: "The novelty of the method and the uncertainty of its practical value would not warrant the alteration of all the ambulance wagons in the service to fit them for transporting in this manner an occasional fractured femur." The Board refused to recommend the introduction of the Langer ambulance wagon into the service in preference to those then in use. At the same time Dr. Langer submitted to the Surgeon General for inspection an army wagon which had been fitted up with twelve beds for transporting patients. Dr. Langer claimed "that this change of the army wagon would not interfere with its design of conveying forage or other articles to and from a camp; that when the wagon is used for carrying forage the twelve beds are packed under a movable bottom, and the railing supporting them is stowed away on the sides, so that the capacity of the wagon box is not impaired; that in ten minutes after the wagon is unloaded it is changed into an ambulance wagon with all the equipments for transport--six patients in a sitting posture, six in a lying, two of which, if necessary, suspended on fracture beds of Dr. Langer's pattern; that there is room for all the equipments of the patients, for a water-keg, and for boxes with provisions and bandages, and that the wagon can be loaded from the front as well 'as the rear." As far as can be ascertained the experiment was tried but once. A drawing of the Confederate field ambulance wagon is copied from Chisolm. No description of the vehicle could be obtained.

8

The History of the English Civil Wars

THE BISHOPS' WARS, 1639 AND 1640

The Bishops' Wars were fought between the Scots and English forces led by Charles I. These conflicts paved the way for the uprising of Parliament that began the English civil wars.

Charles I was attempting to enforce Anglican reforms onto the Scottish church. However the Scots were opposed to this, and even wanted to destroy the control that bishops had over the church. To this end, Charles' reforms were rejected by the Scottish Assembly at Glasgow in 1638.

Charles was furious that the Scots had rejected his proposals, and hastily formed an English force with which to march on Scotland in 1639. He did not have the funds for such a military expedition, nor confidence in his troops, so he was forced to leave Scotland without fighting a battle.

The unrest continued in Scotland, and when Charles discovered that they had been plotting with the French he again decided to mount a military expedition. This time, Charles called Parliament in order to get funds (1640).

When parliament formed, they immediately wanted to discuss grievances against the government, and were generally opposed to any military operation. This angered Charles and he dismissed parliament again, hence the name "Short Parliament" that it is commonly given.

Charles went ahead with his military operation without Parliament's support, and was beaten by the Scots. The Scots, taking advantage of this, went on to seize Northumberland and Durham.

Charles found himself in a desperate position, and was forced to call parliament again in November, 1640. This parliament is known as the "Long Parliament".

The Civil Wars 1642-51

The tension between Charles and Parliament was still great, since none of the issues raised by the Short Parliament had been resolved. This tension was brought to a head on January 4th, 1642 when Charles attempted to arrest five members of parliament. This attempt failed, since they were spirited away before the king's troops arrived.

Charles left London and both he and parliament began to stockpile military resources and recruit troops.

Charles officially began the war by raising his standard at Nottingham in August, 1642. Robert Devereux (3rd Earl of Essex) was made parliamentary commander.

At this stage of the wars, parliament had no wish to kill the king. It was hoped that Charles could be reinstated as ruler, but with a more constructive attitude to parliament.

The majority of the country was neutral in the civil wars, and both sides only had about 13,000 men in 1642.

The areas of Royalist support tended to be the North, West and Wales. Parliament were supported by the richer South and East, including London. Parliament also held most of the ports, since the merchants that ran them saw more profit in a parliament-lead country.

Parliament definitely had access to more resources than the king, and could collect taxes. Charles had to depend on donations from his supporters to fund his armies. The first war stretched from 1642 to 1646, beginning with the king's raising of the standard.

Charles marched on London, hoping for a quick victory that would negate the benefits of parliament's resources. He was met at Edgehill (Oct 23 1642) by Essex and a battle was fought. This battle proved inconclusive, but failed to stop Charles' advance. He was met by another force at Turnham Green, however, and was forced to turn away from London.

Charles withdrew to Oxford, where his headquarters was based for the rest of the war.

In 1643, many battles were fought all over the country.

The royalist forces won at Adwalton Moor (Jun 30), taking control of Yorkshire. They also won at Lansdown and Roundway Down (Jul) in the South-West, allowing Prince Rupert to take Bristol.

The forces of parliament won at Winceby (Oct 11), taking Lincoln, but on the whole had the worst part of military actions for the year.

At Newbury (Sep), a large battle took place that was inconclusive. After this testing of the major armies, both sides sought allies elsewhere.

Parliament drew up the "Solemn League & Covenant", which promised the Scots religious reforms in return for their help.

Charles negotiated a cease-fire in Ireland that freed English troops for action on the mainland.

In 1644, military actions were more balanced. Parliament won at Marston Moor (Jul 2), allowing them to take York with the Scots' help. They lost at Lostwithiel in the South-West, and withdrew from Newbury after a second inconclusive battle.

In 1645, the New Model Army was formed by Fairfax. This army won two important victories, at Naseby (Jun 14) and at Langport (Jul 10), effectively destroying all of Charles' armies.

In 1646, Charles had little choice but to disband his remaining forces. Oxford surrendered, and Charles fled North seeking refuge with the Scots, bringing the first war to a close.

Charles was ransomed by parliament, and held at Holmby House whilst parliament drew up proposals. In the mean time, parliament began to disband its army.

However, the army was unhappy about issues such as arrears of pay and living conditions, and resisted the disbandment.

Eventually the army kidnapped Charles in an attempt to win a bargaining piece. However, Charles escaped to the Isle of Wight.

Increasingly concerned, the army marched to London (Aug 1647) and debated proposals of their own at Putney.

Charles took advantage of this shift of emphasis away from him to negotiate a new agreement with the Scots, again promising church reform (Dec 28 1647). This agreement lead to the second war.

A series of royalist rebellions and a Scottish invasion (Jul 1648) took place. However, all were defeated by the now powerful standing army. This new betrayal by Charles caused parliament to debate whether Charles should be returned to power at all. Those who still supported Charles' place on the throne tried once more to negotiate with him.

The army, angry that parliament were still considering Charles as a ruler, marched on parliament and conducted "Pride's Purge" (named such since the commanding officer of the operation was Sir Thomas Pride). 45 MP's were arrested, 146 were kept out of parliament, and only 75 were allowed in, and then only to do the army's bidding.

This rump parliament was ordered to set up a high court of justice in order to try Charles I for treason in the name of the people of England.

The trial of the king (Jan 1649) found Charles guilty as charged, and he was beheaded on January 30th.

Oliver Cromwell then lead the army in quelling revolts in Ireland and Scotland (1649-50) to finally restore an uneasy peace.

Charles II was then crowned in Scotland, claiming that the throne was rightfully his. He marched with the Scots on England. Cromwell beat the Scottish forces at Dunbar (Sep 3 1650), but could not prevent Charles II marching deep into England.

Cromwell finally engaged the new king at Worcester (Sep 3 1651) and beat him. Charles II fled abroad, ending the civil wars.

The Commonwealth was then established, with Oliver Cromwell as Lord Protector of England.

THE SOLEMN LEAGUE AND COVENANT

In the last few months of 1643, John Pym sought to establish an alliance with Scotland in order to balance Charles I's superior forces.

After ten days of debate, the Solemn League and Covenant was signed in Margaret's Church, Westminster, on September 25th.

The agreement gave each side what it wanted. Parliament wanted troops to support its military endeavours, and Scotland wanted religious reform that favoured its own church. Parliament had already abolished bishops, but Scotland wanted more than that.

Charles had made a truce with the Irish, which endangered Parliament (by freeing troops for use in England) and angered Scotland (since the Irish were not considered religious or God-fearing).

As a part of this agreement, Parliament rose monies in London to support an army of 21,000 men from Scotland. This new force marched South on January 19th, 1644.

THE TEXT

The text of the Solemn League and Covenant was divided into six points, which are summarised below.

The first dealt with the reform of the churches, and the keeping of the present Scottish church.

> "...prefervation of the Reformed Religion in the Church of Scotland...reformation of Religion in the kingdoms of England and Ireland...indeavour to bring the Churches of God in the three kingdoms to the neereft coniunction and Uniformity in Religion."

The second specifically stated that the hierarchy of ecclesiastical rule would be abolished.

> "...indeavour the extirpation of Popery...Church government by...all other Ecclefiafticall Officers...and whatfoever shall be contrary to found Doctrine."

The third is interesting, since it shows the sincerity with which the parliamentarians wished to re-establish Charles' rule, but on their own terms. It states that parliament will be defended, but also that the king and the king's authority should be defended as well.

> "...endeavour...to preferve the Rights and Priviledges of the Parliaments...and to preferve and defend the king's Majefties person and authority."

The fourth point justifies the war by ordering the seeking out of all who oppose the reforms.

> "...endeavour the difcovery of all...Incendiaries, Malignants or evill Inftruments... hindering the Reformation of Religion, dividing the king from his people, or one of the kingdoms from another..."

The fifth point restates that the three kingdoms of England, Ireland and Scotland remain as a union at peace.

> "...indeavour that [the three kingdoms] may remain unioyned in a firm Peace an Union."

The sixth, and final, point confirms the alliance by stating that those who sign will assist and defend each other.

> "...affift and defend all thofe that enter in to this League and Covenant."

THE NEW MODEL ARMY

In the closing stages of 1644, Oliver Cromwell realised that the existing parliamentary armies were less than ideal. Using his influence in parliament, he proposed the Self-Denying Ordinance. This stated that any member of the House of Commons or the House of Lords holding a military commission should resign it.

This was intended to remove the aristocratic leaders, such as the Earl of Essex , and the Earl of Manchester, from the armies, allowing true military leaders to take their place.

In addition to this, the armies were to be combined and reorganised into the "New Model". The personal regiments would be split up and pay standardised. Food and provisions of clothing would be guaranteed to all in order to encourage soldiers to agree to the changes.

The "Soldier's Catechism" was drawn up, which laid down rules and regulations, as well as correct drill procedures, in order that the soldiers would know what was expected of them.

This army was proposed in February 1645, and began to come into being in April 1645. Conscription was necessary to make up the numbers envisaged, although this was for a small percentage of the army.

Significantly, the phrase "the protection of his Majesty's person" was not included in the description of the task of this army, although "the defence of the King and Parliament" remained.

The Army

Sir Thomas Fairfax was appointed the new Lord General of the army. He had no political connections, and was a good soldier, making him ideal for the post.

The army consisted of a total of 22,000 men, broken down in the following way:

Type	No of Regiments	No in Each Regiment
Cavalry	11	600
Infantry	12	1200
Dragoons	1	1000
Artillery	N/K	N/K

The infantry were issued with red uniforms to replace their existing regiment's colour. Cavalry were issued with light headpieces, armour front & back, and a buffcoat of leather.

The pay was set at eight pence a day for infantry, and two shillings a day for cavalry. Those in the cavalry had to provide their own horse.

Promotion was now done strictly on military prowess, and no longer on a family or monetary basis.

Interestingly, although supposedly unable to hold his military commission, due to the Self-Denying Ordinance, Oliver Cromwell continued to lead cavalry, and was eventually excepted by Parliament and made General of Horse in June 1645.

HOLMBY HOUSE

Holmby House, or Holdenby House as it is sometimes known, is where Charles I was kept in "protective custody" after being ransomed from the Scots in 1647. Holmby house is near Althorp in Northamptonshire, Charles being escorted there from Nottingham by Sir Thomas Fairfax himself.

Charles was escorted, and kept, well. His popularity was still high - everyone wanted him to be in power, but only if they could control him.

Charles remained at Holmby House until 4 June 1647, when a party of 500 cavalry lead by Cornet Joyce came to escort him to a meeting of the army at Newmarket. The army were meeting to discuss the demands that they should make of parliament refering to pay and indemnity.

THE TRIAL OF CHARLES I

The trial was arranged so as to be as public as possible. The intention was to justify the execution of Charles I in the eyes of the people, many of whom did not wish to see the king dead.

Sir Thomas Fairfax also did not want to see him dead, and protested that killing Charles would only lead to further problems with his successor, then Prince of Wales. However, his protestations fell on deaf ears.

No English laws could be discovered in all history that dealt with the trial of the monarch. The order convening the court was written by a Dutch lawyer, Isaac Dorislaus, and dated back to the Roman era, wherein the Praetorian Guard (a military body) could leagally overthrow a tyrant. The rump parliament elected a court of commissioners 135 strong on 1 Jan 1649. However, only 68 of these obeyed this summons. None of the existing high court judges agreed to preside over the court, and a lawyer called John Bradshaw was elected president.

The House of Lords threw this ordinance out the very next day. However, parliament re-enacted the ordinance on the 4th, although only 46 MP's were now in the house, and only 26 of these voted for the ordinance.

The king himself, although forced to attend, refused to acknowledge the court, considering it completely illegal. Fairfax refused to attend, and strove to save the king from execution, but could not do so without dividing the army against itself, which could have led to further hostilities.

Apart from the commissioners and the king, the hall was crowded with soldiers to guard against possible attacks. Bradshaw himself apparently wore an iron hat, fearing for an assassination attempt. Ironically, though, the pubilc were not allowed into the hall until after the charge had been read, since it was so sketchy, and the public so supportive of the king, that it was considered too dangerous.

Charles was found guilty, and sentenced to death on 26 Jan. On the 30th, he was lead from St. James' Palace to Whitehall to be executed. At 1.00pm he was beheaded in front of a crowd kept back by thick ranks of soldiers. His last words, printed and sold on that very day, were:

> "I have delivered my conscience; I pray God you do take those courses that are best for the good of the kingdom and your own salvation."

A contempory diarist wrote that when his head was held up "...there was such a groan by the thousands then present...", since none were happy to see him dead.

ARMOUR

The majority of soldiers wore very light armour - simply a thick buff leather coat or tunic. This was capable of protecting the wearer from some sword thrusts, although it had little effect against a musket ball or cannon shot.

For those who were equipped a little better, mainly the pikemen since they were required to engage the enemy closely, steel helmets would be worn, as would back and breast plates. These helmets or "pots", were a slightly angular round helmet with a straight ridge around the edge, which would be level with the center of the ear. "Back" and "breast" came in many designs, but were basically metal plates shaped to fit the torso, fastening together on either side.

Cavalry tended to have a little extra in the way of leg protection, and sometimes thigh protection. The danger of sword thrusts to the leg is greater for a cavalry trooper, so thick leather boots and thigh covers were often worn.

A few heavy cavalry regiments wore full articulated plate armour, with lobster-tail helmets and nose guards that covered them from head to toe.

This was very expensive, and extremely hot in the summer, but afforded excellent protection. Sir Arthur Haselrigg survived three point-blank pistol shots and several sword thrusts at the battle of Roundway Down , causing Charles I to joke: "[had he] been victualled as well as fortified he might have endured a siege."

Still, the majority of soldiers disliked heavy armour. It was particularly uncomfortable during long marches, or in the summer months.

MUSKETS

There were two main types of musket in use during the civil wars - the matchlock and the flintlock.

Both types of weapon were up to 5 ft long, and were effective up to 300 yds. They might not kill at that range, but most musket injuries were fatal eventually. Although they were hugely inaccurate at maximum range, formations in the civil wars were too large for it to make much difference. When used as a sharpshooter's weapon, the effective range was halved, or even less.

Muskets were muzzle loaded, and the process was very slow. First, powder was dropped down the barrel and tapped down with a scouring stick (wooden rod). Then the lead ball would be dropped down, and wadding of some kind added to hold it in place. This would be rammed down to ensure the best range.

The different types of musket had different firing mechanisms, which are described below.

Matchlock

The matchlock mechanism consists of a serpent (a movable armature) that is brought down onto a pan when the trigger is pulled. When loaded, powder would be put in the pan (which could be covered to protect the powder). A match (flax soaked in saltpetre) would be kept lighted at both ends, and when ready to fire would be pressed into the serpent. When firing, the match would come down into the open pan to ignite the powder. The flame from this would travel along a small tube into the main charge, firing the musket.

Flintlock

Flintlock mechanisms are easier to use, but more expensive to produce. A flint is brought down sharply onto a metal tray. When loaded, the tray has powder in it, which is ignited by the sparks. The flame then travels to the main charge in a similar way to the matchlock. The main advantage of this weapon, is that there is no need to keep match lighted in order to fire it. In fact, the troops guarding the powder stores were issued with these weapons to prevent sparks from matches igniting the precious powder.

PIKES

The pike was a primitive weapon, consisting only of a sixteen foot long wooden shaft, steel shod at the tip. Its advantages lay in the ease in which it could be manufactured, and the minimal training needed to ready men for its use in combat.

Although all pikes should have been sixteen feet in length, industrious soldiers often sawed off a few feet at the end to make it easier to carry on marches. This was strongly discouraged by officers, since it gave the regiment a disadvantage in combat.

> "...few exceed fifteen feet; and if officers be not careful to prevent it, many a base soldier will cut some off the length of that, as I have often seen."

Artillery

Artillery pieces varied in size from the big siege guns to very light cannon that were wheeled around by infantry regiments.

They were loaded with charges rammed from the front, making their rate of fire very low. Big guns would fire about ten rounds every hour.

Large guns were usually placed before or at the start of a battle, and then would not be moved until it was over. These would be at the back of an army, on ground that gave best opportunity to fire at the enemy's positions.

These bigger guns tended not to be placed too far above the battlefield, since depressing the barrels caused problems. The ball could roll out, or when fired would not travel as far as expected.

Lighter pieces were positioned between regiments or brigades, and could be loaded with shrapnel. Shrapnel could consist of all kinds of junk metal that could be gathered, and was effective against enemy troops at close range.

Cavalry

Cavalry regiments were about 400 men strong, although there was much variety between regiments. These would have been divided into six troops of 60-70 men each.

Cavalry troopers usually wore armour in the form of back and breast plates, and a pot helmet. Often a buff coat would be worn underneath this, and some kind of thigh protection - perhaps just long leather boots.

Some regiments wore heavier armour, such as Haselrigg's Lobsters who wore full plate. This was expensive and hot, so it was limited to a select few.

Cavalry weapons consisted of a couple of pistols, and perhaps a carbine, plus a sword or cutlass. The pistols would probably be fired only once in the battle, since they were difficult to reload.

There were two main tactics used by cavalry, the Dutch and the Swedish methods.

The Dutch, apparently used by the parliamentarians at the start of the war, was to advance at a trot. The pistols would be fired at the enemy infantry when in range, and then the cavalry would wheel away. Then they would return with drawn swords and initiate a melee.

The Swedish, introduced by Prince Rupert, involved charging at the gallop. Pistols would be fired at the last moment before contact was made, and then a melee would ensue. This became the prefered tactic for both sides.

During the English Civil Wars, the cavalry tended to fight their own battle. Only when the opposing cavalry had been driven off would the remainder turn and help their infantry. In fact, the royalists were notorious for pursuing a beaten cavalry force for miles, leaving the infantry unprotected on the battlefield.

Once the pistols were fired, cavalry were very ineffective against infantry with pike support. Casualties amoungst horses were severe, and several troopers got through two or three horses in a single battle.

Dragoons

Dragoons were essentially a form of mobile infantry. Their mounts were inferior to the cavalry's horses, and were not suitable for the battlefield. Dragoons would ride to the battle and then dismount and fight on foot.

Dragoons were principally deployed on the extreme flank of an army. They would snipe at passing troops using flintlock muskets. Since cavalry was usually deployed on the flank, they would normally fire at the opposing cavalry as it charged past.

Dragoons were not always used in battles, even major ones, but were incorporated into the New Model Army as a regiment 1,000 strong.

Infantry

Infantry regiments in the English Civil Wars were supposedly 1,200 men strong, although many were understrength due to casualties, sickness or lack of recruiting. These would be divided into companies. Roughly speaking, there were 10 companies of 120 men each, but each regiment tended to have its own structure.

Each regiment would contain both musketeers and pikemen. Usually these were divided in a rough ratio of 2:1 pike to musket at the start of the war, although each regiment was different. By the end of the war, this ratio had reversed, as most commanders prefered the versitility of the musket. In addition to these main weapons, most men would carry a secondary weapon, such as a sword or axe for close-quarters fighting.

When on the field of battle, the pike would be positioned in the centre, with musketeers on either side. If it was a major battle, then three or more regiments would join to make a brigade. In this case the brigade's pike would be in the middle, and the musketeers would be divided on both sides, companies would be kept together, but the regiment would be split.

Tactics usually involved the musketeers firing a few volleys into the enemy ranks, and then the opposing formations advancing to meet each other at "push of pike", where each attempted to push the other back physically.

When engaged in "push of pike", there was no room to make use of a weapon, so after the initial contact was made, very few casulaties occured. However, if one side turned and ran, or collapsed upon itself, then large casualties could result.

"Push of pike" was not always reached. Sometimes the morale of one side would be such that it would withdraw or rout before contact was made. At other times, both sides might be wary, and stand apart, jabbing with the pikes as best they could.

If attacked by cavalry in the absence of infantry, then the pikemen would shelter the musketeers, forming the equivalent of a square, but more like a blob. The pikes would protude, keeping the horse away, and musketeers would take opportunities to fire out at any target that presented itself.

ADWALTON MOOR

Date: 30th June 1643

Location: Birkenshaw, Yorkshire

Parliamentarian Commander: Ferdinando Fairfax, 2nd Baron of Cameron

Royalist Commander: William Cavendish, Duke of Newcastle

Victor: Royalists

Newcastle's army outnumbered the parliamentary forces in the North, where support for Parliament was scant. With this in mind he marched on Bradford, intending to catch their army in a siege.

Fairfax, knowing that he could not survive such a siege, struck out to meet him, even though he was outnumbered by at least two to one.

The two armies met on the ridge overlooking Adwalton Moor. The terrain was favourable for Fairfax, since the hedges and lanes that stretched across the ridge made it difficult for the royalist cavalry to make contact with the enemy.

The parliamentary forces drove the royalist skirmishers away, and then set up a defensive position that offset the difference in numbers between the armies, trying to funnel the attackers into a narrow front.

> "...found sharp entertainment, and those that were not yet [engaged], as hot welcome from the musketeers that flanked them in the hedges."
>
> 'Stuart Tracts 1603-1693', H.C.Firth (1964)

The parliamentary army drove off several assaults whilst in this defensive stance, but the discipline of the troops was to let Fairfax down.

On seeing yet another royalist assault beaten back, a large part of the force took it upon themselves to chase the enemy. However, once out of their defenses, they began to feel the pressure of the Royalist's greater numbers.

Eventually these troops were beaten back, and found that they had been out-flanked by the royalist cavalry. Attacked from both sides they routed, and the remaining forces were forced to withdraw to Bradford to await the inevitable.

This defeat left Parliament with only one remaining stronghold in the North, at Hull.

ALTON

Date: 12th December 1643

Location: Alton, Hampshire

Parliamentarian Commander: Sir William Waller

Royalist Commander: Ludovich Lindsay, 16th Earl of Crawford

Victor: Parliamentarians

By December 1643, the Royalist position in the South of England was strong. Hopton had forced Parliamentarian forces out of the West Country, and was pushing East into Sussex. However, his forces were now spread thinly by necessity. Hopton's main garrisons were at Arundel and Winchester, with a smaller garrison at Alton under the command of Lord Crawford. Sussex was important to Parliament, since the iron foundries of the Sussex Weald produced much of Parliament's armaments.

Crawford commanded 300-500 horse and the infantry regiment of Colonel Richard Bolle. His forces had built fortifications in the form of a half-moon and breast works.

Crawford was said to have sent a request to his opponent, Waller, for "a runlet of sack" (wine), presumably in jest, promising a fat ox in return. Waller, being a gentleman, obliged by sending the wine and asked for his ox. Crawford, however, said that Waller would have to come and fetch it himself.

Waller was only too happy to march on Alton, since he had been planning an attack anyway. Taking advantage of a heavy frost that hardened the usually muddy winter ground, he marched with 5000 men to Basing and then South to Alton.

Upon the arrival of Waller's army, Lord Crawford attempted to leave Alton with his cavalry for Winchester, to the West. He was turned back by Sir Arthur Haselrigg's "Lobsters" - Parliamentarian heavy cavalry. He did manage to escape to the South, however, leaving Bolle to defend the town with only his infantry.

Waller's forces had not fully arrived at this point, and he wished to wait for the London Regiments before attacking, so he lined his forces along the hedges before the town. Musketeers from both sides began an exchange that would clearly not settle the matter. The Parlimentarian artillery added its weight to the barrage a little before the London Regiments and 4 companies of the Farnham Castle garrison attacked.

The weight of this advance, centered on the Royalist fortifications, was enough to breach the line. The Green Auxiliaries marched on into the town, setting fire to a thatched building in order to smoke out some of the Royalist defenders. A 2 hour street fight began, with the Parliamentarian forces slowly forcing the Royalists back. In order to minimise friendly fire both sides had passwords - the Royalists "Charles" and the Parliamentarians "Truth and Victory".

Colonel Bolle and his remaining defenders were eventually forced into the Church, where they were killed in a last stand behind a barricade, supposedly of dead horses.

> "...laying about them stoutly with Halberts, Swords and Musket-stocks, while some threw hand grenades in at the Church windows, others attempting to enter the Church being led in by Sergeant-Major Shambrooke... who in the entrance received a shot in the thigh..."

'A True Relation of the Trained Bands of Westminster', Elias Archer

Waller recovered his wine and also took some 500 prisoners, many of which joined the Parliamentarian cause. When Charles I heard of Bolle's death he asked for a mourning scarf since, he said, "I have lost one of the best commanders in this kingdom".

Hopton could ill afford to lose so many troops, and his position in the South was now threatened. Waller marched on to Arundel and began a seige of the castle. Arundel fell to Parliament on 6 Jan 1644, stablising the power balance in the South.

The Battle of Dunbar

Date: 3rd September 1650

Location: Dunbar, East Lothian

Parliamentarian Commander: Oliver Cromwell, General of Horse

Royalist Commander: Sir David Leslie

Victor: Parliament

Now that Charles II was in Scotland, parliament wanted to quell the rebellious Scots. Sir Thomas Fairfax did not fully object to Charles II becoming king, and knew that the campaign would be hard, so he sent Cromwell as commander of the army.

Cromwell assembled his forces at Berwick, and then crossed the border in July. His army marched to the outskirts of Edinburgh.

Leslie was put in charge of a hastily recruited army to oppose Cromwell. Although a much larger force, this was poorly trained and most of the officers had no experience.

Cromwell was held outside Edinburgh, and eventually retreated to Dunbar for supplies. The weather was worsening, and Cromwell's army suffered greatly from sickness.

Cromwell marched on Edinburgh again, but was out manoeuvered by Leslie, and forced back to Dunbar.

Leslie now pressed his advantage, and marched to a position south of Dunbar. This blocked Cromwell's route back to England, and was easily defensible against the much reduced English force.

The ministers of the Scottish Kirk then decided that Cromwell must be prevented from escaping by sea, and ordered Leslie to attack. Dutifully, Leslie brought his army down the slopes to approach the town. Seeing this movement, Cromwell formulated a plan that relied on suprise to give the English an advantage.

During the night, Cromwell changed the deployment of his army. On his right, a force of dragoons and artillery were left to hold the flank. The majority of his troops were then concentrated on the right flank.

At dawn, in pouring rain, the first English wave attacked. Cavalry on the left and infantry in the centre caught the Scottish unexpectedly, but were held by the greater number of opponents and the advantage of higher ground against them.

However, the Scottish right flank was now confined to a narrow piece of ground by the terrain. A second wave of cavalry, lead by Cromwell, turned the Scottish cavalry back and into their own infantry.

Attacking the disordered infantry, Cromwell systematically rolled up the Scottish right flank. Seeing this, the rest of the

Scottish army broke and ran. Some 3,000 Scots were killed, and 10,000 captured in a little over an hour of fighting. The Scottish army was destroyed.

Cromwell was then able to march on Edinburgh, and succeeded in taking the city. Edinburgh castle still held out, but royalist resistance was now confined to the north.

Edgehill

Date: 23rd October 1642

Location: Kineton, Warwickshire

Parliamentarian Commander: Robert Devereux, 3rd Earl of Essex

Royalist Commander: Charles I, King of England

Victor: Inconclusive

Charles marched his army from Shrewsbury on 12th October, intending to make straight for London. However, Essex also marched for London from Worcester, almost parallel to Charles' route.

On the 21st October they were but 7 miles apart. Realising the danger of marching on without checking Essex' advance, Prince Rupert persuaded Charles to deploy on the slopes of Edgehill.

Essex, not having realised that the opposing army was so close drew up quite a distance from the slopes during the day. The battle would not commence until afternoon.

Both armies arranged their infantry in the centre, with cavalry on both sides. Dragoons were positioned on the flanks to guard against flanking manouevers.

The main Royalist horse, under Rupert, was on the right, opposite Sir James Ramsey's horse. On the Royalist left was Henry Wilmot who was opposite Fielding's horse. Unlike the Royalists, Essex kept a reserve of two horse regiments under the command of Stapleton and Balfour.

The Royalists had five brigades of infantry in their centre, opposite Essex's three brigades and two regiments. The number of troops overall, though was between 13 and 14 thousand each.

Charles I rode past his army in order to raise morale before the battle. This resulted in a cheer from the Royalist ranks. The parliamentary army responded with artillery fire, which began a period of about an hour of artillery fire from both sides.

Prince Rupert initiated the battle proper by charging his cavalry brigade at the Parliamentary cavalry opposite. At the sight of this, Sir Faithful Fortescue tore off his orange sash and rode to join the Royalists! Demoralised, the remaining cavalry routed and rode through the infantry that were supporting them. Four infantry regiments then broke and ran.

Meanwhile, on the other flank, Wilmot also charged the Royalist horse at the opposing cavalry. He too succeeded in routing his opposition, although the infantry remained untouched.

In an error that was to prove critical, both cavalry brigades then continued their pursuit, running down the routed troops. This action took them far from the battlefield, and many of Rupert's horse occupied themselves sacking the town of Kineton.

This left the Royalist army with no cavalry whatsoever! The parliamentarian reserve, though, was as yet unscathed. Two cavalry regiments lead by Stapleton and Balfour we able to assist the infantry without fear of cavalry assault.

The Royalist foot in the centre attacked, but were held by their opposites, with no side gaining an advantage. This did not last, though, since Balfour charged his cavalry into their rear, and the whole brigade was routed with heavy casualties.

Essex, keen to press the attack whilst he had cavalry superiority, ordered a general advance. Again, this was held by the opposing troops. Yet again, the cavalry harassment of the Royalist rear caused the troops to give ground.

The Royal Foot Guards were broken by repeated combined cavalry and infantry attacks, and the royal standard was taken by Essex' Lifeguard.

Although the number of Royalists running was increasing, an ordered withdrawal of two regiments enabled a new defensive line to be created. Although Essex could have attacked again, it was getting dark, Rupert's cavalry were returning to the field and everyone was exhausted from the fighting, so he decided to disengage.

Both sides camped on the battlefield. Apparently, a Royalist officer infiltrated the Parliamentarian camp by wearing a stolen orange sash and retrieved the royal standard for the king.

In the morning, the Royalists moved up Edgehill, and were not pursued. The battle of Edgehill, which could have gone either way, remained inconclusive.

The Battle of Langport

Date: 10th July 1645

Location: Langport, Somerset

Parliamentarian Commander: Sir Thomas Fairfax, Commander-in-Chief

Royalist Commander: Lord George Goring, General of Horse

Victor: Parliament

After the battle of Naseby and the retaking of Leicester, parliament ordered Fairfax to relieve Taunton, under siege by Goring.

Fairfax marched south through Salisbury and Dorchester, which he reached on 3 July.

Goring, hearing of Fairfax's advance, lifted his siege and withdrew north to Ilchester and Langport. These towns both had bridges across the river Yeo within them, and these would allow Goring to withdraw further to the stronghold of Bridgwater.

Goring, however, had no intention of holding these important points, he sent his artillery and baggage on to Bridgwater and withdrew from Ilchester to concentrate his forces at Langport.

Fairfax crossed the Yeo unopposed at Ilchester, and then swung north to Langport.

Goring had occupied a strong defensive position. To attack, Fairfax would have to cross a narrow ford and then assault uphill.

Fairfax began by silencing Goring's remaining two artillery pieces with his own batteries.

Musketeers then thinned the royalist troops defending the ford with volleys of fire. Cavalry lead by Major Christopher Bethal then charged quickly through the ford before the royalists had properly recovered their positions.

Charging uphill on the other side they were held by the royalists, but more horse and infantry were now rushing to support them, and Goring's forces began to crumble.

Demoralised, the royalists fled the field. As Goring retreated west, his forces deserted in droves, and his army virtually ceased to exist.

Lostwithiel

Date: 31st August - 2nd September 1644

Location: Lostwithiel, Cornwall

Parliamentarian Commander: Robert Devereux, 3rd Earl of Essex

Royalist Commander: Charles I, King of England

Victor: Royalists

Essex marched West into royalist Devon, hoping to relieve some of the besieged ports in Devon and Cornwall. He reached Lyme and relieved the town in June. He then marched on to Plymouth, which he relieved on 23rd July.

Sir William Waller was supposed to be occupying Charles I's army, but was outmanoeuvered by Charles. Charles then pursued Essex Westward, reaching Exeter on 26th July.

Essex knew about this, but continued on regardless - reaching Bodmin whilst driving Sir Richard Grenville out of the way. Grenville had a small royalist army, but would not consider engaging Essex until Charles arrived with reinforcements.

Realising that Charles was getting closer, Essex moved to Lostwithiel and Fowey, where he could keep in contact with the parliamentarian navy. Essex hoped to be reinforced or shipped off by the navy if Charles got too close.

Charles then contacted Essex in an attempt to arrange a peace treaty. Essex replied that he could not speak for Parliament alone, so a treaty was out of the question.

Essex was outnumbered, and sent word that Waller should conduct a diversionary action. However, he did not realise that Waller's force was too weak to be effective.

Charles first cut Essex off from the landward exits by taking Respryn Bridge, to the North (Aug 12).

He then took Bodinnick and Polruan Castle. These were on the Eastern side of Fowey estuary - across from Essex. With artillery stationed there, Charles prevented parliamentary ships from supporting Essex.

Finally, St. Blazey, to the West, was taken (Aug 26), completely surrounding Essex.

The first contact between the two armies occurred on August 31st, when Sir William Balfour attempted to break out with Essex' cavalry. He was successful, reaching Plymouth with light losses.

Royalist troops attacked and took Lostwithiel, driving Essex' infantry back to Castle Dor - an old earth-works.

Charles then assaulted this position. After some hard fighting, some of Essex' regiments broke. Charles then used this gap to cut off the Fowey road, completely encircling Essex.

Essex and Lord Robartes, realising that everything was lost, slipped away and sailed to Plymouth in a small boat. Phillip Skippon was left in charge, and surrendered on September 2nd.

The army, now some 6,000 strong, was disarmed and allowed to leave. They marched to Southampton and Portsmouth, but only a thousand arrived - the others dying of starvation and exposure on the way.

Charles now had control of the West re-established, taking Plymouth a few days later.

Marston Moor

Date: 2nd July 1644

Location: Long Marston, Yorkshire

Parliamentarian Commander: Alexander Leslie, Earl of Leven

Royalist Commander: Prince Rupert

Victor: Parliament

On the 30th June, Prince Rupert had crossed the Pennines with a force that was intended to relieve York, under siege from Leven and Edward Montague, Earl of Manchester.

Manchester had set Lieutenant-General Oliver Cromwell the task of patrolling the area, so he was forewarned of Rupert's proximity.

Not wanting to be caught between two enemy forces, the allied parliamentary army marched out to Long Marston (July 1) to intercept Rupert.

Rupert sent a cavalry screen ahead to Marston Moor, to be observed by the allies. However, he took the major part of his army North, and then East, bypassing Manchester and reaching York without hindrance.

Leven and Manchester moved South, expecting Rupert to march that way. Lieutenant-General Sir Thomas Fairfax was left with a small cavalry force to cover their manouever.

When Fairfax saw that the royalist cavalry were being reinforced in strength, he sent for Leven asking that the army be returned - fearing that it might be attacked whilst in order of march.

Rupert had sent Lord George Goring into York, demanding that Lord William Cavendish, Duke of Newcastle, meet him at Marston Moor to engage the enemy. Newcastle was not happy with this order, but agreed to comply when he was told that Rupert had a letter from Charles I ordering the battle. The letter was ambiguously worded, but Newcastle was not to know that.

The combined allied army outnumbered the royalists considerably, although the number of cavalry was almost equal. Rupert, however, remained undaunted.

The forces of parliament were positioned to the South, along a ridge overlooking the moor. On their right were cavalry commanded by Sir Thomas Fairfax. In the centre were the infantry of Leven and Manchester. On their left flank were the rest of the cavalry under Cromwell and Sir David Leslie.

The royalists, on the moor itself, had Goring's horse opposite Fairfax and Sir John Byron's horse opposite Cromwell. Prince

Rupert was in the rear with a reserve of cavalry. Holding the centre were the infantry of Newcastle and Lord James Eythin.

The royalist force thought it too late to mount an attack, and were unprepared when Leven ordered an advance (between 6 and 7 p.m.).

Byron's horse, however, were able to meet Cromwell at the charge, and initially had some success against the troopers. Rupert rode up in support, hoping to press this advantage. However, Leslie came in on the flank and the royalist cavalry were routed. This was the first time that Rupert's cavalry had been beaten in the war!

Manchester's infantry made use of this victory to press home an attack on Eythin's infantry from their flank. Unsupported, the royalists were forced back, but did not break.

On the other flank, parliament were not faring so well. Fairfax suffered some casualties from musket fire, and his cavalry were disordered by difficult terrain. When contact was made with Goring's cavalry, the parliamentarians were quickly routed.

Goring could not prevent his cavalry from giving chase off the field, and some occupied themselves with looting the baggage train, rather than returning to support their infantry.

Those few horse that did remain gave Leven's infantry a hard time. Manchester, whose infantry had not suffered that badly, sent some of his men to the right in support, and the line was stabilised.

Leslie's horse had now driven Rupert's cavalry off the field, and had rallied. They came in on the rear of Newcastle's 'Whitecoats'. These withdrew slightly to White Syke Close, which was easier to defend, and held their ground well.

Cromwell and the remainder of Fairfax's horse then rode to the rear and assisted Leslie in attacking the royalist infantry. In the face of this new threat all resistance crumbled or was smashed, the 'Whitecoats' dying to a man since they refused to surrender.

After their disastrous defeat, Newcastle and Eythin fled to Scarborough and sailed to the continent, fearing that all was lost. Rupert, who was made of sterner stuff, took what troops remained

West and South to Lancashire, but his reputation of invincibility was ruined.

York surrendered on July 16th, with no way of resisting any further siege. This left the North totally under Parliament's control, a complete reversal from the previous year.

The Battle of Naseby

Date: 14th June 1645

Location: Naseby, Northamptonshire

Parliamentarian Commander: Sir Thomas Fairfax, Commander-in-Chief

Royalist Commander: Charles I, King of England

Victor: Parliament

In the North, Prince Rupert was attacking the city of Leicester, which he sacked on 31 May. Charles marched to Leicester in order to combine their forces.

Meanwhile, Fairfax was besieging the Royalist city of Oxford, where Charles had his headquarters. Charles decided to march south with his combined forces in order to lift the siege.

Charles reached Daventry on 7 Jun, and Fairfax lifted his siege. Fairfax, though, had not been interested in Oxford as much as Charles' army itself, and immediately marched north-east in an attempt to engage it.

The royalist outposts clashed with Fairfax's cavalry on 12 Jun, alerting Charles to the proximity of the parliamentarian forces.

Charles marched north again, having broken the siege he had no wish to engage Fairfax unnecessarily. Fairfax pursued them, and Charles found that he could not outdistance him. Rather than continue the exhausting march, Charles turned his army to fight.

The royalists deployed in a good defensive position at Market Harborough on 14 Jun, and scouts were sent out to determine Fairfax's position.

The scouts failed to find him, but Rupert took it upon himself to scout in person, not believing the army scouts' report. Rupert did find the parliamentarians, near Naseby,and sent word that the army should advance to meet them. This was a dubious order, since it allowed Fairfax to pick his ground, rather than forcing him to advance onto the royalists' own ground.

Fairfax deployed the majority of his forces behind the brow of the ridge of Mill Hill, hiding his troop concentrations from the royalists. The parliamentarian cavalry were on each flank, with Sir Henry Ireton on the left and Oliver Cromwell on the right. Phillip Skippon, in command of the infantry , was in the centre.

Fairfax positioned his dragoons, under Okey, to the left and slightly ahead of his main strength. In this position, they were able to fire across at any cavalry charges.

The royalists were deployed in a similar manner, save for dragoons. Lord Astley commanded the foot in the centre. Sir Marmaduke Langdale commanded the left flank and Rupert the right, both cavalry. Charles himself commanded the reserves to the rear and centre.

The royalists attacked first. Rupert charged his horse across and into Ireton. Although they suffered from the dragoons' fire, they beat Ireton's horse back.

In the centre, the infantry met and the parliamentarians were again pushed back.

Rupert, as was now typical, allowed his cavalry to continue the charge past the parliamentarian rear, and onto the baggage train, where they were checked by the defenders' fire. The damage had been done to the left flank, though, and it began to give ground.

On the right flank, however, Cromwell had timed his charge well. The royalist horse were slowed by marshy ground, and the impetus of Cromwell's charge routed them off the field. Showing the discipline of the New Model Army, his troops then divided. Some continued the chase, to ensure that the opposing cavalry would not return, but the greater part turned on the royalist infantry.

The royalist left began to give ground under this new assault, and Charles lead the reserve backwards, under advice that he would be "riding to his death" had he supported his flank.

Okey's dragoons mounted their steeds and, with the support of a few of Ireton's horse that had rallied, attacked the royalist right. This attack checked the advance of the royalist foot.

With no horse to defend them, the royalist foot were subjected to attacks from all sides, and the army began to disintegrate - most of them surrendering.

The vast majority of the royalist foot were killed or captured. These included some 500 officers, the artillery and the baggage train.

> "...after 3 hours fight, very doubtfull att last routed his Armie, killed and tooke about 5000. Very many officers but of what quallity wee yett know not, wee tooke alsoe... all his gunns, beinge 12 in number..."

Oliver Cromwell after the battle.

Charles fled the area, allowing Fairfax to continue on to Leicester and retake the city.

The First Battle of Newbury

Date: 20th September 1643

Location: Newbury, Berkshire

Parliamentarian Commander: Robert Devereux, 3rd Earl of Essex

Royalist Commander: Charles I, King of England

Victor: Inconclusive

Essex had bravely marched from London, through enemy territory to Gloucester in order to relieve the besieged city. Charles, who had been besieging the city, withdrew, unwilling to be caught between two enemies.

Having resupplied the garrison, Essex then attempted to elude Charles and return to London.

Prince Rupert caught Essex at Aldbourne Chase and made a short attack. He did not have enough men to make much difference, but did slow Essex down, and confirm his probable route.

Charles managed to get to Newbury before Essex, forcing the parliamentary army to sleep in the open, since they had hoped to billet in the parliamentarian town. Charles deployed his army across Essex's route, South of Newbury. Essex would have liked to avoid a fight, but to his North was the River Kennet, and to the South marshy ground that would have been dangerous to travel through.

Charles' main force was either side of Skinners Green with Rupert's cavalry on their left flank.

Perhaps overconfident, Charles allowed Major-General Phillip Skippon to occupy Round Hill for parliament, on which he established an artillery battery defended by infantry.

Each side had four brigades of infantry. Charles had more horse, but Essex had the Trained Bands in reserve.

The royalists, realising the strength of Skippon's position, began by assaulting Round Hill. Sir Nicholas Byron lead an infantry brigade, with his nephew, Sir John Byron, supporting with cavalry.

The great number of heavily defended hedgerows slowed them down considerably. The fighting went on all across the hill, with confusion on both sides.

John Byron managed to establish a foothold on the hill, but was held up by a large hedge with only a small gap to allow progress. Lord Falkland, Charles' Secretary of State was killed at this gap. Why he was so far forward is questionable, but some say that he was disillusioned with the war, and wished to die.

Eventually the royalists withdrew, having suffered greatly. Later on, another assault was mounted. This time John Byron and Sir Thomas Aston's cavalry spearheaded the drive. Together, they succeeded in pushing Skippon back from the summit, but he had brought up some Trained Bands in support, so they could make no further progress.

The cavalry suffered greatly from fire directed at them by the fresh troops. Fortunately for them, their infantry reached the summit and relieved them of its defence.

No futher attacks were made by either side, only exchanges of musket and artillery fire.

To the South, Rupert lead his cavalry in a charge against Sir Phillip Stapleton's cavalry. He was repulsed with the help of parliamentarian infantry. A second charge was also driven back. However, a third charge finally routed the opposing cavalry. Rupert's cavalry gave chase, and suffered massive casualties from musket fire in the narrow lanes that they found themselves in.

The North was relatively quiet, although a parliamentary force that attempted to ford the river was driven back.

When night fell, the battle began to die down, until everything was quiet.

The royalists were dangerously short of ammunition, but had held the ground that barred Essex' route forwards. A heated debate took place in the royalist camp as to whether to stay or move to resupply. Eventually, Charles decided to withdraw into the town.

Come morning, Essex was suprised to find that he was unopposed. He quickly took advantage of the situation to move past Newbury and on to Reading.

The Second Battle of Newbury

Date: 27th October 1644

Location: Newbury, Berkshire

Parliamentarian Commander: Edward Montague, Earl of Manchester

Royalist Commander: Charles I, King of England

Victor: Inconclusive

Charles had not managed to re-engage the remainder of Sir William Waller's army, and Waller withdrew to Basingstoke. Here he combined with Manchester on Oct 17th.

Charles then deployed defensively to the North of Newbury, hoping that the parliamentarians would not engage their strong position, allowing Prince Rupert to rejoin them.

Manchester replied to this by deploying along Clay Hill ridge, to the North-East. He then sent out patrols to gauge the royalists' strength (Oct 25).

Not much information was gleaned, although it was obvious that the royalists were well dug in. Some artillery exchanges occured whilst the commanders discussed the position. It was decided that Waller would take his army, which comprised some two thirds of the total strength, on a night out-flanking manoeuvre, a good 15 miles in length. Manchester would then attack simultaneously, catching the royalists from both sides.

This was very risky, since it divided their force critically, and was difficult to co-ordinate but could prove decisive if it caught the royalists unaware. Despite the risks, Waller set out on Oct 26th.

Waller suprised a royalist outpost early on the 27th, and defeated it after a fight. The royalists now were aware that their rear was threatened, but appeared not to consider this a serious threat, since nothing was done to reinforce the West.

Manchester attacked fairly early in the day, but was repulsed easily by a swift counter-attack.

It wasn't until the afternoon that Waller deployed to the West of the royalist positions.

Waller's attack took Prince Maurice by suprise, but favourable terrain allowed the royalists to beat back the initial assault. Waller attacked again, and this time pushed forward into the village of Speen.

Sir William Balfour routed the royalist cavalry in the South, and a counter-attack by The Earl of Cleveland was repulsed. Further advance was hindered by fire from Donnington castle, which was above them to the north.

Oliver Cromwell, however, was beaten back on the Northern flank, hindering the progress of the infantry.

Manchester then attacked in the East, with some success initially. However, a counter-attack was organised and it drove Manchester's smaller force back.

Night had fallen by now, and the fighting died down. Both sides were unhappy with the events of the day, with the royalists between two forces, and the parliamentarians having suffered heavy losses.

Charles decided that his position was untenable, and organised the withdrawal of his army by moonlight towards Oxford. Waller and Cromwell were keen to pursue Charles in the morning, but Manchester decided that the army was not up to it, and Charles was allowed to continue unmolested.

Roundway Down

Date: 13th July 1643

Location: Devizes, Wiltshire

Parliamentarian Commander: Sir William Waller

Royalist Commander: Lord Henry Wilmot, Earl of Rochester

Victor: Royalists

Lord Hopton's army, still badly weakened from the fighting at Lansdown, retired South-East to Devizes. Waller, knowing that he had an advantage, took every opportunity to harass Hopton's rear.

Upon reaching Devizes, Hopton sent his cavalry on a mission to Oxford to get help. Devizes was unfortified and would not withstand a siege for long. The cavalry set off towards Salisbury, to make the parlimentary troops think that they were fleeing, then turned towards Oxford.

Waller, knowing that Hopton was in a bad position, took his time in besieging the town. He rested and fed his troops well, whilst using his artillery to weaken the defenders.

However, with the news that Lord Wilmot was returning with more cavalry, Waller hastily drew up his forces on Roundway Down, to the North of Devizes.

Waller deployed with his infantry in the centre and cavalry on both flanks, as was normal. He outnumbered the royalist force considerably, and their horses were tired from the 40 mile ride, so Waller had some reason to be optimistic.

Sir Arthur Haselrigg's 'Lobsters' rode out to meet Wilmot's own brigade. Wilmot responded by charging. For some reason, the charge was not met at the charge, which put Haselrigg at a disadvantage, and he was beaten back.

However, Haselrigg rallied his men and went forward again. A second charge, by Wilmot and Sir John Byron, was too much for the troopers, though, and they fled to the West.

Wilmot now co-ordinated his three brigades and charged the remaining parliamentary horse. They could not withstand his charge, and routed off the field. Unaware of the sharp drop on the other side of Oliver's Castle, to the West, many were killed as they rode over the ridge.

Waller's infantry, however, were more resistant to the cavalry, and stood firm. The royalist cavalry could not penetrate their ranks, and could not win the day without support.

Support, though, was forthcoming. Hopton, realising the position, sallied forth from Devizes. This new attack from their rear by infantry caused the parliamentary line to break up. Waller's remaining forces disintegrated under the combined attack, and his army practically ceased to exist.

As a result of this loss, Waller was unable to replace the Earl of Essex as Lord General of the parliamentary army. Also, with no parliamentary forces left in the West country, the royalists had won an important victory.

Turnham Green

Date: 12th- November 1642

Location: Turnham Green, West of London

Parliamentarian Commander: Robert Devereux, 3rd Earl of Essex

Royalist Commander: Charles I, King of England

Victor: Parliament (No battle fought)

Having fought an inconclusive battle at Edgehill, the Earl of Essex moved back to Warwick. This left Charles I with a clear route to London.

Charles marched for London, first capturing Banbury and then entering Oxford, where he was greeted by cheering crowds (Oct 29).

From Oxford, Charles moved East to Colnbrook, which he reached on the 11th November.

Charles had advanced cautiously, not knowing where Essex was, but this had allowed Essex to pass his army on the way, and reach London before him. Essex was able to muster a large defensive force at Turnham Green. Essex also left two regiments at Brentford, not far to the West, which Charles took on the 12th November. This action, and the sacking that followed it, roused the people of London. By the time that Charles was ready to march on, a force of 24,000 men awaited him at Turnham Green.

Charles had no chance against a force twice his size, so he turned South to Kingston. However, Sir James Ramsey with a force of 3,000 men were resting in Kingston before moving to cover the Southern approach to London. Unable to rest his army, Charles withdrew to Reading.

Finally, realising that his chance to take the capital had passed, Charles returned to Oxford, where he established his headquarters for the rest of the war.

WINCEBY

Date: 11th October 1643

Location: Winceby, Lincolnshire

Parliamentarian Commander: Lord Edward Montague, Earl of Manchester

Royalist Commander: Sir John Henderson

Victor: Parliament

Manchester had completed the capture of King's Lynn (Sep 16), and marched North to join Sir Thomas Fairfax and Colonel Oliver Cromwell in their siege of Bolingbroke Castle.

Sir John Henderson, royalist governor of Newark, then took a large body of horse to relieve the garrison at Bolingbroke.

He was discovered by a small party of horse under Fairfax (Oct 10), who were driven off. Manchester decided that, despite the odds, it would be better to attack before they arrived at Bolingbroke, where they could be trapped between the two forces. He sent his cavalry, under Cromwell and Fairfax to intercept Henderson.

They met at Winceby, and a cavalry duel began.

Cromwell charged first, leading his men to the attack. In the second defensive volley from the royalists, Cromwell had his horse shot from under him, and only rejoined the battle when he found another horse. Meanwhile, the charge had disordered the royalists, but not broken them. Fairfax then lead a second charge into their flank. This charge had the desired effect, and the royalist force broke and ran.

Since there was no infantry support, the parliamentary forces had little to do but chase the fleeing royalists, and the casualties suffered by Henderson were heavy. In comparison, the parliamentary casulaties were very light.

This action ensured that the siege at Bolingbroke was not broken. It also reinforced Cromwell's reputation as a leader of cavalry.

The Battle of Worcester

Date: 3rd September 1651

Location: Worcester, Hereford & Worcester

Parliamentarian Commander: Oliver Cromwell, General of Horse

Royalist Commander: Charles II, King of England (in exile)

Victor: Parliament

Charles marched south into England with a mostly Scottish army. Sir David Leslie would have prefered to stay in Scotland to fight Cromwell on his own terms, but Charles was adamant that the fight be carried to his own country.

Cromwell sent John Lambert to harass the Scots on their march, whilst he took a parallel route south. A new parliamentarian force was gathered in the South by Charles Fleetwood, and the three forces combined at Warwick on 24 August.

Charles arrived in Worcester on 23 August, and decided to rest and resupply his army. Fortifications were erected to defend against attack.

Cromwell's force now outnumbered the royalists 2 to 1. Fleetwood and Lambert were sent to cross the Severn to the south, with the intention of working north towards the city. Cromwell drew the rest of his forces up to the East of the city, and began an artillery bombardment.

Charles sallied out against Cromwell's artillery battery, but was driven back without taking any guns.

The approach from the south was barred by the river Teme. A mixed parliamentarian force under Deane was to attack Powick Bridge, which was defended by Keith.

Meanwhile, Lambert would attempt a crossing on a temporary bridge of boats farther east. He was opposed by Pitscottie.

Despite many attacks, the parliamentarians could not push the royalists back from the bridges.

However, Cromwell constructed a second bridge of boats across the Severn. Leading his infantry across, he attacked Pitscottie in the flank. Together with Lambert, Cromwell pushed the royalists back from their bridges.

Keith was now forced to withdraw by the threat from his flank, but the poor discipline of the Scots turned this into a rout that could not be stopped by the reserves behind them.

Charles, seeing that Cromwell had weakened his northern troops, attacked to the east. His assault drove the parliamentarians back, and Cromwell was forced to recross the river to support them. After three hours of fighting, Cromwell eventually drove the royalists back into the city.

By now the royalist cause was lost. Units attempted to flee north, but were captured by parliamentarians that now surrounded the city.

Despite this, Charles managed to escape, leaving his bodyguard to hold off pursuit. He spent six weeks wandering through England before finding a boat that would take him to France. The civil wars had ended.

The English Civil War Society

The English Civil War Society (ECWS) is a fun-orientated group that enables interested people to re-create parts of the English Civil Wars.

This does not just mean battles, but also demonstrations of the everyday aspects of life in the 17th century - known as "Living Histories".

The English Civil War Society of America

The English Civil War Society of America (ECWSA) is an American organisation that recreates the experience of fighting within the English Civil Wars. I haven't been to America myself, but the ECWS run joint events with the ECWSA about once a year.

Information on ECWSA was provided by Capt Bob Giglio, commander of the King's Lifeguard of Foot.

The Sealed Knot

The Sealed Knot is Europe's largest re-enactment society, with upwards of 6,000 members. Their aim is to re-create events of the English Civil Wars. Not just battles, but also 'Living History' re-enactments of life in the 17th century.

The Siege Group

The Siege Group are based within the UK, and mainly present small skirmishes and sieges that would have taken place, quite detached from the main battles. They draw on the local history of the venues they attend and try to fit it in with the chronlogy of the battles that took place nearby. Sometimes, though not often, local restrictions prevent the use of cannon or musket-fire. But the camp or garrison, together with a household, continues to draw interest with the presentation of daily 17th Century life.

9

Glossary of Terms for Civil War Era

Abatis: Rows of trees felled in the direction of the enemy with the smaller branches removed, the remainder sharpened to a point to create a defensive obstacle against advancing troops.

Advanced Works: Fortifications located beyond the glacis, but still within musket or rifle range of the main works.

Accouterments: Refers to the basic equipment of the infantry soldier; such as the cartridge box, belts, bayonet scabbard, haversack, knapsack, canteen, etc. When a soldier is under arms, he is said to be armed and accoutered.

Anchoring Gad: A device consisting of a three to four foot long "rope," made from twig fibers, and attached to a gad and an anchoring picket. This was used to secure the fascine to the parapet wall.

Anchoring Picket: A stake driven into the parapet as it was built to tightly hold the ropes or anchoring gads, which held fascines, gabions, and hurdles in place as revetments.

Approaches: The lines of entrenchments or ditches by which besiegers approach a fortified position. The principal trenches are called the first, second, and third parallels.

Armory: A storehouse where arms were stored and repaired. The individual who made repairs to the weapons was called an armorer.

Army: The body of troops of various corps (infantry, cavalry, artillery, and engineers) organized and commanded by a general.

Arsenal: A facility where arms were made, repaired, and stored, along with other types of military equipage.

Artillery: This term includes all kinds of military cannon, mortars, howitzers, etc., and all munitions and implements required for their operation. Attack:

Any type of movement upon the enemy. In siege warfare the term attack implies the works constructed by the besiegers. When an assault was partially made, with the intent of deceiving the enemy and diverting attention, it was called a false attack or a feint.

Banquette: The inside step at the base of a parapet wall that allowed a soldier to stand, load and fire over the crest of the parapet while being sheltered.

Banquette Slope: An access ramp to the banquette.

Barbette Battery: Cannons (referred to as guns) were said to be in barbette when they were mounted so as to be able to fire over the crest of the parapet, providing a wide range of fire. In this position the firing angle of the guns was not limited, as in firing through embrasures. The disadvantage of firing in barbette was the increased exposure of the artillery crew to direct enemy fire.

Barricade: To obstruct the avenues of access, as roads, streets, etc. This was accomplished by overturning wagons, placement of large stones, abatis; and ditches.

Bastion: A projection from a main work (or field fortification) containing two faces and two flanks that provide flanking fire to the front of the main work.

Bastion Fort: A polygon work with bastions at the corners. These eliminate dead spaces and angles in the main work.

Bastioned Front: An area of the work between the capitals of two adjacent bastions.

Battalion: Battalions consisted of approximately 500 men or one half the strength of a 1000 man infantry regiment. The term battalion was used loosely during the Civil War. Occasionally two companies (200 men) were referred to as a battalion, while the whole regiment was often mistakenly called a battalion. It was commonly accepted, however, that a regiment was composed of two battalions.

Battle: A contest between two large bodies of hostile troops. The term battle usually applies to a larger and more significant contest than a skirmish or an affair or engagement.

Battlefield: The area over which two large bodies of hostile troops engaged in combat. During the Civil War military site surveys conducted in Tennessee, battlefields were divided into two categories, small or large engagements. Small engagements involved a relatively small number of troops, while large engagements were fought by units the size of a division or greater, approximately 12,000 troops or more.

Battle Order: In the use of tactics, the order of battle referred to the arrangement or formations of troops drawn up in a line of battle, ready to meet the enemy. The theory of military formations was defined in all the U.S. and Confederate drill manuals of the day and was derived almost exclusively from translations of French manuals dating back to the Napoleonic era. Scott' s Infantry Tactics of 1835 was updated by Hardee's Rifle and Light Infantry Tactics in 1855, and in 1862 both of the above were combined in Silas Casey's, Evolution of a Brigade and Corps D'Armee. Casey's manual soon became the most popular on the subject. The usual order of battle began with a skirmish line, generally two companies, deployed 400 to 500 yards in front of the main line of battle. These were positioned at wide intervals and were used to locate the enemy or protect the main line from surprise. As the war progressed, frequently half of the regiment would form as skirmishers. The main line of troops (usually composed of six companies) was next in line and was drawn-up in two lines or ranks, for both attack and defense. The double line formation allowed the maximum number of muskets to fire and made it possible for officers to better control their men in the confusion of battle. A brigade might occupy less than 500 yards of front. To the rear of the main battle line (300 yards) two companies were placed in reserve.

Berm: A narrow shelf between the parapet and the ditch (or exterior slope and the scarp), which prevented the parapet from collapsing into the ditch.

Bivouac: A temporary encampment for one night or longer with troops using tents or other types of hastily constructed shelters or lean-tos of wood branches or other types of available natural cover.

Blockhouse: In Tennessee, blockhouses were wooden defensive structures that served primarily to guard railroad trestles. They were constructed of heavy vertical timbers and incorporated flat overhead ceilings of heavy timber, usually covered with a thick layer of dirt and capped with sloping board and batten roofs to shed water. The exterior walls contained loopholes for the firing of weapons, and these were located just above an embankment made from dirt removed from a surrounding ditch. As the war progressed, horizontal timbers were added to double the thickness of the walls to enable them to withstand artillery fire. Most of the blockhouses constructed in Tennessee were square, rectangular or cross-shaped.

Bombproof: A structure built of wood and earth that could withstand artillery fire.

Boyau: In siege work fortifications a boyau trench was constructed to allow troops to move from one parallel trench to another. They were usually made in zigzag form to provide protection from enemy fire.

Breach: An opening in an enemy wall or position usually made by artillery fire, for the purpose of allowing entry by attacking troops. During the Battle of Franklin, Tennessee in 1864, Confederate infantry, without the aid of supporting artillery, breached the federal entrenchments.

Break Joints: In sod revetments, each layer of sod overlapped the joints of the prior layer, adding strength to the sod wall.

Breastwork: A hastily constructed parapet that was breast high and usually did not include a banquette or step at the base of the parapet.

Bridge Head: A work composed of one or more redans or bastions that protected a bridge from enemy fire. It was also known by its French name, the tete-du-pont.

Brigade: A military unit, ideally consisting of four regiments, or approximately 4,000 soldiers, though during the Civil War actual numbers varied. Brigades were commanded by brigadier generals.

Camp: A temporary place for the repose of troops, whether for one night or a long period of time.

Cantonment: Refers to the quartering of troops in temporary structures, sometimes distributed among towns or villages, or when placed in huts at the end of a campaign.

Capital: An imaginary line that bisects the salient angle, dividing a work into two symmetrical parts.

Caponnier: A work projecting perpendicularly from the main work to provide flanking fire in the ditch and along the front. The work could also be bomb proofed and contain loopholes and serve as a line of communication or a passage to another work.

Casemate: A bombproof structure made of timber and earth and constructed of post and beam form, used to house artillery. In permanent fortifications it could also be used as quarters for the garrison, a powder magazine, a hospital, or as a last place of refuge within a fortification if overrun by the enemy.

Cavalier: An elevated artillery position within a fort, commanding its interior and the surrounding countryside. This was sometimes constructed on the terreplein of a bastion or curtain.

Cheek: This refers to the sides of an embrasure and was often revetted with fascine, gabions, or sand bags.

Chevaux-de-frise: An obstacle made of a wooden shaft or body from which wood projections or spears radiated in four directions. They were used to obstruct passages, protect a breach in the line, or form an impediment to cavalry.

Citadel: A small and strongly enclosed work, located in the interior of a fort, used as a final place of defense. Sometimes referred to as the keep.

City-class Ironclad: The United States Navy created these vessels as their first operational ironclads. They were designed with a single paddle wheel located mid-ship and enclosed within the protection of the ship's armament. There were a total of seven ironclads built by the U.S. during the war and all of them were named after cities. They were also known as "Pook's Turtles" (after the designer) or sometimes as "Eads Ironclads"(after their builder).

Company: The smallest tactical unit of soldiers, usually containing 50 to 100 men, commanded by a captain.

Commanding Position: A position that overlooked another position or surrounding country and enabled an army to give a plunging fire.

Corps: A military unit of two to four divisions, commanded by a major general in the Union armies or by a lieutenant general in the Confederate armies.

Cottonclad: Many Union and Confederate vessels were given extra protection by stacking cotton bales on their decks as barricades against small arms and light artillery fire. Larger vessels were known to have carried over 900 bales. Some Confederate "cottonclads" used compressed layers of cotton between the heavy walls of their gundecks. Most of the Confederate cottonclads were reinforced on the bow and also carried an iron prow for ramming.

Counterscarp: A wall located on the far side of the parapet ditch, opposite the exterior slope and scarp wall of the parapet. If the entrenchment is constructed with a glacis, the counterscarp wall will also include a banquette, interior slope, covered way and glacis slope. Most of the entrenchments constructed in Tennessee were built without the use of a glacis.

Covered Way: In permanent fortifications, a narrow walkway between the counterscarp and the glacis that covered troop movements and provided an outer line of defense for infantry. Very few of these entrenchments were constructed during the war. Union Fort Negley in Nashville was the largest inland masonry fortification built during the war, and it contained covered ways.

Cremaillere or Indented Line: A zigzag line of field fortifications. This type of earthwork was placed between two advanced works that were too far apart to protect each other as well as the space between them.

Cross Fire: Rifle or cannon fire delivered from two or more directions against the same target or point of ground in front of a work.

Crow's Foot: A star-shaped obstacle (also called Caltrop) made of iron prongs that radiate in all directions. When placed on the ground, at least one point will always point upward, forming an obstacle for troops and especially cavalry. They appeared in warfare as early as the Bronze Age and are still in use.

Cunette: A small ditch within the main ditch that acted as a drain or run-off for water.

Curtain: A section of the rampart that existed between two bastions and connected the flanks of the bastions.

Dead Angle or Space: Any angle or ground in front of a fortification that could not be covered by musket or artillery fire.

Defilading: The process of constructing the profile of a parapet to protect its interior from enfilading and plunging fire. Defiladement of fortifications consisted of either raising the parapet, constructing traverses, or excavating the terreplein below the line of sight of the enemy, located on a commanding height. A work constructed in this manner was said to be defiladed.

Defile: A narrow passage or road.

Demilune: A French engineers term meaning half moon. Such works were often constructed in early Renaissance defenses. The demilune was a crescent-shaped outer work created to protect a bastion or a fort's curtain wall. In later fortifications, demilune became synonymous with ravelin, a v-shaped outer work.

Detached Works: Fortifications constructed beyond musketry or rifle range of the main work but serving as part of the overall defenses of the main work.

Direct Fire: To fire perpendicular to the curtain wall or line of works; to fire into the front of an enemy.

Ditch: An excavation made in front or behind an earthwork providing the earth for that work. When the ditch is located in the front it serves as an obstacle to an attacker and when dug in the back, it affords the defender a secure position.

Division: A military unit consisting of approximately three brigades or 12,000 men. As with other units, actual numbers varied during the course of the Civil War.

Earthworks: A generic term applied to fortifications that were built for temporary use, especially those constructed of earth.

Embrasure: An opening in a parapet wall through which an artillery piece or other weapon could be fired.

Embrasure Battery: A battery that fired through embrasures in the parapet wall and provided more protection to the guns and crews than barbette style batteries. The drawback was a severely reduced field of fire for the guns.

En Barbette: The arrangement of cannon to fire over the parapet wall and not through embrasures. This provided a wide field of fire but afforded little protection for the gun crew (see Barbette Battery).

Encampment: A place where troops temporarily camped. Civil War troop movements resulted in numerous short-term encampments of over night or several days duration. Long-term encampments are considered to be camps with durations of weeks, months, or even years.

Enfilade Fire: A sweeping rifle or artillery fire delivered along the length of the parapet from a direction that was parallel to the front of the target so that it crossed the target from one flank to the other.

Engineers: In 1861 the engineers of the Union army were organized in two small but highly professional bodies - the Corps of Engineers and the Corps of Topographical Engineers. In 1863 these were merged and became known collectively as the Corps of Engineers.

Entanglement: An obstruction, usually abatis. Occasionally telegraph wire "entanglements" were strung close to the ground to trip attackers. Wire entanglements were created by union troops to help deter Confederate attacks on Fort Sanders in Knoxville in 1863.

Entrenchment: A temporary fortification or fieldwork composed of a ditch and parapet.

Epaulement: An earthen wall constructed on the open ends or flanks of a battery fortification to protect the flanks from enemy fire. Some sources use the term to denote both the front and flanks of the parapet of a battery.

Exterior Ditch: The ditch on the outer side of the parapet, between the parapet and the enemy.

Exterior Slope: The outer side of the parapet that faced the enemy. The exterior slope extended from the superior slope to the berm.

Face: The two sides of a work that converge to form a salient angle. The faces of field works were the stretches of parapet extending from one angle in the work to the next and were designed to provide a direct fire on an attacking body of troops as they advanced up the glacis.

Fascine: A long cylindrical bundle of closely-bound thin saplings. The saplings were usually referred to as green brushwood and were approximately one to two inches in diameter. Fascine was used as revetment for sustaining the slopes of a battery or parapet wall or to cover excessively wet ground. The most common type of fascine (one of three types below) was called battery or long fascine (also called saucissons) and was made in bundles 18 feet long by ten inches in diameter, weighing about 140 pounds. Trench fascine was made four to six feet long and was used for crowning a line of gabions in a sap or trench. These were made by sawing the long fascine into three parts. Water fascine, used as cover for marshy ground, was 18 inches in diameter and six to nine feet in length. Fascine could also be used as fill for crossing an enemy ditch during an attack. Five men could construct long fascine in one hour, including the cutting of wood.

Fascine Choker: A device composed of two five-foot-long wooden poles with one end of each connected to a chain and used to tighten the fascine into bundles by looping the chain around the saplings and tightening with leverage from the poles. The fascine were then tied with tough withes or gads, prepared by twisting small sapling so as to render them flexible or easily bent into knots.

Fascine Horse: A "machine" used to hold saplings in a bundle to form fascines. Driving stakes into the ground, obliquely, in pairs so that each pair crossed at the same height made the horse. They were then firmly lashed together to form an X-shaped support and repeated every eighteen inches until the desired length of the horse had been attained.

Field Engineering: The practice of making temporary military fortifications and military roads, the planning and construction of military bridges, and the attack and defeat of military works. This included all the various duties of engineer troops, either in the operation of a campaign, or in the dispositions on the battlefield.

Field Fortification: Field fortification was the art of engineering and strengthening a position for temporary use with available materials. Military engineers developed field works along the same principals as permanent fortifications, but were given greater latitude in their application in the field.

Field Works: Most field works were commonly called entrenchments during the Civil War. These were temporary fortifications constructed of available materials and used to defend important positions, or bodies of troops, against a sudden assault from superior forces. Field works were usually confined to a single campaign and used to strengthen positions that were to be occupied for short periods of time. Most field works could be constructed by troops in a single day. Field works can be divided into two major categories: Major field works were constructed to serve as both protection and as an obstacle, while minor field works were intended only for protective cover. The primary distinguishing feature was the placement of the ditch. Major field works contained a ditch around the exterior of the parapet, whereas minor works usually had no exterior ditch or a ditch on the interior of the parapet. As per the regulations of the day major works included redans, lunettes and redoubts, while minor works usually referred to rifle pits, blockhouses, and stockades.

Flank: The right or left side of a position or body of troops. Flanks are also the re-entering sides of a lunette or bastion.

Flying Bridge: A floating vessel (usually some type of wooden raft) that was propelled from one bank to the other by the current of the stream. The usual procedure to create a "ferry" of this kind was to attach the head of the boat, by means of a cable and anchor, to some point near the middle of the stream. By steering obliquely to the current, the boat could cross from shore to shore along the same arc.

Flying Sap: Refers to the rapid construction of the type of siege trenches referred to as saps.

Fort: An enclosed work of higher class than a field work, consisting of either a detached work or a work constructed within the framework of a large fortified area. During the Civil War the term was often used to mean any important position, no matter what type of military engineering was used in its construction.

Fortification: The military art of strengthening a position to resist an attack from a superior force. If the fortification was to be placed in a position of great importance and the materials were of durable quality, it is called a permanent fortification; if not it is called a field or temporary fortification. A position can be strengthened by the use of natural resources such as rivers, forests and hills or by artificial means using earth, timber, and stone for temporary or permanent works.

Fougass: Fougass was a small mine placed in a pit or shaft dug in the ground. It could be hidden in the ditch of a work with a thin covering of dirt or debris. It could also be placed and detonated anywhere advancing troops were forced to cross. An obstacle was often placed over it, such as chevaux de frize or abatis, in order that the attackers were occupied long enough for the charge to be detonated by means of a long fuse. Sometimes a fougass was made by using several loaded artillery shells placed in a watertight box with a charge of powder under them. Another type of mine used during the war was the contact mine. It consisted of a small powder charge with a mercury fulminate detonator arranged to explode under the pressure of a man's foot. The term "torpedo," as it was used in the 1860s, referred to another type of explosive mine fired by use of mechanical or electrical detonators. Both sides denounced mines as illegal and immoral at different times but continued to use them, though few were ever manufactured.

Fortress: A fortified town or city, or any large fortification so strongly fortified as to be capable of resisting a large and sustained attack. Fortress Rosecrans in Murfreesboro, Tennessee, was one of the largest earthen fortifications in the state and contained over 200 acres within its walls.

Fraise: A fraise is an obstacle formed by means of constructing a palisade, placed horizontally or slightly inclined at the edge of the berm of a ditch, so as to be concealed by the counter scarp crest.

Gabion: Stout, rough, cylindrical baskets, open at top and bottom used to revet the interior slopes of batteries or the cheeks of embrasures, to form the parapet of trenches, and to form free-standing defensive works. Gabions were made of various dimensions and heights according to their use. The open-end basket was woven from twigs and small branches and was filled with dirt.

Gabionnade: A fieldwork constructed of gabions.

Gads: These were also called withes and were used to tie fascine bundles. They were made of tough twigs or sapling rods and were to be "no smaller than your little finger and no larger than your thumb." They were prepared by twisting by hand, in order to make them supple, then "tying" them around the fascine bundles.

Gallery: A covered passage way usually in the counterscarp and used as a ditch defense. The gallery was about six feet high and four feet wide.

Glacis: A mound of earth placed in front of the ditch. The function of raising the ground in front of the rampart was to eliminate any dead space and to allow a sweeping fire form the parapet. The Glacis also caused shots from enemy cannons to ricochet over the main works. It was seldom used in field works due to the time and energy needed for construction.

Gorge: The open-ended side of the rear of a lunette or redan or the opening in an enclosed work. If the work was detached or isolated, the gorge may have been fortified with a stockade wall.

Gunboat: The term gunboat was used broadly during the Civil War to describe any armed vessel that was not a ship of the line, a frigate, or a sloop. The term included all ocean-going ships and steamers that could operate for long periods of time at sea. It also included Union and Confederate ironclads and monitor class vessels with V-shaped hulls of the ocean going type. These ships were handicapped by not being able to sail far from the protection of a friendly harbor. The term gunboat also includes all of the flat-bottomed armored ships that navigated the inland waterways and were predominately propelled by either side wheels or stern paddle wheels.

Head Log: Logs placed horizontally on top of an earthwork and raised three to four inches above the work allowing a soldier to fire a rifle through the opening without exposing his head to enemy fire. Log supporting struts were often placed beneath the head log and back across the top of the trench to keep the head logs from rolling into the trench if hit by enemy artillery fire. This type of defensive work was used with deadly effect by entrenched federal troops at the Battle of Franklin, Tennessee.

Headquarters: Refers to buildings or field sites occupied by commanding officers and their staff for one night or up to several months.

Hurdle Revetment: A wicker or woven sapling wall, 3 to 4 feet high and 6 to 9 feet long, constructed between upright poles. Hurdles were used as revetments in temporary works, and were placed on the steep interior slope or used on the walls of traverses. Hurdles were also used to form a dry footing in trenches during wet weather.

Indented or Cremaillere Line: A continuous line of alternating (zigzag) long and short faces constructed perpendicular to each other. The reenterings were arranged so as to provide for crossfire in front of them.

Inundations: Water inundations were created by damming streams that passed in front of a field fortification. This type of obstacle was rarely used during the Civil War, but at Knoxville, Tennessee, sections of the Federal defenses were partially protected by damming several creeks.

Interior Slope: The angle of the parapet wall extending between the superior slope and the banquette.

Ironclad: A ship or boat that was sheathed in thick iron plate. Ironclad ships were in use in Europe before 1861, but not until the American Civil War did any ironclad vessels fight one another.

Keep: The final stronghold in the interior of a complex fortification. Often referred to as the citadel.

Loopholes: Small openings in a wall through which a weapon

could be fired. Most frequently seen in blockhouse and stockade construction.

Lunette: An earthen fortification similar to a redan in construction and function, with the addition of two flanking walls on either side of the open gorge.

Magazine: A bombproof compartment designed to safely store and contain gunpowder and fixed ammunition.

Merlon: A portion of the parapet wall between two embrasures.

Military Crest: The military crest of a ridge is a position that allows troops to see all the ground in front of them. The topographical crest of a ridge is the highest point on the ridge and allows for a favorable position for distant observation but would not allow troops to see the foreground and fire upon an enemy. Therefore, on a convex slope, the military crest is below the topographical crest.

Military Foundry: Foundries were used for the manufacture of cast iron or bronze cannons or other metal military products, such as munitions, small arms, swords, and belt buckles. In Tennessee several civilian foundries were converted into military use by the Confederacy, the T. M. Brennan Foundry in Nashville being one of them.

Military Hospital: During the surveys of Civil War military sites in Tennessee, military hospitals were categorized as short term and long term. The first refers to buildings that were used as temporary hospitals following a battle, as well as tent hospitals, known as "brigade depots" or "forward dressing stations." The latter were located as close as possible to battle fronts, and the wounded from the field were brought there by stretcher-bearers. Soldiers treated in these front line hospitals were often placed in ambulance wagons or train cars and transported to larger field or divisional hospitals further in the rear. Wounded soldiers from brigade depots or divisional hospitals were often transported to "general" or "base" hospitals, which were usually permanent buildings located in larger cities.

Military Railroad Depot: Military depots usually consisted of collections of warehouses built for the storage of large quantities of military goods. Supplies were shipped by river, train, or wagon to these depots, usually located in larger cities and guarded by extensive fortifications. During the Civil War, Nashville, Johnsonville, and Murfreesboro, Tennessee, became major Federal storage facilities.

Military Saltpeter Mine: A military controlled mining operation for extracting saltpeter from the floors of caves. This material was refined and became a major component in the manufacturing of gunpowder.

Military Shipyard: Civil War era military shipyards were designed for the construction and maintenance of vessels such as gunboats, transports, and barges. Most were located in large cities on major waterways. In Tennessee, important military shipyards were located at Nashville, Johnsonville, Chattanooga, and Memphis.

Mitre: Another name for a priest cap or swallow tail earthwork.

Mouth: The narrow opening of an embrasure at the interior slope of a parapet.

Oblique Embrasure: An embrasure that intersects a parapet at an acute angle.

Obstacle: A device or material, such as abatis or chevaux-de-frise, placed in front of a fortification or a passage to hinder attackers by breaking up the orderliness and momentum of an attack. It delayed enemy troops at a point in the field where defenders could most effectively sweep the enemy with gunfire.

Palisade: Pointed stakes placed in the ground at an angle facing the enemy. The stakes were 6 to 8 inches in diameter and 6 to 10 feet long. A small ditch, about 2 feet 6 inches in depth and width, was dug for the palisade line. A large lintel or beam, called a riband, was nailed to the bottom of the palisade stakes, sunk into the ditch, filled with earth, and packed. When finished, at least 7 feet of palisade was angled above ground. Another riband was sometimes attached to the upper portion of the palisade stakes, about 18 inches from the pointed ends, to provide additional strength. The palisade was usually placed in front of a ditch or the base of a slope, as an obstacle. Today the terms stockade and palisade are sometimes used interchangeably, but during the Civil

War, palisade referred to the above described angled defensive configuration, while stockade referred to vertical post defenses.

Pan coupe: A pan coupe was constructed by modifying a lunette or redan fortification by the addition of a small face (or flattened point) constructed across the salient angle, allowing a wider range of fire.

Parallels: Trenches constructed parallel to enemy works to contain reserve troops and artillery during a siege. Successive parallels were dug, each being nearer to the work and connected by saps.

Parapet: The wall of the rampart that troops stood behind to defend the fortified position. In field works, the height of the parapet was recommended at about 7 feet, the thickness of the parapet varied according to the kind of fire it was intended to resist. If the parapet was out of the range of enemy artillery (about 800 yards), then it was constructed to resist only musketry or rifle fire, a thickness of 2½ feet. To withstand artillery fire the thickness of the wall was 6 to 10 feet.

Permanent Fortifications: Fortifications designed for long-term occupation and constructed of durable materials. Fort Negley in Nashville and Fortress Rosecrans in Murfreesboro, Tennessee, are two examples.

Picket Stake: A stake driven through fascine or other forms of revetment in order to secure them to the interior slope of the parapet wall.

Pioneers: Soldiers equipped with axes, saws, spades, mattocks, pickaxes, billhooks and other tools for clearing the way before an advancing army or to entrench. Pioneers were sometimes detailed from different companies of a regiment and formed under a non-commissioned officer.

Pisa: A form of sun-dried brick revetment made of ordinary earth mixed with clay and sometimes with chopped straw. The mixture was kneaded with water and laid wet, 12 inches thick by 2 feet broad and well packed. To protect the face from weathering, grass seeds or oats were sown, but were not to be cut when the stalks matured.

Plane of Sight: An imaginary line sighted by an engineer that represented the converging enemy's fire into the interior of a work.

Platform: A foundation, usually built of timber, which supported an artillery piece and kept it from miring into the dirt surface of the terreplein.

Plongee: The downward slope of the superior slope of the parapet; also the downward slope of the sole or floor of an embrasure.

Plunging Fire: An annihilating fire from a high or commanding position. River batteries were often positioned on high ground to obtain a plunging fire that would strike the vulnerable and unarmed decks of gunboats and other river transportation.

Pontoniering: The construction of temporary military bridges or ferries by engineers, aided by a detachment of sappers. The bridges were made using wooded pontoon skiffs (called bateau by French engineers), which were transported on carriages, or by using wooden raft frames covered with a vulcanized India rubber canvas. During the Civil War these devices were generally called pontoons, but the engineer corps continued to refer to them by the older spelling "pontons."

Postern: A covered passage beneath the rampart that provided communication from the interior into the ditch. The passage from the covered way into the surrounding countryside, usually in front of the works, was called the sally port.

Priest Cap: An earthwork resembling the capital letter "M," having an indented salient that forms two small redans. It was seldom used as a detached work, but was often constructed at the end of a main line of defenses. One example of this type fortification is recorded in Tennessee.

Profile: A wooden outline, or frame of poles and laths nailed together, usually constructed on the ground and raised to a vertical position to simulate the dimensions of the desired earthen fortification to be built. Dirt would then be excavated from the ditch and thrown back into the profiled framework and compacted until it filled the dimensions of the profile. The parapet was then ready to be finished with a suitable revetment.

Railroad Guard Post: This refers to posts that protected vulnerable points along the rail system such as bridges, trestles, or depots. These were often defended using stockades, blockhouses, or earthworks such as redoubts and entrenchments.

Ram: A ship or boat equipped with an armored prow for ramming another ship was called a "ram."

Ramp: An inclining passage from the interior of a work to the terreplein, allowing troops and artillery access to the parapet wall.

Rampart: A broad wall or embankment forming the main body of a fortification and consisting of a terreplein and a parapet.

Rampart Plane: That part of the rampart that is visually in line or in the same plane as a point in the rear of the work and the commanding heights in the front of the work. The plane represents the converging fire along the length of the rampart.

Rampart Slope: The side of the rampart between either the banquette or the terreplein and the rear of the work, constructed with a slope of forty-five degrees.

Ravelin: A large V-shaped outwork composed of two faces forming a salient angle, constructed outside the ditch. It was used to cover the curtain wall, the gate, or the flank of a bastion. It was sometimes referred to as a demi lune . Two ravelins were used in the construction of Fort Negley at Nashville.

Redoubt: An earthwork that is enclosed on all sides. The overall configuration may be square, polygonal, or circular. Redoubts on level ground were generally square or pentagonal. On a hill or rising ground their outlines often followed the contour of the summit of the hill. Tennessee redoubts were often relatively small detached works used to fortify hilltops or to strengthen main lines of defense.

Redan: A V-shaped earthwork, open at the rear, the opening being referred to as a gorge. In Tennessee examples occur both as detached works and as portions of defensive lines.

Re-entering: An angle or line that points inward or toward the interior of the work. Almost all flanks joined faces of field works at re-entering angles.

Regiment: A military unit composed of ten or more companies, usually about 1,000 men at the start of the Civil War. Regiments were commonly thought to consist of two battalions. As the war progressed regiment size was often under strength, with considerably less than 1,000 men, in some reported instances as low as 375.

Relief: The height of the work. High or bold relief refers to a tall or commanding work; low relief refers to a work that is low in height.

Retrenchment: A retrenchment was a parapet or trench constructed in the rear of the forward parapet of a field work that defending troops could fall back to when driven from the outer works. It was a second line of defense that could be used to prevent enemy forces from entering the interior of a field fortification or penetrating through a line of works. Retrenchments were used in the works at the Battles of Franklin and Nashville and at other Civil War sites across Tennessee.

Reverse Fire: A fire that strikes the rear of a work or a fire that hits the interior slope of a parapet at an angle greater than thirty degrees.

Revetment: Material used to sustain an embankment when the slope is steeper than the natural slope. Revetments were constructed with materials such as wood, stone, sandbags, sod, gabions, or fascines, held in place with wooden picket stakes.

Riband: A thick plank or log nailed horizontally to the base of a row of palisades and placed in the ground to strengthen the palisades. Another riband was sometimes placed about 18 inches from the pointed ends or tops of the palisades to also provided more stability.

Ricochet Fire: Ricochet artillery fire was delivered at a low elevation toward a parapet so that shot would pass over the parapet wall and bound along the interior of the work.

Rifle Pit: Rifle pits were relatively simple to construct, requiring no engineering expertise. They could be thrown up quickly almost anywhere and provided fairly efficient protection against small arms and some light artillery fire. Some of the entrenchments had an interior or exterior ditch, but it was not intended as an obstacle for the enemy. Rifle pits can be subdivided into two distinct types of works defined by their lateral extent (rather than their profiles) and function. Skirmish pits were small, detached works providing cover for one or two or small groups of troops. They were placed on the flanks of a fortified or unfortified position to provide cover for skirmishers or pickets. Rifle trenches were extended lines of rifle pits that were used to connect major field works and cover the front of infantry troops deployed in a position. The term rifle pit was a "catch-all" phrase used during the war, and its true definition was commonly misinterpreted when describing types of infantry field works. Both subdivisions were used in many locations throughout Tennessee. Fort Donelson National Battlefield in Dover, Tennessee, contains excellent examples of both types of rifle pits as described above (see also "Entrenchment").

Salient: Part of a work that projects outward from the main work.

Salient Angle: A projection of a work that forms an angle.

Sally Port: An opening in a work that allowed access into the work and was used by troops to make a sally or sortie out of the work.

Sandbag: A canvas bag (sometimes tarred) measuring roughly 14 inches by 30 inches an d filled three-fourths full with earth to form a quick defensive structure or a revetment.

Sap: Armies advanced on enemy works by the construction of approach trenches, referred to as saps, the work being carried out by sappers (the term sap derives from the French word sappe, meaning spade or shovel). A large sap roller was placed at the head of the sap (or trench) and advanced foot by foot as gabions were placed on the side towards the besieged work and filled with dirt. These protected the workmen from enemy fire. When enemy fire was slack many gabions could be placed and filled at the same time, this procedure being known as a flying sap. If two gabion parapets were placed one on each side of the trench, this was called a double sap.

Sappers: During the sixteenth and seventeenth centuries a system of siegecraft was developed by French Field Marshal Vauban that provided a systematic approach for attackers and their artillery to enemy fortifications by means of entrenchments.

Under the cover of artillery fire, the attacking troops dug "saps," or approach trenches, toward the enemy (thus the origins of the word "sapper" for certain kinds of engineers). During the American Civil War, detachments of sappers, miners, and pontoniers were used in advance of the infantry to open and repair roads, establish pontoon bridges, and occasionally to lay siege to fortified positions.

Sapping: This is a general term applied to the operation of forming trenches, along which troops may approach an enemy work without being exposed to enemy fire. Construction of the trench could be carried out night and day without cessation.

Sap-Roller: A device that was placed at the head of the trench being dug by a squad of sappers and pushed ahead of them (using specialized tools) to provide cover from enemy fire. It consisted of two large concentric gabions, 6 feet in length, the outer one having a diameter of 4 feet, the inner one a diameter of 2 feet 8 inches. It was made shot proof by filling the space between the gabions with small pieces of hardwood, cotton, straw, or some similar type material.

Saucisson: The largest type of fascine measuring 10 inches in diameter and 18 feet long, used in constructing batteries and magazines.

Scantling: A small-sized timber for construction, similar to a stud or rafter.

Scarp: The inner slope of the ditch under the berm.

Side Wheeler: A vessel propelled by steam-powered paddle wheels on either side of the hull.

Signal Station: Usually located on prominent hilltops, signal stations were set up to form an interlocking grid throughout the theater of war. Their primary function was to pass messages by semaphore (or "wig wag"), but their localities also offered ideal views of enemy movements. Most of the signal stations had signal towers of wood or used large trees to support observation platforms. In a few cases strategically located buildings, such as the Tennessee State Capital building in Nashville, were occupied as signal stations.

Simple sap: A trench constructed on ordinary soil beyond the range of the enemy's artillery grape shot was called a simple sap or ordinary trench. The earth was thrown up on the side towards the enemy, so as to form a kind of parapet to cover the men in the trench. The work was done by working parties detached from various military units, supervised by engineer troops.

Skirmisher: Skirmishers were used in advance of the main body of advancing troops. They fought on open ground, taking advantage of the terrain. When formed into line of battle, a regiment might fight with all its companies abreast, forming one long double line of men, or one or more companies might be held back as reserves. One or more companies were usually sent forward as a skirmish line. In a divisional attack, whole regiments might be assigned as skirmishers. As the war progressed skirmish lines grew heavier, in some cases consisting of half the regimental strength, the remainder being held in line of battle as reserves. Skirmish lines might be 400 to 500 yards in advance of the main formation.

Small Pickets: An obstacle made of pickets or sharpened branches two and a half feet long and driven into the ground one foot apart in quincunx order.

Sod revetment: Sod or turfs used for the formation of the interior slopes of parapets and the cheeks of embrasures. The sod was to be cut from good grass, with thickly matted roots, and was to be mowed and watered before it was cut. Sod was cut in two sizes with the typical pattern consisting of headers that were 12 inches square by 4½ inches thick and stretchers that were 18 inches long by 12 inches broad and 4½ inches thick. For the first layer the sod was laid horizontal, grass side down, with two stretchers and one header alternating and packed firmly with a mallet. When this was completed a second layer with the grass side up was laid on the first, positioned so as to cover the joints. In hot weather the revetment was to be watered frequently.

Sole: The bottom or floor of an embrasure.

Splay: The widening effect of an embrasure.

Sortie: A secret movement of troops made by a strong detachment of troops in a besieged position, to destroy or retard the enemy's approaches.

Star Fort: An enclosed work composed of salients and re-entering angles. It was an ineffective design for defenses as the flanks did not receive sufficient flank protection.

Strategy: The art of creating a plan of campaign, combining a system of military operations to attain certain goals, such as the character of the enemy, the nature and resources of the country, and the means of attack and defense.

Stern-Wheeler: A flat-bottomed steamer propelled by a single paddle wheel located in the stern of the vessel.

Stockade: Stockade, or picket, was an early frontier term that described a relatively simple enclosure designed in a German cross or square shape, often with bastioned corners. Vertical log walls usually contained loopholes for firing. Troops often dug outer ditches and heaped the earth against the exterior walls to add strength to the stockade. Before blockhouses became common in Tennessee in 1864, Federal troops relied primarily on stockades to protect railroad trestles.

Superior Slope: The top of the parapet extending from the interior slope to the exterior slope.

Swallow Tail: A priest-cap or mitre type of earthwork.

Tactics: As opposed to strategy, tactics is the art of handling the movement of armies upon the battlefield within sight of the enemy.

Tambour: A loop-holed stockade with two faces forming a salient angle, constructed to defend the gorge of a small field work or to guard the doorways of a fortification or fortified building.

Temporary Fortifications: Fortifications built for a battle or a campaign and constructed of available materials; usually constructed in a single day.

Terreplein: The name given to the floor or level ground surface inside a fortification, located between the banquette slope and the interior slope of a rampart.

Tete du pont: A detached fortification designed primarily to cover a bridge, usually constructed as a redan.

Tinclad: A river gunboat that was minimally armored with

thin sheets of iron plating no more than 5/8 inch thick. Some tinclads were reinforced by two layers of plating but were still only protected from small arms fire and were susceptible to artillery shells that sometimes penetrated entirely through the vessel. Most tinclads were stern-wheelers and the exposed wheel could be disabled if hit by enemy fire. This flaw soon lead to a new class of vessel, the "city-class ironclad."

Traverse: An earthen wall or embankment, perpendicular to the main rampart wall, that provides protection from enfilading fire. In the construction of artillery batteries, splinter-proof traverses were placed alternately between the cannons to limit the destructive effect of a shell exploding within the battery. These rectangular earthen traverses were usually reveted with fascine, gabion or sand bags.

Tread: The top platform of the banquette.

Trench: A common name for a parapet and ditch; also the parallels or zigzags constructed by besiegers in an attempt to capture enemy works.

Trestle bridge (for infantry): A bridge principally used for crossing a small stream not more than eight feet in depth. In shallow water, they also served to connect floating bridges with the shore.

Trestle bridge (railroad): Military Bridges of the American Civil War were usually constructed with unskilled laborers, supervised by officers trained in such construction, using materials obtained on or near the site. The illustration depicts a military railroad bridge in Virginia that was 80 feet high and 400 feet long. A Civil War era guide to building military railroad bridges (Military Bridges: Designs for Trestle and Truss Bridges, 1864) was published by Colonel Herman Haupt, Chief of U.S. Military Railways.

Trous de loup: An obstacle consisting of a sharpened stake placed in an inverted pyramid or cone-shaped pit, some six feet in diameter and about the same number of feet in depth. They are usually placed in "checkerboard" rows a few yards in front of the ditch and concealed by some type of slight covering. An identical type of defensive tool, substantiated by recent archaeological findings, was used by Roman legions in 52 BC at the siege of Alesia in Britain. Trous de loup derives from the French, meaning wolf holes.

Vertical Fire: Artillery mortars generally used vertical fire to reach their targets. Fire was said to be vertical when it was delivered at a high angle.

Withes: Wooden twigs twisted together to form a rope for tying a fascine, also known as gads (see Gad).

Works: The term works was commonly used by Civil War era military personal in reference to any type of earthen field works or field fortifications.

Zigzag: A line of defiladed approach trenches, built by besiegers in an attempt to move toward enemy works while under the protection of a parapet. The zigzag trenches could eventually lead to the capture of the besieged position.

Bibliography

Ashton, S.R.: British Policy Towards the Indian States, 1905-1939, London, Curzon, 1982.

Brierly, L.: The Law of Nations, New York, Oxford University Press, 1955.

Dixit, Prabla: Communalism: A Struggle for Power, New Delhi, Orient Longman, 1981.

Greer P.: Transforming Central Government: the Next Steps Initiative, Buckingham, Open University Press, 1994.

Huntington, S.P.: The Soldier and the State, N.Y., Vintage Books, 1964.

Jones, W.H.: The Government and Politics of India, London, Hutchinson, 1971.

Keane J.: Democracy and Civil Liberty, London, Verso, 1988.

Mackenzie, D.: Knowing Machines: Essays on Technical Change, London, Mit Press, 1996.

Mary, W.: Asian Power and Politics: the Cultural Dimensions of Authority, Cambridge, Belknap Press, 1985.

Nair, A. M.: An Indian Freedom Fighter in Japan, Bombay, Orient Longman, 1983.

Posen, B.R.: The Sources of Military Doctrine, Ithaca, 1984, Cornell Univ. Press.

Rosen, P.: Societies and Military Power: India and its Armies, Ithaca, Cornell University Press, 1996.

Simon, D. : Public Administration, New York, Knopf, 1950.

Victor G. : Law as a Political Instrument, New York, Random House, 1955.

Index

♦♦♦